DESTINATION HIKES
IN AND AROUND SOUTHWESTERN
BRITISH COLUMBIA

STEPHEN HUI
Foreword by **Cecilia Point**

DESTINATION HIKES

In and Around Southwestern British Columbia

Swimming Holes • Mountain Peaks • Waterfalls • and More

GREYSTONE BOOKS
Vancouver/Berkeley

*For my son, Ollie, who loves a good transit hike as much as I do,
and for all of my trail partners, old and new*

21 22 23 24 25   5 4 3 2 1

Greystone Books Ltd.
greystonebooks.com

Cataloguing data available from Library and Archives Canada
ISBN 978-1-77164-530-0 (pbk.)
ISBN 978-1-77164-531-7 (epub)

Editing by Lucy Kenward
Copy editing by Erin Parker
Proofreading by Alison Strobel
Indexing by Stephen Ullstrom
Cover and text design by Nayeli Jimenez
Cover photograph by Colin Knowles
Photographs by Stephen Hui, except where credited otherwise
Cartography by Steve Chapman, Canadian Map Makers

Printed and bound in Singapore on ancient-forest-friendly paper by
COS Printers Pte Ltd.

Greystone Books gratefully acknowledges the Musqueam, Squamish, and
Tsleil-Waututh peoples on whose land our office is located.

Greystone Books thanks the Canada Council for the Arts, the British
Columbia Arts Council, the Province of British Columbia through the Book
Publishing Tax Credit, and the Government of Canada for supporting our
publishing activities.

Canadä

PREVIOUS SPREAD: *A rock arch partially conceals a waterfall on the Echo Lake Trail.*

Hiking, scrambling, and all forms of outdoor recreation involve inherent risks and an element of unpredictability. Many of the hikes in this guidebook are not for novices and may not be safe for your party. There are dangers on every trail, route, and road, and conditions can change at any time. While every effort has been made to ensure accuracy, this book may contain errors. You assume full responsibility for your safety and health in the backcountry. The author, publisher, and distributors accept no liability for any loss, damage, injury, or death arising from the use of this book. Check current conditions, carry the 10 essentials, exercise caution, and stay within your limits.

CONTENTS

HIKES NORTH OF VANCOUVER

North Shore

A secluded swimming hole worth sweating for
Thread your way to solitude on the summit
First stop: a giant western red cedar
After the Grouse Grind, keep going for superb city views
Get up close and personal with Vancouver's rock stars

Squamish

Swim and soak up the Howe Sound views
Gain a unique perspective of Stawamus Chief Mountain

FOREWORD

by Cecilia Point

ʔa səy̓eḿ nə syey̓ə
ʔenθə Cecilia Point
*təniʔ cən ʔə ƛ̓ x*ʷ*məθk*ʷ*əy̓əm*
*ʔəḿi ce:p k*ʷ*ətx*ʷ*iləm*

UPON BEING INVITED to write the foreword to this hiking guide, I decided that a protocol welcome to Musqueam territory was required. While this informative book focuses on trails scattered in and around the wider Coast Salish territories, Musqueam territory is generally the gateway to this region.

The purpose of a protocol welcome is, for us, the original people of the land, to open the floor for the hosts of an event to do their work. Its purpose is also to give the visitor a sense of where they are, the place they're in, its history, and the people who have resided here for thousands of years. What better way, I thought, to open a book that invites people to take a journey in Coast Salish territories?

In the Musqueam language, hən̓q̓əmin̓əm̓, the beginning of this foreword says:

Respected friends and relatives
My name is Cecilia Point
I'm from Musqueam
Welcome to our territory

The Musqueam people have long believed that our original ancestors descended from the sky wrapped in clouds. These first beings were transformed by *χe:ls* (the transformer) into mountains, trees, rocks, bodies of water, animals, and humans. This is why we have such a strong connection to this place. The animals and various parts of the landscape are our ancestral relatives.

The first people of this area view local places and their names in a very different light than colonial occupants and visitors to this land. Many places in the region are commonly known by newer names given by European visitors to commemorate European people or places. Meanwhile, our names for these places are thousands of years old, with histories of their own.

For example, the waterway we long called staɬəw̓ is now known as the Fraser River, after Simon Fraser, a fur trader and explorer for the North West Company who visited the region in the early 1800s. In fact, Fraser and his party were the first white people seen by many of the Coast Salish peoples.

Ch'ich'iyúy, or the Twin Sisters, is what my teʔə (granny) from the Skwxwú7mesh (Squamish Nation) long called a distinctive pair of peaks overlooking Vancouver. A B.C. Supreme Court judge renamed them The Lions in the late 1800s—possibly in reference to a particular set of statues in London.

A very important place name is c̓əsnaʔəm, an ancient Musqueam village at the mouth of the Fraser River. Significant activity took place at this site between 5,000 and 2,500 years ago. In the early 1900s, the area was named Marpole after a Canadian Pacific Railway executive.

When I think of our territory, I can't help but think about my great grandpa mənel̓ (James Point) of xʷməθkʷəy̓əm (Musqueam). He was a young man at the turn of the century (1900) and lived to be 104 years of age. Like his ancestors before him, he walked in his territory every day of his life and saw drastic changes take shape before his very eyes. He recalled how, in the old days, young men, runners, travelled between our villages to announce visitors approaching by land or water. He told of sʔi:ɬqəy̓, the two-headed serpent who shaped the area we now live.

I also think of my granny χʷlayχʷlet (Valentina [Tina] Cortez), who lived to the age of 92, of the Skwxwú7mesh in North Vancouver. When she was a young girl, her mother brought her across the inlet to our longhouse in xʷməθkʷəy̓əm for a potlatch. At the end of the evening, her mother departed, telling her daughter she was now married to this man, cəlsəmqəm (Tony Point), my grandfather.

When I met the author, Stephen Hui, to discuss this book, we talked about our different experiences growing up in the metropolis of Vancouver. I was raised in East Vancouver and Richmond. As children, my siblings and I would run through the grass in our bare feet. We caught fish in the river—on one occasion, we caught swiw̓ə (eulachon) with our hands—and we spent many summer days picking wild berries.

Now, as a mother of two grown kids, I walk with my family on the river dikes near my home in Richmond. We are treated to amazing views of the mountains and can often see all the way across the water to Vancouver Island. I tell my children to squint their eyes to block out the buildings and picture what our ancestors saw as they went about a typical day, either on foot or by canoe. When we walk into the mountains, I tell them about how my dad enjoyed taking us out of the city and into the woods to set up camp in the wilderness.

My heart is filled when I meet someone like Stephen who resides in my territory. He has a genuine appreciation for the beauty of this place. Like me, Stephen grew up in the Metro Vancouver area (Burnaby and Coquitlam, in his case), but he loves to explore the wildness and nature that still exists in the region. When he shares his experiences, I feel Stephen brings me with him, and I can't help but join in his enjoyment of the spectacular views that he captures through his photography—the magnificence and impressiveness of the landscape and the many places that appear undisturbed. Indeed, his imagery makes me think of how this place looked to my ancestors before contact with Europeans.

So when you go hiking in Coast Salish territories, I'd love for you to think of our ancestors venturing into the woods to strip cedar for making baskets, hats, or clothing, or of the p̓q̓ə́lqən (mountain goats) which used to populate this area and whose wool we used in our swə́qw'elh (blanket) weavings. As well, I hope you will take time to think about what Musqueam people have asked of visitors arriving all these years: Think of the ancestors from the past seven generations, the original caretakers of the land, and look after this place for the next seven generations to enjoy. Delight in your journey with Stephen, as he takes you on the trails and gives you a true sense of place.

A member of the Musqueam Nation, Cecilia Point is a political activist who stood for more than 200 days at her people's ancestral burial site to protect it from development in 2012. She works for the Indigenous Tourism Association of Canada and lives in Richmond, B.C.

INTRODUCTION

WANDER THROUGH BRILLIANT wildflower meadows and scramble up a craggy peak to a historical fire lookout (Hike 53). Paddle across a mighty river and discover a series of sublime waterfalls in a granitic canyon (Hike 8). Commune with old-growth giants and swim with rainbow trout in a refreshingly remote lake (Hike 31). Follow in the footsteps of Indigenous traders and gold prospectors, and bask in the alpenglow of high peaks and glaciers (Hike 54).

These are just four of the 55 hiking adventures described in this guidebook. The focus of *Destination Hikes In and Around Southwestern British Columbia* is trails and routes to enticing and intriguing destinations in the Coast Mountains and Cascade Range and around the Salish Sea, in southwestern British Columbia and northwestern Washington.

Vancouver, the nucleus of this cross-border guide, lies in the Indigenous territories of the Musqueam (xʷməθkʷəy̓əm), Squamish (Sḵwx̱wú7mesh), and Tsleil-Waututh (səl̓ilw̓ətaʔɬ) First Nations. The area covered spans the territories of many First Nations among the Coast Salish, Nlaka'pamux, St̓át̓imc, and Syilx peoples, who have stewarded these lands and waters since time immemorial. Among the destinations are sites of cultural, historical, and spiritual importance to First Nations—locations with long-standing names in Indigenous languages, such as hən̓q̓əmin̓əm̓, Lhéchelesem, Lushootseed, Nlaka'pamuchin, SENĆOŦEN, Sḵwx̱wú7mesh sníchim, and Ucwalmícwts. Respect these special places.

All of the trips featured in this book are distinct from those of the companion volume, *105 Hikes In and Around Southwestern British Columbia*. Although *Destination Hikes* explores some of the same regions as *105 Hikes*, it ventures into fresh terrain, including Nanaimo and Galiano Island in B.C. and the Cascade River in Washington, and offers greater coverage of trails near

Abbotsford and Chilliwack. The selected hikes include exceptional places that visitors won't want to miss and local favourites worth returning to again and again. The trips vary widely in quality and difficulty, but they generally fit within the following parameters (with a few exceptions):

- Offer one or more of the following features: waterfalls, big trees, wildflowers, swimming, coastal views, mountain views, history, or geology. (For more details, see How to Use This Guide.)

- Are accessible as a day or weekend trip from Vancouver.

- Are doable in a day on foot, though some are better suited to overnighters.

- Take a minimum of 3 hours (with at least 150 m [490 ft] of elevation gain) and a maximum of 12 hours.

- Require no more than Class 3 scrambling. (In the Yosemite Decimal System, Class 1 denotes foot travel; Class 2 involves some use of hands; Class 3 entails easier climbing that's typically tackled unroped; Class 4 indicates steeper, more exposed climbing, where a belay is recommended; and Class 5 applies to technical climbing on vertical or nearly vertical rock.)

Every hike is accompanied by a Stop of Interest to add value to your trip. Ranging from birding hot spots and hidden waterfalls to museums of local culture and historic sites, these are recommended side quests in the vicinity or on the road to the trailhead. (For a full list, see the Stops of Interest appendix.)

I've hiked every trail in the book, and I've striven for accuracy in my descriptions. However, little is static in the backcountry. Conditions vary depending on the weather, time of day, season, and year. Trails are rerouted, bridges get washed away, logging obliterates paths, signs fade, markers disappear, and roads are deactivated.

It doesn't help that B.C.'s provincial parks are starved of funding, short on rangers, and threatened by boundary amendments from time to time. Established in 1995, Pinecone Burke Provincial Park still lacks trailhead parking lots and toilets, and proper signage. Trail maintenance in Golden Ears Provincial Park is largely thanks to the tireless efforts of Ridge Meadows Outdoor Club volunteers. The Canadian Parks and Wilderness Society and the Federation of Mountain Clubs of B.C. are advocating for increases to base funding and rangers at B.C. Parks.

Semaphore Lakes (Hike 15), Eaton Lake (Hike 31), and Ghostpass Lake (Hike 36) deserve to be permanently preserved as wild places. For years, conservation and recreation organizations, including the Wilderness Committee, have sought the protection of the Silverdaisy "donut hole" surrounded by

E.C. Manning and Skagit Valley Provincial Parks; those efforts resulted in a halt to logging in 2019. The Lummi Nation, Upper Similkameen Band, Upper Skagit Tribe, and other Indigenous governments on both sides of the Canada-U.S. border have declared their opposition to mining and logging in the headwaters of the Skagit River.

Like many a guidebook author before me, I hope that your enjoyment of the outdoors will propel you to speak out in support of our parks—present and future. Please share any trail and access updates, as well as your feedback on this guide, via *105hikes.com*. Now take a hike!

SAFETY MATTERS

YOU'VE SEEN THIS news story before. A lost or injured hiker is stuck in the backcountry after dark. The call comes in to 911. Search-and-rescue volunteers spring into action and bring the hiker out. Experts dispense safety tips. The online mob has a field day at the rescued hiker's expense, regardless of the facts.

Yes, there's no shortage of unprepared and ill-equipped hikers on the trails. However, let's not kid ourselves. Regardless of skill or experience, all of us have the potential to be the subject of a search-and-rescue incident. Fortunately, you can do much to prevent disaster and increase your chances of survival should you get into trouble.

CARRY THE 10 ESSENTIALS:
1. *Navigation* (map, compass, GPS)
2. *Headlamp* (extra batteries)
3. *Sun protection* (sunglasses, sunscreen)
4. *First aid* (bandages, blister pads)
5. *Knife* (repair kit, duct tape)
6. *Fire* (waterproof matches, lighter)
7. *Shelter* (tent, emergency blanket)
8. *Extra food* (energy bars, trail mix)
9. *Extra water* (purifier)
10. *Extra clothes* (rain gear, insulating layers)

Leave a trip plan: Before you go hiking, inform a reliable person of your destination, route, equipment, and expected return time—to help search-and-rescue teams find you in the event of an emergency.

A warning on the Statlu Lake Trail.

Consult road and trail reports: B.C. Parks posts updates on road and trail conditions on provincial park websites. The U.S. Forest Service does the same for national forests, as does the National Park Service for North Cascades National Park. Trip reports posted on hiking websites, such as the Washington Trails Association's, may also offer useful observations about conditions.

Check the avalanche forecast: During the snow season, Avalanche Canada and the Northwest Avalanche Center issue bulletins for B.C. and Washington, respectively. If venturing into avalanche terrain, everyone in your party should have the three avalanche essentials—a transceiver, probe, and shovel—and know how to use them.

Note sunset time: It's easy to get lost or injured in the dark, even with a headlamp. Set a safe turnaround time and stick to it.

Bring bear spray: This is bear country. Pepper spray is considered the best deterrent against an aggressive black or grizzly bear. (Use bearproof canisters to store food and other wildlife attractants 100 m [110 yd] away from campsites.)

Hike with a group: Stay together to reduce the likelihood of getting lost. Groups of three or more are less likely to be attacked by a bear.

Save the cellphone for emergencies: Most of these hikes go out of cellphone range. Unless you carry a personal locator beacon or satellite messenger, however, you'll probably need to seek reception and call for help in an emergency. Keeping your cellphone warm, dry, and powered off helps ensure you have enough battery life to make the all-important call.

GET INFORMED

AdventureSmart
adventuresmart.ca

Avalanche Canada
avalanche.ca

B.C. Search and Rescue Association
bcsara.com

Federation of Mountain Clubs of B.C.
mountainclubs.org

Leave No Trace Center for Outdoor Ethics
lnt.org

Northwest Avalanche Center
nwac.us

Washington Trails Association
wta.org

OUTDOOR ETHICS

SUBALPINE MEADOWS TRAMPLED by careless feet. Graffiti carved in rock and trees. Campsites littered with toilet paper. Off-leash dogs fouling water and disturbing wildlife. Conservation officers being forced to kill problem bears.

These are but a few of the consequences of irresponsible behaviour in the outdoors. Let's agree to try our best not to spoil the backcountry for wildlife—and our fellow humans. Pack it in, pack it out. A little knowledge of outdoor ethics and etiquette goes a long way.

LEARN THE SEVEN PRINCIPLES OF LEAVE NO TRACE:
1. *Plan ahead and prepare*
2. *Travel and camp on durable surfaces*
3. *Dispose of waste properly*
4. *Leave what you find*
5. *Minimize campfire impacts*
6. *Respect wildlife*
7. *Be considerate of other visitors*

Respect the posted regulations: These rules are in place to safeguard the natural and cultural values of protected areas. Adhere to fire bans. Drones, mushroom picking, smoking, and vaping are prohibited in the backcountry of provincial parks.

Use toilets where available: Where facilities don't exist, bury poop and toilet tissue in a cat hole 15–20 cm (6–8 in) deep and 70 adult paces away from water, trails, and campsites. Don't bury tampons. In some places, it's mandatory to pack out poop and toilet paper.

Never feed or approach wildlife: You've heard the old maxim: "A fed bear is a dead bear." The same is true of cougars, coyotes, and other wild animals

Minimum impact tips at Elsay Lake.

that become habituated to people.

Keep dogs on leash (or at home): Even on leash, dogs disrupt the natural patterns of wildlife. Off-leash dogs can harass, injure, and kill wild animals. B.C. Parks discourages taking dogs into the backcountry due to the potential for conflicts with wildlife, including bears. Dogs must be leashed in many provincial parks, and are prohibited in Garibaldi Provincial Park and most of North Cascades National Park. Pack out dog poop; don't leave it in plastic bags along the trail.

Stick to established trails: Stay on designated trails to avoid damaging sensitive environments, such as slow-growing subalpine meadows. Shortcutting switchbacks degrades trails, soil, and vegetation. Respect restoration area closures.

Avoid hiking in large groups: In the U.S., regulations limit the size of parties to 12 in wilderness areas. Consider this a general rule for the backcountry. Large groups are more likely to disturb wildlife and cause environmental damage.

Be inclusive: Everyone should feel welcome in the outdoors, but that's not always the case, especially for marginalized people. In 2018, outdoor retailer Mountain Equipment Co-operative (MEC) took responsibility for decades of marketing that "perpetuated the vastly incorrect notion that people of colour in Canada don't ski, hike, climb, or camp." Fat Girls Hiking, which has chapters in Vancouver and Seattle, is an organization taking on body-shaming and social stigma in the backcountry. Are you an ally?

Yield to other trail users: Let faster parties pass. On narrow paths, downhill hikers should step aside for those travelling uphill. On multi-use trails, mountain bikers yield to hikers and both give way to horse riders. However, it's often easier—and courteous—for hikers to step aside for bikers too.

Use headphones for music: Just because you're listening to Taylor Swift doesn't mean everyone else has to as well. Respect the outdoor experiences of other hikers, who may—shockingly—prefer to hear the sounds of nature.

HOW TO USE THIS GUIDE

THE 55 HIKES in this book are categorized by regions north, east, west, and south of Vancouver and arranged by distance from the city. Each numbered trip comes with feature icons, statistics and ratings, hiking and driving directions, a topographic map, photographs, and a Stop of Interest. Where available, I've included public transit options. (Note: Trails are not described in winter conditions.)

For kid-friendly recommendations and trails good most of the year (without snowshoes or traction aids), consult the Hikes at a Glance table. Statistics are compiled in the Hikes by the Numbers appendix. What follows are explanations of the feature icons, statistics, and ratings used in this guide.

FEATURES

Every hike has its particular rewards. Icons draw your attention to the special features of each numbered trip.

 Waterfalls: Water plunges or cascades over a steep drop, visible from the trail or a viewpoint.

 Big trees: Old-growth trees exhibit impressive diameter or height.

 Wildflowers: Alpine or subalpine meadows produce colourful blooms seasonally.

 Swimming: The hike begins, passes, or ends at a lake or other swimming hole.

 Coastal views: The hike offers vistas of the Salish Sea—comprising the Strait of Georgia, Juan de Fuca Strait, and Puget Sound.

Mountain views: The hike offers vistas of the Coast Mountains, Cascade Range, or Vancouver Island Ranges.

 History: Historical or heritage aspects add value to the hike.

 Geology: The landscape exposes interesting geological processes or phenomena.

STATISTICS

Distance: The length of the hike as described is provided in metric and imperial units.

Time: Everyone hikes at their own pace. Once you've completed several of the hikes in the book, you'll get an idea of how your times compare to the estimates listed. I've indicated whether a given time (and distance) refers to an out-and-back trip or a loop, lollipop, circuit, etc. The estimates include enough time for an average hiker to take short breaks for snacks, lunch, and viewpoints.

Elevation gain: The net elevation gain is simply the difference between the highest and lowest points encountered on the hike. Although both metric and imperial elevations are noted in the text, the maps show contour lines in metric only.

High point: This statistic represents the highest elevation above mean sea level attained on the hike—often, but not always, a summit.

Maps: The small maps in this guide are no substitute for large, printed maps. For each hike, the relevant map sheets from Natural Resources Canada's National Topographic System (NTS) or the U.S. Geological Survey (USGS) are noted, as are other recommended topo maps.

Trailhead: The geographic position of the start of the hike is given in degrees, minutes, and seconds using the World Geodetic System 1984 (WGS84) datum. The trailhead is often, but not necessarily, near the parking area.

RATINGS

This book and the companion volume, *105 Hikes In and Around Southwestern British Columbia*, share the same rating system for difficulty. A "best quality" star ★ indicates a given hike is among the most scenic and satisfying experiences in the book. Both the difficulty and quality ratings are inherently subjective, but might help you select the right trip for a given day.

The Wedgemount Glacier behind Wedgemount Lake.

● **Easy:** Minimal distance and elevation gain on well-marked trails.

■ **Moderate:** A workout with decent distance and/or elevation gain on reasonably obvious paths.

◆ **Difficult:** Strenuous due to large distance and/or elevation gain, some route-finding challenges, and/or easy scrambling with little exposure.

◆◆ **Advanced:** Extremely demanding with tricky route-finding, substantial off-trail travel, and/or exposed scrambling—for experienced parties only.

KEY TO MAP SYMBOLS

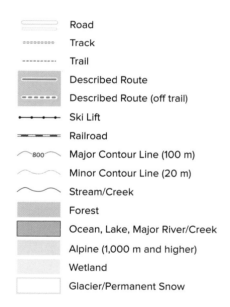

P Parking

Toilet

Camping

Waterfall

Viewpoint

Ferry Dock

Bus Stop

Backcountry Hut

Chalet/Lodge

4WD 4 Wheel Drive Road

⚠ Warning

No Entry/Restricted Access

99 Primary Highway

▲ Mountain Peak

→ Direction of Travel/ Off-Map Destination

Road

Track

Trail

Described Route

Described Route (off trail)

Ski Lift

Railroad

800 Major Contour Line (100 m)

Minor Contour Line (20 m)

Stream/Creek

Forest

Ocean, Lake, Major River/Creek

Alpine (1,000 m and higher)

Wetland

Glacier/Permanent Snow

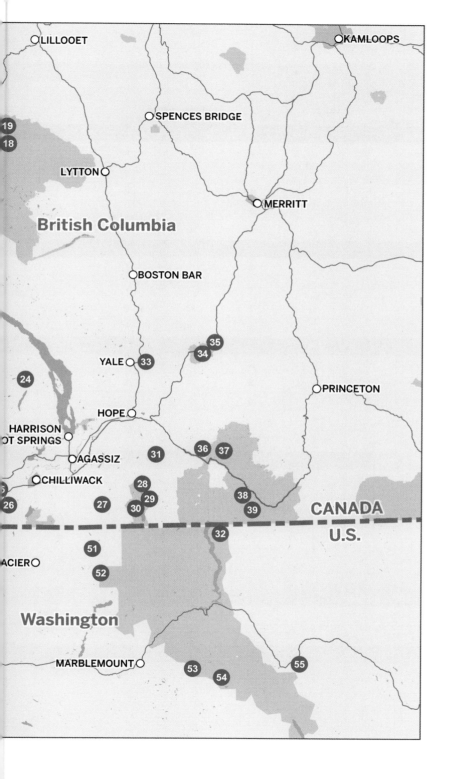

Hike	Best Quality	Difficulty	Waterfalls	Big Trees	Wildflowers
HIKES NORTH OF VANCOUVER					
North Shore					
1. Elsay Lake		◆		●	
2. South Needle		◆		●	
3. Kennedy Falls		■	●	●	
4. Dam Mountain		■			
5. Twin Sisters (The Lions)	★	◆◆	●		
Squamish					
6. Petgill Lake		■			
7. Slhánaẏ		◆			
8. Echo Lake	★	◆	●	●	
9. Crooked Falls		◆	●	●	
Whistler					
10. Helm Lake	★	■		●	●
11. Cheakamus Lake	★	●		●	
12. Singing Pass		■			●
13. Decker Mountain	★	◆◆			●
14. Wedgemount Lake	★	◆	●		●
Pemberton					
15. Semaphore Lakes	★	■	●		●
16. Marriott Basin	★	◆◆			●
17. Blowdown Pass		■			●
18. Gotcha Peak	★	◆◆			●
19. Gott Peak	★	◆			●
HIKES EAST OF VANCOUVER					
Port Moody and Coquitlam					
20. Diez Vistas Trail		■			
21. Dennett Lake		◆	●		
Maple Ridge to Harrison Hot Springs					
22. East Canyon Trail		■		●	

Swimming	Coastal Views	Mountain Views	History	Geology	Kid-Friendly	Good Most of the Year	✓
•	•	•					
	•	•					
			•		•	•	
	•	•					
	•	•	•	•			
•	•	•		•		•	
	•	•		•		•	
•		•		•			
		•				•	
•		•		•			
•					•		
				•	•		
		•					
•		•		•			
•		•					
•		•					
•		•			•		
•		•					
•		•		•			
•	•	•	•			•	
•			•				
•		•			•	•	

Hike	Best Quality	Difficulty	Waterfalls	Big Trees	Wildflowers
23. Mount Nutt Viewpoints		■			
24. Statlu Lake	★	◆	●	●	
Abbotsford					
25. Chadsey Lake		■	●		
26. Taggart Peak		■			
Chilliwack					
27. Pierce Lake		◆		●	●
28. Greendrop Lake	★	■	●		
29. Flora Pass	★	■			●
30. Radium Lake		■		●	●
Hope and Fraser Canyon					
31. Eaton Lake		■	●	●	
32. Hozomeen Lake	★	●			
33. Mount Lincoln		■			
Coquihalla Pass					
34. Yak Peak	★	◆			●
35. Zoa Peak	★	■			●
E.C. Manning Provincial Park					
36. Ghostpass Lake		◆◆	●	●	
37. Punch Bowl Pass		■		●	●
38. Poland Lake		●			●
39. Derek Falls		●	●		●
HIKES WEST OF VANCOUVER					
Howe Sound and Sunshine Coast					
40. Mount Killam		■		●	
41. Mount Elphinstone		■	●	●	
42. Mount Hallowell		■	●		
Gulf Islands					
43. Mount Galiano	★	■			
44. Bodega Ridge	★	●			

Swimming	Coastal Views	Mountain Views	History	Geology	Kid-Friendly	Good Most of the Year	✓
		●					
●		●					
●					●	●	
		●				●	
●		●					
●		●			●		
		●					
●		●					
●		●			●		
●		●	●		●		
		●	●			●	
		●		●			
		●			●		
●			●				
		●	●				
●		●			●		
		●			●		
●	●	●				●	
	●	●					
	●	●	●				
●	●	●	●	●	●	●	
	●	●		●		●	

Hike	Best Quality	Difficulty	Waterfalls	Big Trees	Wildflowers
Nanaimo					
45. Extension Ridge		●	●		
46. Mount Benson		■			
HIKES SOUTH OF VANCOUVER					
Bellingham					
47. Lookout Mountain		●	●		
48. Lost Lake		●	●	●	
49. Chuckanut Ridge		■		●	
50. North Butte		■			
Mount Baker Wilderness					
51. Welcome Pass	★	■			●
52. Lake Ann	★	■	●		●
Cascade River to Washington Pass					
53. Hidden Lake Lookout	★	◆			●
54. Cascade Pass	★	■	●		●
55. Blue Lake	★	●			●

Swimming	Coastal Views	Mountain Views	History	Geology	Kid-Friendly	Good Most of the Year	✓
•	•		•	•	•	•	
•	•	•	•			•	
	•				•	•	
•			•	•	•	•	
	•	•	•	•		•	
•	•	•	•	•	•	•	
		•					
•		•		•	•		
		•	•	•			
		•	•	•	•		
•		•	•	•	•		

ELSAY LAKE

A secluded swimming hole worth sweating for

Distance: 18 km (11.2 mi)
Time: 10.5 hours (out and back)
Elevation gain: 610 m (2,000 ft)
High point: 1,260 m (4,130 ft)

Difficulty: ♦
Maps: NTS 92-G/7 Port Coquitlam; Trail Ventures BC North Shore
Trailhead: 49°22'03" N, 122°56'57" W

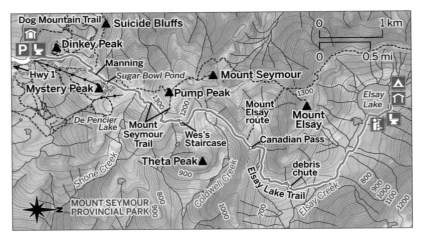

DOWN FOR a daunting challenge? The strenuous hike to Elsay Lake, in the territories of the Musqueam, Squamish, and Tsleil-Waututh First Nations, will test your mettle. A marvellously rugged affair with plenty of boulder fields and abrupt elevation changes, the Elsay Lake Trail (best hiked late June to October) starts out higher than its objective, meaning you'll save most of the climbing for the way back. Tackled more often by backpackers than day hikers, the trail grants access to the wild backcountry and big trees of Mount Seymour Provincial Park and a swim in the remote bowl guarded by Mount Elsay and Mount Bishop. This trip is for experienced hikers only.

GETTING THERE
Vehicle: On Trans-Canada Highway 1 in North Vancouver, north of Iron-workers Memorial Second Narrows Crossing, take Exit 21 (eastbound) or 22B

Mount Elsay towers over Elsay Lake.

(westbound). Head east on Mount Seymour Parkway. In 4.3 km (2.7 mi), turn left on Mount Seymour Road. Drive 13 km (8.1 mi) up to the ski area in Mount Seymour Provincial Park. Winter tires or chains required October to March. Park as close as you can to the top (toilet available). (Use Parking Lot 2 for overnight trips. The gate beyond is closed from dusk till dawn.)

THE HIKE

From the B.C. Parks kiosk at the top of Parking Lot 4 (1,067 m/3,500 ft), set off north on the well-trafficked Mount Seymour Trail, left of the Manning ski run and Mystery Peak Express chairlift. Go by the memorial to North Shore Rescue team leader Tim Jones (1956–2014). Ignore leftward turnoffs for Dog Mountain, Dinkey Peak, and First Lake. Turn left to merge with the ski run below the top of Mystery Peak. Shortly thereafter, exit to the left and drop to Sugar Bowl Pond. The trail passes Brockton Point, then swings east of Pump Peak.

One hour in, reach a signed junction (49°23′10″ N, 122°56′10″ W) at the Mount Seymour Trail's 2.6-km (1.6-mi) mark. Go right for the Elsay Lake Trail. In winter, this rough trail (adopted by the Vancouver Korean Hiking Club) is closed due to extreme avalanche hazard. Plunge down Wes's Staircase along a rockslide—following orange markers on trees, small cairns with flagging tape, and old paint splashes and faded arrows on boulders.

A half-hour from the junction, start a descending traverse of the wide bowl containing the headwaters of Coldwell Creek. With the cliffs of Pump

The B.C. Parks shelter at Elsay Lake.

Peak, Tim Jones Peak (ewəyəɬəm in hən̓q̓əmin̓əm̓, the language of the Tsleil-Waututh Nation), Mount Seymour, and Runner Peak looming above, cross three steep boulder fields separated by trees. Spot American pikas and dark-eyed juncos lurking, and fireweed, green false hellebore, and pink monkey-flower blooming.

After 1 hour on the Elsay Lake Trail, make an ascending traverse of a fourth boulder field with smaller rocks. Back in the trees, pass a big old-growth fir. The first large orange diamond on the left indicates the easy-to-miss turnoff for the Mount Elsay route (49°23′53″ N, 122°55′48″ W). Stick with the Elsay Lake Trail, however, through Canadian Pass. Descend to cross the south fork of Elsay Creek. From a small lake to the left, the rockslide leading to the Mount Elsay–Runner Peak col is visible.

The increasingly muddy trail bears right and downstream. A cornucopia of mushrooms—Cascade russula, violet cort, woolly chanterelle, etc.—adorn the forest floor. Pass a large cedar and score vistas of Indian Arm (Sḵlilutulh to the Squamish Nation, Tsleil-Wat to the Tsleil-Waututh) as the trail goes round the east flank of Mount Elsay. Make an awkward descending traverse of a boulder patch. On the far side, exit to the left following ribbons. The sometimes-overgrown path negotiates more boulders as it enters the main Elsay Creek valley.

Three-and-a-half hours from the parking lot, the trail meets a narrow debris chute and plummets straight down it. Cairns and flagging mark the sequel to Wes's Staircase. Below, a blue sign for Elsay Lake (2.1 km/1.3 mi away) welcomes you back to the woods near the low point of the hike. The undulating, root-infested path turns up-valley in the lush forest, passing through devil's club, encountering a big fir, and pulling alongside the wide channel of Elsay Creek. Beware of wasps.

Beyond the Elsay Lake Trail's 5.5-km (3.4-mi) marker, switch to river left on boulders, if it's safe to do so, heeding markers on the opposite bank. (River directions are given from the perspective of looking downstream.) Cross a few tributaries and follow planks over a wetland to reach the muddy shore of Elsay Lake (750 m/2,460 ft). Mount Elsay rises precipitously to the south, its summit fortified by cliffs. The Episcopal Bumps (Rector, Curate, and Vicar peaks) stand west across the big lake.

Continue right along the shore for 500 m (0.3 mi), passing an outhouse, using a log crossing, and encountering massive blowdowns. Finally, arrive at the musty A-frame shelter (49°25′08″ N, 122°56′16″ W) maintained by B.C. Parks, after 5 hours of hiking (longer with overnight gear). A folding table, rusty chairs, and locked storage chests line the main floor, while a ladder provides access to the narrow loft. It's preferable to pitch a tent nearby. Sit on the porch or cool off in the lake before tackling the 5-hour, 9-km (5.6-mi) uphill journey back to the trailhead via the debris chute and Wes's Staircase.

Bikes, drones, fires, hunting, smoking, vaping, and flower and mushroom picking are prohibited on the Elsay Lake Trail. Camping is allowed north of Brockton Point. Dogs must be leashed; however, B.C. Parks advises that pets are "not suitable" for the backcountry due to wildlife concerns. Make sure to carry plenty of water. Pack it in, pack it out.

STOP OF INTEREST
CATES PARK/WHEY-AH-WICHEN

Located at Roche Point on Burrard Inlet, Whey-ah-Wichen (həṅq̓əmiṅəṁ for "facing the wind") is an ancestral village site of the Tsleil-Waututh Nation. Today, Cates Park is cooperatively managed by the Tsleil-Waututh and the District of North Vancouver, and home to a First Nations dugout canoe race every July. Explore the remains of the old Dollar Mill's waste burner, look across the water to Burnaby Mountain (Lhuḵw'lhuḵw'áyten to the Squamish Nation), and spot great blue herons and pelagic cormorants from the beach (no dogs allowed). Find the park entrance on Dollarton Highway, 5.3 km (3.3 mi) east of Trans-Canada Highway 1.

SOUTH NEEDLE

Thread your way to solitude on the summit

Distance: 18 km (11.2 mi)
Time: 8 hours (reverse lollipop)
Elevation gain: 1,060 m (3,480 ft)
High point: 1,163 m (3,820 ft)

Difficulty: ◆
Maps: NTS 92-G/6, 92-G/7; Trail Ventures BC North Shore
Trailhead: 49°21'01" N, 123°00'52" W

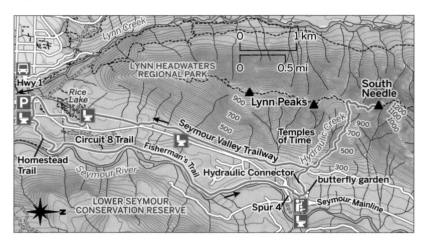

THE NEEDLES consist of three peaks on the Seymour River–Lynn Creek divide, which is best known for the Lynn Peak Lookout, a bustling workout hike. A visit to the relatively remote South Needle may beckon experienced hikers with its promise of solitude, big trees, and panoramic views. Although a rough route extends north along the ridge from the lookout, the South Needle is best accessed via Hydraulic Creek in the Lower Seymour Conservation Reserve. The Middle and North Needles entail serious scrambling and bushwhacking; neither of those objectives are described in this guide.

GETTING THERE

Transit: Take TransLink Bus 209, 210 (Upper Lynn Valley), or 228 (Lynn Valley) to Underwood Avenue at Evelyn Street. Walk east via Evelyn Park and Evelyn Street. Cross Lynn Valley Road, staying outside of the Lynn

Headwaters Regional Park gate. Descend Rice Lake Road, cross Pipeline Bridge, keep left, and ascend the wide gravel path to reach the Rice Lake gate and parking lot in 800 m (0.5 mi).

Vehicle: Westbound on Trans-Canada Highway 1 in North Vancouver, north of Ironworkers Memorial Second Narrows Crossing, take Exit 23B. Head east on Main Street, which becomes Dollarton Highway. Turn left on Riverside Drive, left on Mount Seymour Parkway, and right on Lillooet Road. (Eastbound on Highway 1, take Exit 21, go left on Keith Road, and turn left onto Lillooet.) Drive 4.8 km (3 mi) farther, following Lillooet left at the Monashee Drive intersection and through the Lower Seymour Con-

Lynn Peaks and Burrard Inlet (Tsleil-Wat) from the summit cairn.

servation Reserve gate, and fork right at road's end for the main parking lot (toilet available). The gate is open between 6 a.m. and 9 p.m. from May to August, and closes as early as 5 p.m. in winter.

THE HIKE

To scale the South Needle, one must travel up the valley of the Seymour River (Ch'ích'elxwi7ḵw Stáḵw to the Squamish Nation, Jol-gul-hook to the Tsleil-Waututh Nation) to the base of the mountain. On foot, head east on the gravel trail behind the kiosk next to the washrooms. In short order, fork left for the bike-free Homestead Trail (1.2 km/0.7 mi) and descend amid tall Douglas-firs. After 15 minutes, hang a left on the Fisherman's Trail (5.1 km/3.2 mi), go through the gate (no dogs beyond this point), and continue upstream on the flat gravel road.

With the river on your right, pass the Circuit 8 Trail turnoff, and cross a debris flow channel and a couple of concrete bridges. The eroding escarpment looming left of the trail poses a high risk for slides. Salmonberries, skunk cabbage, and Steller's jays are common sights, as are cyclists and joggers. The river remains closed to salmon fishing in the wake of the 2014 Seymour Canyon rockslide downstream.

Lynn Peaks, Lynn Creek (Kan-ul-cha), and Mount Fromme from the summit.

Eventually, the trail rises to cross the Spur 4 road and pass through a few speed-control gates. Follow a gravel road left to arrive at the Mid Valley lookout, after an hour on Fisherman's. Two Adirondack chairs face Dog Mountain, an open shelter (a legacy of the 2005 superhero film *Elektra*) offers a reprieve from wet weather, and an outhouse awaits your deposit. Spot the Hydraulic Connector (800 m/0.5 mi) across the Seymour Mainline, and follow signs west to the Hydraulic picnic area, 15 minutes away. On the way, detour right to visit the butterfly garden, planted on a site used by the Royal Canadian Mounted Police for bomb disposal until 1991.

Emerge on the Seymour Valley Trailway, after 1.5 hours of easy hiking. (Alternatively, cycling this paved path cuts the approach time to 30 minutes.) Across it, find the start of the decidedly steep and rough route up the mountainside, on the north side of Hydraulic Creek (250 m/820 ft; 49°23'39" N, 122°59'54" W). The path sets off northwest through salmonberry bushes and mossy woods—unmarked at first, then confirmed by yellow squares.

In 10 minutes, a few pink ribbons with faded writing affixed to a snag indicate the leftward turnoff for the Temples of Time grove. Its vanishing trails and elusive old-growth giants are better left for another day. So don't hop the creek; continue tackling the relentless incline, chasing orange flagging in the dappled light. Cross a small debris flow channel with a huge western red cedar on the far side. Devil's club and red elderberry grow in the understory, and bunchberry on the forest floor. As you near the crest of Lynn Ridge, the grade eases and the canopy opens.

Reach a three-way junction (49°24′01″ N, 123°00′56″ W), 2 hours from the Hydraulic Creek bridge, and turn right (north) for the South Needle, less than 1 hour away. Admire the amabilis firs. You'll need to use your hands and watch your footing during the scrambly ascent. Sidehill around the penultimate bump. Follow the spine of the rocky ridge—side paths lead to cliffs—earning views down both sides. A cairn marks the open summit (49°24′19″ N, 123°00′52″ W), 3 hours up (2.6 km/1.6 mi) from the Seymour Valley Trailway.

The Middle Needle dominates the northern scene. To the south, survey the pair of knolls officially named Lynn Peaks, bald eagles soaring over the valleys of the Seymour River and Lynn Creek (X̱a7élcha Swa7lt to the Squamish, Kan-ul-cha to the Tsleil-Waututh), Burrard Inlet (Slíl̓utulh to the Squamish, Tsleil-Wat to the Tsleil-Waututh), Vancouver, and the Salish Sea. Mount Fromme, Grouse Mountain (Mumtem in the Sḵwx̱wú7mesh language), Dam Mountain (Hike 4), Goat Mountain, and Crown Mountain rise to the west. Mount Elsay, Runner Peak, and Mount Seymour lie due east, in the Fannin Range.

Retrace your steps to the Hydraulic Creek bridge. An hour's walk (5.7 km/3.5 mi) on the Seymour Valley Trailway returns you to the Rice Lake gate and parking lot.

Formerly known as the Seymour Demonstration Forest, the Lower Seymour Conservation Reserve lies in the territories of the Musqueam, Squamish, and Tsleil-Waututh First Nations, and downstream of Seymour Lake, a drinking water reservoir. No camping, fires, or smoking. Beware of bears and cougars, and make sure to carry sufficient water as the ridge is dry.

STOP OF INTEREST
MAPLEWOOD FLATS

The Conservation Area at Maplewood Flats (2649 Dollarton Highway) in North Vancouver is a birding hot spot known as St'itsma to the Squamish Nation and Squatzi to the Tsleil-Waututh Nation. Managed by the Wild Bird Trust of B.C., the wildlife sanctuary protects intertidal mud flat, salt- and freshwater marsh, meadow, and forest habitats. Stroll wheelchair-accessible trails, visit the Coast Salish plant nursery, and keep your eyes peeled for ospreys and barred owls, as well as black bears, Columbian black-tailed deer, northern river otters, ochre sea stars, and Pacific tree frogs. (Dogs must be leashed and are not permitted beyond the Westcoast Bridge.)

KENNEDY FALLS

First stop: a giant western red cedar

Distance: 10 km (6.2 mi)
Time: 5 hours (out and back)
Elevation gain: 140 m (460 ft)
High point: 450 m (1,480 ft)

Difficulty: ■
Maps: NTS 92-G/6 North Vancouver;
Trail Ventures BC North Shore
Trailhead: 49°21'35" N, 123°02'08" W

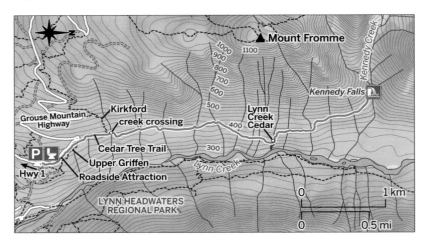

FORMERLY KNOWN as Timber Mountain and Dome Mountain, Mount Fromme is the centre of the local mountain-biking universe and lies in the territories of the Musqueam, Squamish, and Tsleil-Waututh First Nations. Due east of higher-profile Grouse Mountain (Mumtem in the Skwxwú7mesh language), Fromme is also worthy of hikers' interest. One destination particularly suited to shoulder season is Kennedy Falls. If a misty waterfall isn't enough of an enticement, perhaps a gargantuan western red cedar will do the trick. Keep an eye out for relics of Lynn Valley's logging past too. Settlers didn't call this area Shaketown for nothing.

GETTING THERE
Transit: Take TransLink Bus 210 (Upper Lynn Valley) to McNair Drive at Tourney Road. Walk southwest on McNair, then north on Mountain Highway (1 km/0.6 mi).

Kennedy Falls in autumn.

Vehicle: On Trans-Canada Highway 1 in North Vancouver, take Exit 21 and go north on Mountain Highway. Or, from Exit 19, head north on Lynn Valley Road and turn left onto Mountain Highway. Drive 2.5 km (1.6 mi) farther to the top, and pull into the Mount Fromme parking lot (toilet available). Check the posted opening and closing times for the gate. (Alternatively, find a legal parking spot below Coleman Street and walk up.)

THE HIKE

From the parking lot, head past the water towers, bike-wash station, interpretative panels, and gate onto the old Grouse Mountain Highway, which opened as a toll road in 1926. (One panel highlights a hiking map published by the B.C. Electric Railway Company in 1934.) Immediately, spot an entrance to the Roadside Attraction trail on the right. Bear left on the multi-use path, paralleling the gravel service road for 10 minutes. Pass the entrance to Upper Griffen, and go right on the Cedar Tree Trail and proceed north. In short order, the Kirkford mountain-bike path strikes off to the left, but you stick with Cedar (hiking-only beyond this point).

Although it enters Lynn Headwaters Regional Park, a sign warns that the trail is unofficial, unmaintained, unpatrolled, and lacking in cellphone coverage. The upcoming creek crossing may stop you in your tracks. At times of heavy rain or snowmelt, the stream can be a raging torrent, making it too dangerous to continue. Ignore various side paths until the trail drops to the right, passing a huge stump with a hollow core. Quaint sections of corduroy road

The Lynn Creek Cedar is likely over 600 years old.

call attention to the history of logging in the area. Horses and oxen towed timber out of the woods on greased skid roads.

A fixed rope helps with the steep descent to a creek crossing upstream of a cascade. Traverse two debris channels in quick succession and negotiate a particularly muddy section. Red-belted polypore and orange jelly are two species of fungi whose fruiting bodies are commonly seen in these coniferous woods.

After 1.5 hours (3.3 km/ 2.1 mi) of hiking, come face to trunk with one of the largest old-growth survivors in the Lower Mainland. As conservationist Randy Stoltmann (see Hike 9) noted in his classic *Hiking Guide to the Big Trees of Southwestern British Columbia*, estimates peg the majestic Lynn Creek Cedar (49°23'03" N, 123°02'21" W) at over 600 years old, 4 m (13 ft) in diameter, and 55 m (180 ft) tall. Elsewhere in Lynn Valley, a Douglas-fir felled in 1902 is touted as a contender for the title of tallest tree ever, with a supposed height of 126 m (415 ft).

Tree hunters may opt to turn around at this point. Falls baggers should head uphill to the left on the well-marked trail. Continue north onto a wide corduroy road. To the east, Lynn Creek (X̱a7élcha Swa7lt to the Squamish Nation, Kan-ul-cha to the Tsleil-Waututh Nation) is audible in the second-growth. Cross a large debris channel. To the right, spy The Needles (Hike 2) and Lynn Peaks through the trees.

As the waterfall comes within earshot, the trail turns upstream and enters the canyon of Kennedy Creek. Cross the final debris channel to arrive at the base of Kennedy Falls (49°23'41" N, 123°02'51" W), 50 minutes (1.7 km/ 1.1 mi) beyond the big cedar. Enjoy the sight of the shadowy, segmented cascade, but watch your step on the slippery rock. Return the way you came.

Camping, fires, and smoking are prohibited in Lynn Headwaters Regional Park. Dogs must be leashed, and human companions must pick up their poop. Black bears and cougars roam here.

LYNN CANYON ECOLOGY CENTRE

Located down-valley from Kennedy Falls, the Lynn Canyon Ecology Centre (3663 Park Road) is loved by kids and adults alike. Opened in 1971 and operated by the District of North Vancouver, the mini museum features informative exhibits about local history, native flora and fauna, forest management, water pollution, the global climate emergency, and more. According to one display, American dippers, black-tailed deer, coastal tailed frogs, and northern flying squirrels are among the animals living in surrounding Lynn Canyon Park (also home to a 50-m [160-ft] high suspension bridge). Stop by, pick up a bird checklist, listen to black bear sounds, learn about the path to decarbonization, and check out the pollinator garden outside. The museum is open daily (except for statutory holidays October to May), and admission is by donation. Find the park entrance at the east end of Peters Road via Lynn Valley Road.

DAM MOUNTAIN

After the Grouse Grind, keep going for superb city views

Distance: 12 km (7.5 mi)
Time: 5 hours (circuit)
Elevation gain: 1,075 m (3,530 ft)
High point: 1,349 m (4,430 ft)

Difficulty: ■
Maps: NTS 92-G/6 North Vancouver;
Trail Ventures BC North Shore
Trailhead: 49°22'16" N, 123°05'54" W

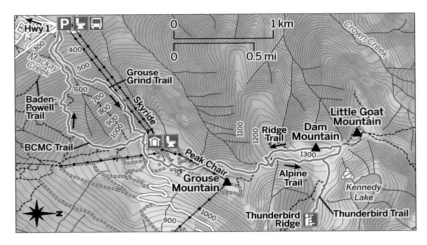

CREATED IN 2017, Grouse Mountain Regional Park's raison d'être is a pair of super-steep and trendy workouts: the Grouse Grind Trail and B.C. Mountaineering Club (BCMC) Trail. For serious hikers, though, either path is simply a means to get up to the ski area without paying for the Skyride aerial tram. The better hiking lies beyond Grouse Mountain (Mumtem in the Skwxwú7mesh language) in Lynn Headwaters Regional Park. A tour of Thunderbird Ridge and Dam Mountain offers a quick sampling of the backcountry's bird sightings and panoramic views.

GETTING THERE
Transit: Take TransLink Bus 232, 236 (Grouse Mountain), or 247 (Upper Capilano) to the Grouse Mountain Skyride's base station. (In summer, the Grouse Mountain resort runs a free shuttle daily to and from Canada Place in downtown Vancouver.)

Crown Mountain and The Camel from Dam Mountain.

A raven on the summit of Dam Mountain.

Vehicle: On Trans-Canada Highway 1 in North Vancouver, take Exit 14. Head north on Capilano Road, which becomes Nancy Greene Way. Arrive at the pay parking lots (toilet and electric vehicle charging station available) at the base of the Grouse Mountain resort (6400 Nancy Greene Way), 4.5 km (2.8 mi) from the highway.

THE HIKE

Don't be fooled by the fashion show at the trailhead (274 m/900 ft). Flip-flops are not suitable footwear for the plunging slopes of Grouse Mountain. Bring plenty of food and water—and, to be safe, the rest of the 10 essentials. Amplified music is not allowed nor considerate of others; put those head-phones on.

Go through the gate (closed at night and most of the winter), being mind-ful of sunset time. Follow the crowd left onto the viewless Grouse Grind. (The Baden-Powell Trail forks right and provides access to the BCMC Trail.) Skirt-ing the headwaters of Mackay Creek (ƛ̓ələmə́lqəʔ to the Musqueam Nation, Tl'alhema7elks to the Squamish Nation), gain 853 m (2,800 ft) of elevation over 2.5 km (1.6 mi), with the help of some 2,830 stairs and no shortage of progress markers. On average, it takes 1.5 hours to reach the chalet (1,127 m/ 3,700 ft) at the top of the Grind. However, the fastest recorded time is 23 minutes and 48 seconds, set in 2010.

From the chalet, a 6.4-km (4-mi) lollipop hike of Thunderbird Ridge and Dam Mountain awaits. Head northeast through the ski area on paved trails, going by the lumberjack show and grizzly bear enclosure. Bypassing the top of Grouse Mountain (1,231 m/4,040 ft), take a gravel road (part of the Snow-shoe Grind in winter) to the left of the Lower Peak ski run. Go under the Peak Chair, and find the Lynn Headwaters hiker registration kiosk.

After gaining some height on Dam Mountain, fork right on the rugged Alpine Trail, saving the summit for the return. Pass ziplines, and turn right on the Thunderbird Trail. Continue east to the subalpine viewpoint. Thunderbird Ridge affords damn fine perspectives of Crown Mountain and The Camel, Goat Mountain, Cathedral Mountain, The Needles (Hike 2), and the Fannin Range to the north and east. Close at hand, a sightseeing tower, with a wind turbine mounted on it, stands on Grouse Mountain.

Double-back to the Alpine Trail, and continue north. In short order, U-turn left onto the Ridge Trail, just shy of Little Goat Mountain. Head south to the rocky summit of Dam Mountain (2.5 hours up; 49°23'39" N, 123°04'52" W). The Vancouver metropolis, Capilano Lake, Burrard Inlet (Slilutulh to the Squamish, Tsleil-Wat to the Tsleil-Waututh Nation), and the Salish Sea spread out grandly before you. Follow the Ridge Trail south, and merge with the Alpine Trail on the way back to the ski area.

Below the chalet, find the steep BCMC Trail popping out of the woods, just east of the Grind's top. Descend the rustic, rooty path for 2.9 km (1.8 mi) under cover of western hemlock, Douglas-fir, and western red cedar trees. Wildlife sightings may include black bears, cougars, snowshoe hares, Pacific sideband snails, and olive-sided flycatchers. Turn right on the Baden-Powell Trail to return to the trailhead.

Grouse Mountain lies in the territories of the Musqueam, Squamish, and Tsleil-Waututh First Nations. Paying customers can board the Skyride to skip the Grouse Grind and/or BCMC Trail. Balloons, fireworks, littering, and smoking are prohibited in Metro Vancouver regional parks, as are feeding wildlife and foraging for fungi and plants. Dogs are not allowed on the Grouse Grind, BCMC Trail, or Skyride. Downhill hiking is not permitted on the Grind.

STOP OF INTEREST
CAPILANO RIVER HATCHERY

The completion of the Cleveland Dam in 1954 decimated the salmon runs of the Capilano River (xʷməθkʷəy̓əma?ɬ to the Musqueam Nation, Xwemélch'stn Stákw to the Squamish Nation) and harmed local livelihoods. In 1971, the Canadian government built the Capilano River Hatchery (4500 Capilano Park Road) to give salmon stocks a boost. Visit the hatchery to see adult chinook (October to November) and coho (June to November) salmon, and steelhead trout (March to April) swim up the fish ladder. Open daily, the hatchery is found downstream of the dam in Capilano River Regional Park, which is accessed from Capilano Road, north of Trans-Canada Highway 1.

TWIN SISTERS (THE LIONS)

Get up close and personal with Vancouver's rock stars

Distance: 15 km (9.3 mi)
Time: 9 hours (out and back)
Elevation gain: 1,430 m (4,690 ft)
High point: 1,654 m (5,430 ft)

Difficulty: ♦♦
Maps: NTS 92-G/6 North Vancouver; Trail Ventures BC North Shore
Trailhead: 49°28'15" N, 123°14'05" W

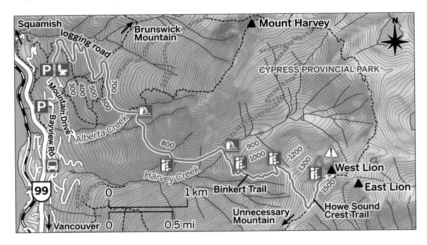

KNOWN AS Ch'ich'iyúy to the Squamish Nation and officially named The Lions, the Twin Sisters are undoubtedly the rock stars of the Vancouver skyline. Poet E. Pauline Johnson (Tekahionwake) famously retells the story of "The Two Sisters" in her 1911 book, *Legends of Vancouver*, based on her conversations with Chief Joe Capilano (Sahp-luk) and Mary Capilano (Lixwelut). The classic hike to the West Lion (best done July to October) leads to the approach ridge just shy of the peak. Most hikers would be wise to stop there. For experienced scramblers only, beyond lies the exhilarating Class 3 climb to the summit.

GETTING THERE

Transit: Take TransLink Bus 262 (Lions Bay–Brunswick) to Crosscreek Road. Walk 1.6 km (1 mi) to the Sunset Drive trailhead.

Pink mountain-heather in the subalpine on the Binkert Trail.

Vehicle: On Highway 99 (Sea to Sky Highway) in Lions Bay, 12 km (7.5 mi) north of Trans-Canada Highway 1 at Horseshoe Bay, take the Lions Bay Avenue exit. Heading east, immediately make a left on Crosscreek Road. On the far side of Harvey Creek, go right on Centre Road, left on Bayview Road, left on Mountain Drive, and left on Sunset Drive. Use the pay parking lot at Sunset's north end (toilet available). Alternatively, find a spot lower down on Mountain Drive or at Lions Bay Elementary School (250 Bayview Road). Beware of no-parking signs.

THE HIKE

From the Sunset Drive gate (220 m/720 ft), enter the Village of Lions Bay's Magnesia Creek (Ḵél'etstn in Sḵwx̱wú7mesh sníchim) drinking watershed and trudge up the rocky logging road. (Fires, smoking, and vaping are prohibited. Dogs must be leashed and poop carried out.) Pass a water treatment plant and keep right, spurning turnoffs for Brunswick Mountain, Harvey's Pup, and Mount Harvey. Note rockfall debris on the road. In 50 minutes, cross Alberta Creek (P'ap'ḵ') on wooden bridge remnants below a waterfall, and enter a pleasant flat stretch. A viewpoint to the right overlooks Bowen Island (c̓əw̓c̓əw̓ʔiqən to the Musqueam Nation, Nex̱wlélex̱wem to the Squamish) and Howe Sound (Atl'ḵa7tsem to the Squamish).

After an hour and a half (4.7 km/2.9 mi) on the old road, scorched wooden signs indicate where the Binkert Trail leaves to the right (835 m/2,740 ft;

The East Lion (Elxwíḵn) from the summit of its sister peak, the West Lion.

49°27′38″ N, 123°12′21″ W). Follow the path—named for trail builder Paul Binkert (1908–1995) and maintained by the B.C. Mountaineering Club—down steps topped with rebar and a short ladder to Harvey Creek. (The road continues up the Harvey basin.) Cross it above a waterfall on a bridge built in memory of Lions Bay Search and Rescue founder Marcel Andrié (1935–1994). The steep and rugged trail bears left and uphill under tall trees, with signs and orange paint sprayed on rock showing the way. (A rope and arrows prevent you from missing this turn on the descent.)

Twenty minutes from the old road, a rockslide affords a vantage of Gambier Island (Cha7élḵnech) and Mount Elphinstone (Hike 41). The halfway mark is spray-painted on a rock, and the merciless switchbacks begin in earnest. Clamber up big roots and rocks. At another viewpoint, look out at Keats Island and up at Unnecessary Mountain. Work steeply up the side of a boulder patch in the woods.

Gain an open shoulder (1,230 m/4,040 ft) with blueberries and an impressive perspective of the West Lion above, after 3 hours. To the north, Brunswick Mountain peeks out behind logging-scarred Mount Harvey. Continue up the demanding route, earning more views. Follow orange ribbons and paint diagonally up sun-baked rock bearing rivulets of water. Pink mountain-heather and subalpine daisies enhance the gorgeous scene. Ascend scree and scramble up to the ridge to intersect the Howe Sound Crest Trail in Cypress Provincial Park (a no-drone zone). Right leads to Unnecessary

Mountain and Cypress Bowl, so turn left and head on up to the West Lion's precipitous doorstep, just past the high point (1,550 m/5,090 ft) of the approach ridge. The hike is rated "difficult" to this point (8 hours round trip). If you are not properly prepared or equipped to do some rock climbing—or it's wet—go no farther. While the imposing summit is 25 adrenaline-filled minutes away, the scramble comes with the risk of a deadly fall. Don a helmet and drop into the dizzying gap separating the ridge and peak, with the aid of knotted ropes. The crux is immediately up and to the right—an exposed, ascending traverse of a down-sloping ledge. On the far side, pick up the flagged route in the trees. Grip roots, grab trunks, and make use of veggie belays to reach the second tricky bit. Climb up the rock and traverse right. Follow cairns to stand atop the West Lion (4.5 hours up; 49°27′28″ N, 123°11′11″ W).

The 360-degree outlook is rapturous. Ravens and sightseeing helicopters soar beneath your feet. Enchantment Lake gleams to the northeast, and the Capilano River (xʷməθkʷəẏəmaʔɬ to the Musqueam, Xwemélch'stn Stákw to the Squamish) drains the valley south. On a clear day, spot Mount Garibaldi (Nch'kaẏ to the Squamish), The Black Tusk (T'ekt'akmúẏin tl'a In7inẏáxa7en to the Squamish), and Mount Baker (χe:tᶿenəxʷ to the Musqueam, Xwsa7k to the Squamish) in the distance.

The East Lion (1,606 m/5,270 ft; Elxwíkn to the Squamish), a more diffi-cult objective, lies in the Capilano drinking watershed and is therefore illegal to climb. Rounded by glacial abrasion, the Twin Sisters are composed of vertically jointed hornblende diorite. Try to imagine the double peak buried by the Cordilleran Ice Sheet 15,000 years ago during the Fraser Glaciation. Take care to descend via the same route.

KELVIN GROVE BEACH

Fancy an après-hike dip? Lions Bay's Kelvin Grove Beach Park offers shore-line access for swimmers and divers. The park entrance is at the foot of Tidewater Way, west of the Kelvin Grove Way exit on Highway 99 (Sea to Sky Highway). The Tidewater Trail leads down to the beach, which faces Bowyer Island (Lhákw'tich to the Squamish Nation) and the sunset. The nearby Kelvin Grove Seamount is home to a glass sponge reef, which provides habitat for California sea cucumbers, longhorn decorator crabs, pygmy rockfish, and squat lobsters.

6 SQUAMISH
PETGILL LAKE

Swim and soak up the Howe Sound views

Distance: 10 km (6.2 mi)
Time: 5.5 hours (out and back)
Elevation gain: 625 m (2,050 ft)
High point: 770 m (2,530 ft)

Difficulty: ■
Maps: NTS 092-G/11 Squamish
Trailhead: 49°38'53" N, 123°12'06" W

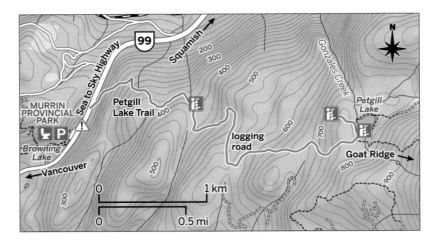

IT'S NOT every day one encounters a hiking trail that boasts a swimming hole at either end. That's far from the only reason to hit the Petgill Lake Trail, in the territory of the Squamish Nation. For one thing, this low-elevation outing furnishes grand views of the head of Howe Sound (Atl'ḵa7tsem in Sḵwx̱wú7mesh sníchim), one of the southernmost fjords in North America. Although logging has considerably altered the trail, Petgill Lake remains a dependable destination, especially for rainy days and shoulder season.

GETTING THERE

Vehicle: On Highway 99 (Sea to Sky Highway), 3 km (1.9 mi) north of Britannia Beach and 8.3 km (5.2 mi) south of Downtown Squamish, turn west into the parking lot at Murrin Provincial Park (toilet available). The gates are closed 11 p.m. to 7 a.m. Overnight parking and highway shoulder parking are prohibited.

Howe Sound (Atl'ḵa7tsem) from the bluff viewpoint near Petgill Lake.

THE HIKE

Accessing the trailhead requires safely crossing the highway—in some ways, the crux of the hike. Find the signed start of the Petgill Lake Trail on the east shoulder, 200 m (0.1 mi) north of the Murrin Provincial Park entrance. Right away, the provincially designated recreation trail demands you scramble up two rocky bits with a chain for assistance on the second. Follow orange squares into a transmission corridor and switchback right to exit. Glance back at the forested hill across the one-time Garibaldi Highway; it's partially composed of dacite lava extruded by a volcano at Watts Point (Sts'íts'a7ḵin) during the Fraser Glaciation.

Scamper up more rock, and enter the tall timber. Switchback up to pass beneath the first of many rock walls. These may bring to mind the famed monolith of Stawamus Chief Mountain (Siyám Smánit), since they share the granodiorite of the Cretaceous Squamish Pluton. Cross a creek choked with woody debris. An arrow points right to an ascending traverse of a rooty ledge.

As the traffic noise fades away, don't linger at two mediocre vistas. After 45 minutes, detour left for a dynamite viewpoint atop quartz-studded rock and amid shore pines. Cloud-permitting, gaze upon the mouth and valley of the Squamish River (Sḵwx̱wú7mesh Stáḵw), Mamquam Blind Channel (ḵ'íyax̱enáy̓ch), The Malamute, and the Chief.

Less than an hour from the highway, drop to cross a creek and turn right on a deactivated logging road (49°38'54" N, 123°11'32" W). Hear but only gain

A sooty grouse on the Petgill Lake Trail.

unsatisfactory glimpses of a waterfall to the left and another to the right, and bypass cutblocks. Go right at a three-way junction. Wood and rock arrows help you stay on track. Hop over streams, and ignore a road on the left. Listen for the hooting of the sooty grouse.

After little more than a half-hour of road walking, hang a left at a boulder blockade to begin the upper trail (49°38'36" N, 123°11'03" W). Follow a whaleback, spot skunk cabbage, and drop into and out of a gully. Avoiding logged areas, ascend to a patch of bare rock. Back in the trees, negotiate a steep-sided gully, climbing up the other side to the right of a prominent wall. The path veers left, away from a clear-cut, and along the base of slabs to reach the crest before the lake.

Stay left at the easy-to-miss junction with the challenging route to Goat Ridge (Ntsewásus). Reach a viewpoint on a ridge overlooking Petgill Lake, which drains into Gonzales Creek (Txwn7us). Unless you plan to take a dip, keep left to skip the lake circuit and make a beeline for the final bluff-top viewpoint (3 hours up; 49°38'50" N, 123°10'12" W), 10 minutes northwest. The wide-angle outlook calls attention to Anvil (Lhaxwm), Bowen (Nexwlélexwem), and Gambier (Cha7élknech) Islands in Howe Sound. To the west, a rock quarry and cutblocks scar the landscape.

Retrace your steps to Murrin, where an optional swim awaits at Browning Lake. To the Squamish people, it's a special place, associated with spirits, pictographs, and hunting. Dogs must be leashed in the park. From May 15 to September 15, pets are banned in the beach area.

STOP OF INTEREST
PORTEAU COVE

For a sea-level perspective on Howe Sound (Atl'ka7tsem to the Squamish Nation), visit Porteau Cove Provincial Park. It sits at one end of a sill, or submarine ridge, left behind by the glacier that inhabited the sound over 10,000 years ago; the Defence Islands (Kw'émkw'em) are positioned at the other end. Inshore, scuba divers explore artificial reefs of concrete, steel, and tires, and sunken shipwrecks. Porteau Cove (Xwáwchayay) itself features a lagoon and a lookout. If you're lucky, you might spot an orca, grey whale, or humpback whale. Find the park entrance on the west side of Highway 99 (Sea to Sky Highway), 8 km (5 mi) south of Britannia Beach (Shishayu7ay). (Dogs must be leashed and are not allowed on beaches.)

SLHÁNAÝ

Gain a unique perspective of Stawamus Chief Mountain

Distance: 5 km (3.1 mi)
Time: 4.5 hours
Elevation gain: 630 m (2,070 ft)
High point: 660 m (2,170 ft)

Difficulty: ◆
Maps: NTS 092-G/11 Squamish
Trailhead: 49°41'42" N, 123°07'49" W

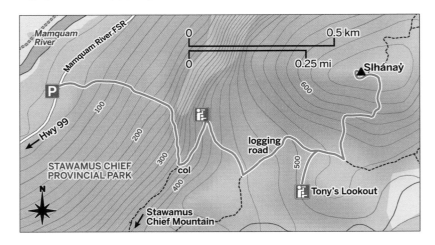

FOR MANY years, the northeastern companion of Stawamus Chief Mountain (Siyám Smánit to the Squamish Nation) was generally known as the Stawamus Squaw. The B.C. government rescinded several official place names bearing that racist and sexist label in 2000. And in 2008, the Squamish bestowed the Skwxwú7mesh toponym Slhánaý ("woman") on the granodiorite horn and cliffs. More trafficked by rock climbers than hikers, Slhánaý (pronounced "sss-thlah-nigh") beckons with its quiet woods and extraordinary outlook on the Chief's north walls.

GETTING THERE

Vehicle: On Highway 99 (Sea to Sky Highway), 1.8 km (1.1 mi) south of Downtown Squamish and 2.4 km (1.5 mi) north of Shannon Falls Provincial Park, turn east onto Mamquam River Forest Service Road. (The turnoff is

Stawamus Chief Mountain (Siÿáṁ Smánit) and Squamish Harbour from Slhánaẏ.

signed "Forestry Rd.") Drive 1.4 km (0.9 mi) on dusty gravel (2WD), and park on the shoulder where a roadside clearing filled with rocks is on the right.

THE HIKE

Spot the climbers' approach trail disappearing east into the woods immediately north of the rocky clearing. Pass a massive boulder on your right, and take a left fork signed for Slhánaẏ. (Right leads to the Poxy Crag and Disaster Response climbing areas.) Follow orange squares up the steep, rooty path, which weaves through mossy boulders.

After a half-hour, reach the base of a multi-pitch rock face, home to Birds of Prey, The Great Game, and other lines. (Please don't distract the belayers.) Bear right to make an ascending traverse beneath the wall. Follow the bouldery path up, outflanking Part Way Wall and climbing to a key junction at the north col of the Chief. Turn left for Slhánaẏ, and the going gets easier.

After an hour (1 km/0.6 mi) on foot, detour left for a stupendous vantage of the Chief and Squamish from atop Slhánaẏ's main crag (400 m/1,310 ft; 49°41'39″ N, 123°07'23″ W). See if you can spot slackliners traversing the North-North Gully of the monolith and kiteboarders catching wind in Squamish Harbour. The glacier-polished granodiorite around you solidified from magma during the Cretaceous Period, when dinosaurs roamed the Earth.

Back in the woods, continue up on a less-obvious single track. Follow orange markers right at a fork with a faint path. Descend slightly to a dark

The Squamish River (Sḵwx̱wú7mesh Stáḵw) meets Howe Sound (Atl'ḵa7tsem).

old logging road, and turn left (49°41′32″ N, 123°07′17″ W). Take note of this indistinct junction for the return. Stick with the road for 10 minutes, spurning paths leaving to the left. At a signed turnoff with pink flagging, head right to gain an unusual perspective of the Chief from a memorial bench at Tony's Lookout. Backtrack to the road, go forth, and quickly find the start of the summit trail, indicated by tapes of multiple colours, on the left.

From this point forth, the flagged path is messy, obstructed by deadfall, and easy to lose. Trudge through second-growth to a gully, exiting to the left. Go left around the summit walls, and clamber up the other side to top out (2.5 hours up; 49°41′44″ N, 123°06′57″ W). Shore pines partially obscure the panorama but not enough to spoil the scene. Looking north, find Cloud-burst Mountain (Xwmitl'm) and two dissected stratovolcanoes—Mount Fee, in the distance, and Mount Garibaldi (Nch'ḵay̓), closer at hand. To the west, the Squamish River (Sḵwx̱wú7mesh Stáḵw) empties into the head of Howe Sound (Atl'ḵa7tsem) and Goat Ridge (Ntsewásus) rises to the south. Retrace your steps to the bottom.

Slhánay̓ is largely protected as part of Stawamus Chief Provincial Park. Camping is allowed at designated sites only (permit required) and fires are prohibited. Dogs must be leashed. Water is scarce; be sure to bring plenty to drink.

Leaving the summit of Sḵ̲wá̓nǎy̓.

SHANNON FALLS

Six times taller than Niagara Falls, Shannon Falls (Kwékwetxwm to the Squamish Nation) cascades 335 m (1,100 ft) over a granodiorite cliff in Squamish. It's particularly spectacular in spring runoff and after heavy rain, when the roaring, rushing water seems to leap from the rock face. A bustling roadside attraction, the waterfall is easily accessed via a short trail. The cliffs in the vicinity constitute an important rock-climbing area. Since the 1970s, ice climbers have front-pointed up Shannon Falls too—on the rare occasion it freezes, that is. The entrance to Shannon Falls Provincial Park is 4.1 km (2.5 mi) south of Downtown Squamish, on the east side of Highway 99 (Sea to Sky Highway). (Dogs must be leashed.)

ECHO LAKE

Chase the best waterfall hike in Sea to Sky Country

Distance: 7.5 km (4.7 mi)
Time: 7 hours (out and back)
Elevation gain: 905 m (2,970 ft)
High point: 910 m (2,990 ft)

Difficulty: ◆
Maps: NTS 092-G/11 Squamish
Trailhead: 49°42'51" N, 123°10'26" W

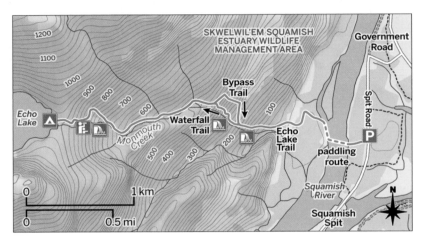

THE ECHO Lake Trail is more than just the best waterfall hike in Sea to Sky Country. It's a bonafide adventure, which requires crossing the powerful Squamish River (Skwxwú7mesh Stákw to the Squamish Nation) to access the trailhead. Paralleling Monmouth Creek all the way up to the cirque lake, the rough and wickedly steep route visits a succession of sublime waterfalls noted for thrilling canyoneering descents. The lower portion of the creek lies within the Skwelwil'em Squamish Estuary Wildlife Management Area and is designated as a Squamish Nation cultural site (Síiyamín ta Skwxwú7mesh).

GETTING THERE

Vehicle: From Highway 99 (Sea to Sky Highway) in Squamish, 44 km (27 mi) north of Horseshoe Bay, head west on Cleveland Avenue. Cross the train tracks, and make a right on Bailey Street, which turns to gravel. Keep right at a fork. Regain pavement on Government Road, and go left on the gravel Spit Road (2WD). After 350 m (0.2 mi), the road turns left onto the Squamish River training berm. Continue south for 820 m (0.5 mi), where an obvious path drops into the woods on the right (49°42'44" N, 123°10'04" W). Park on the opposite shoulder.

Waterfall-sculpted granodiorite on Monmouth Creek.

THE HIKE

The first order of business is to canoe across the big river. River paddling skills are essential. If you don't have access to a canoe, rentals are available in Squamish. (Alternatively, Squamish Watersports runs a shuttle boat to the trailhead on Saturdays and accepts private bookings.)

From Spit Road, follow the path—over deadfall and across a muddy channel—160 m (0.1 mi) west to the canoe put-in. Spot a cluster of several log pilings off the west bank, a tad upstream, below the south end of a wooded island. The 10-minute, 400-m (0.2-mi) paddle is easiest at high tide; low tide means a faster current and possibly portaging a gravel bar. The takeout is right behind the pilings. Stash your boat near the clearing behind the bank.

Orange diamonds on alders indicate the trailhead at the clearing's upstream edge. Go west on the rocky floodplain and over a creek on a soft log. Swing south as the Echo Lake Trail nears a B.C. Hydro transmission line (don't jump the creek on your left), then follow pink flagging west across the right-of-way. Draw parallel to Monmouth Creek. Begin the steep ascent, breathing in the lush rainforest of Douglas-firs, western red cedars, and mossy boulders. Stay on river left all the way up.

Encounter the first of myriad waterfall viewpoints after a half-hour of hiking. Search for a rainbow in the mist generated by three tiers of horsetails. Continue up the rooty path to a waterfall that's sculpted the mid-Cretaceous phaneritic granodiorite into a work of art. Under a second set of power lines, glance back to see Stawamus Chief Mountain (Siyáṁ Smánit), flanked by

The view from the outlet of Echo Lake.

Slhánaẏ (Hike 7) and Goat Ridge (Ntsewásus), with Sky Pilot Mountain in the background. Watch your step on the slippery rock.

At 1.1 km (0.7 mi), orange diamonds fork in the woods on the uphill side of the transmission corridor (200 m/660 ft). If you are comfortable with devilishly steep terrain and scrambling up rocky gullies and ledges, choose left for the Waterfall Trail and the most dazzling stretch of the canyon. (Right is for the less scenic but more forgiving Bypass Trail, which is recommended for a safer descent.) A keyhole waterfall is the first spectacle. Then you must carefully cross a sketchy earth bridge over a chasm. Up next is the pièce de résistance—a waterfall, partially concealed by a surreal rock arch, plunges into a green pool. Roots and fixed chains ease your passage to the junction above, where the ascent and descent trails reunite (420 m/1,380 ft; 49°42′56″ N, 123°11′17″ W). For a shorter hike, turn around here; the best falls are behind you.

The grade relents, and the trail descends a bit to return to the creek. On the far bank, outcrops of columnar-jointed aphyric andesite lava are exposed. According to geologists, when the Monmouth Creek volcanic complex erupted, most likely during the Fraser Glaciation, the Squamish River valley was filled by ice more than 1 km (0.6 mi) thick. Less old but still ancient are giant fire-scarred firs and a massive trailside cedar. Spotted coralroot and jellied bird's nest fungi are found on the forest floor.

The steepness returns, and with it the first of the upper waterfalls. Cross a landslide zone. View a colossal cascade from below and beside it. Ascend inclined rock following small cairns, and score an excellent vantage of Squamish. Just when your thighs can't scream any louder, reach a fork (49°42′50″ N, 123°12′26″ W). Head left to enjoy the pleasing view from the Echo Lake outflow. Then return to the fork and scamper up the rock to find a couple of tiny tent sites and the lakeshore (3.5 hours up). Contemplate a swim, and gaze across the bowl to Mount Murchison and Mount Lapworth. Alec Lake lies hidden beneath Murchison.

Follow the diamonds—yellow for the way down—back to the trailhead, via the Bypass Trail. Camping, fires, and off-leash dogs are prohibited from the riverbank to the top of the bypass. Respect the land—leave no trace.

STOP OF INTEREST
EAGLE RUN

Brackendale Eagles Provincial Park protects floodplain habitat for wintering bald eagles that flock to the Squamish River (Sḵwx̱wú7mesh Stákw to the Squamish Nation) valley to feast on spawning chum and pink salmon. Between November and January, Squamish's Eagle Run dike and viewing shelter (opposite 41015 Government Road, north of the Squamish Spit), across the river, is a birdwatching hot spot. Don't disturb the eagles; dogs should be leashed and drones left at home. Eagle nests are protected under B.C.'s Wildlife Act.

9 SQUAMISH
CROOKED FALLS

Ancient giants, thundering water

Distance: 6 km (3.7 mi)
Time: 4.5 hours (out and back)
Elevation gain: 465 m (1,530 ft)
High point: 520 m (1,710 ft)

Difficulty: ◆
Maps: NTS 92-G/14 Cheakamus River
Trailhead: 49°54'38" N, 123°19'23" W

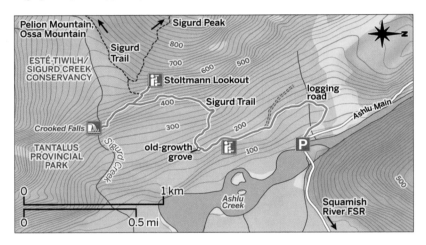

AN IMPRESSIVE waterfall is even more so when it's not just a hop, skip, and jump from the road. Nevertheless, the rain-friendly hike to Crooked Falls is about both the low-elevation destination *and* the not-so-long journey. There are ancient trees to hug and luxuriant moss to feel. The Sigurd Trail takes you into the Esté-tiwilh/Sigurd Creek Conservancy—part of the Squamish Nation's Esté-tiwilh Wild Spirit Place (Esté-tiwilh ḵwéḵwayex kwelháynexw ta Sḵwx̱wú7mesh Temíxw), set aside as a spiritual and cultural sanctuary.

GETTING THERE
Vehicle: On Highway 99 (Sea to Sky Highway), 10 km (6.2 mi) north of Downtown Squamish, turn west onto Squamish Valley Road (opposite Alice Lake Provincial Park). In 3.7 km (2.3 mi), bear left at the Paradise Valley Road fork, and drive through the Squamish Nation's Cheakamus reserve. (Respect

The plunging waters of Crooked Falls.

the speed limit.) At 23 km (14 mi), continue onto Squamish River Forest Service Road (2WD), with its gravel and potholes. Turn left onto Ashlu Main, at 24 km (15 mi), and cross the Squamish River. Once over the Ashlu Creek bridge, the road curves right. Park on the right shoulder, before the run-of-river powerhouse, 26 km (16 mi) from the highway.

THE HIKE

A rough logging road leaves the west side of Ashlu Main under the first wooden power-line pylon after the Ashlu Creek bridge. Keep left at an early fork and step over small streams. In 800 m (0.5 mi), spot the trailhead on the left, with its yellow signage and bare kiosk, at a rightward bend in the road.

The Sigurd Trail, maintained by the B.C. Mountaineering Club, starts off south on a mellow old road in mixed woods. In a few minutes, deviate left for a bluff viewpoint that overlooks the confluence of Ashlu Creek, a favourite of whitewater kayakers, and the Squamish River (Skwxwú7mesh Stákw). Cloudburst Mountain (Xwmitl'm) looms across the valley. A few minutes later, there's a partial view from the trail.

Where a sign points right, the trail says *hu*y *melh halh* ("goodbye" in Skwxwú7mesh sníchim) to the old road and heads steeply up into the conifers. Follow orange squares to another partial view, where the path bends right and approaches a creek. Enter a grove of old-growth giants. Stately Douglas-firs and western red cedars tower over huge, moss-blanketed

A mossy boulder in the Esté-tiwilh/Sigurd Creek Conservancy.

boulders. The rugged, rocky, and rooty trail rises below overhanging outcrops in the lush forest. Cross a debris chute, switchback around a massive downed fir, and pass beneath imposing rock walls.

Reach the signed Crooked Falls junction (2 hours up; 49°53′57″ N, 123°19′36″ W), 1.6 km (1 mi) after the trailhead kiosk. With the waterfall 15 minutes away but already within earshot, go left on the challenging spur. Clamber over and under deadfall. With the falls becoming visible through the trees, bear left (mind the drop-off) to descend to the viewpoint, 300 m (0.2 mi) from the junction. From the besprinkled ledge, behold the breathtaking power of water and gravity. Watch your footing on the slippery ground. Don't break out the sandwiches yet, unless sogginess appeals. Return to the falls junction.

The hike's final reward lies 15 minutes farther. Switchback up the Sigurd Trail to the next junction. Following a 1930s trappers' trail, the rough route continues up the Sigurd Creek valley, granting mountaineers access to Pelion and Ossa Mountains in the Tantalus Range (Tsewílx̱) and Tantalus Provincial Park. However, go right and climb the messy dead-end path, littered with blowdowns, for 100 m (0.1 mi) to the Stoltmann Lookout (49°54′02″ N, 123°19′42″ W). Take a gander at The Table and Mount Garibaldi (Nch'ḵaẏ), both volcanoes, to the east, before retracing your steps to Ashlu Main.

A metal plate at the lookout commemorates environmentalist Randy Stoltmann (1962–1994), who campaigned to save old-growth forests from logging and was the impetus for the B.C. Big Tree Registry. In the 1990s, the Western Canada Wilderness Committee rallied for the preservation of the Sims Creek, Clendinning Creek, upper Elaho River, and upper Lillooet River (Lilwatátkwa) valleys—calling the expanse the Randy Stoltmann Wilderness Area. In 2008, the B.C. government set aside part of the area for the Upper Elaho Valley Conservancy.

Esté-tiwilh/Sigurd Creek Conservancy, also created in 2008, is off-limits to industrial development and protects habitat for grizzly and black bears, elk, mountain goats, and grey wolves. It is co-managed by the Squamish Nation and B.C. Parks. Esté-tiwilh translates to "the great beauty and power that surrounds us and that we should strive to be in harmony with." B.C. Parks discourages dogs in the backcountry. There are no facilities; please use Leave No Trace practices.

STOP OF INTEREST

SQUAMISH SPIT

Every summer, windsurfers and kiteboarders flock to the Squamish Spit. The end of the spit—actually a training berm built by B.C. Rail in 1972 to pave the way for an unrealized coal port—offers an incredible 360-degree view of the Squamish River (Sḵwxwú7mesh Stáḵw to the Squamish Nation) estuary. Located near the proximal end of the spit, the interpretative Chelem Trail (1.1 km/0.7 mi) highlights the natural and cultural significance of the fluvial-to-tidal transition zone. From Highway 99 (Sea to Sky Highway), 2.8 km (1.7 mi) north of Downtown Squamish, head west on Centennial Way. Continue onto Government Road and follow it south to Spit Road, where you go right. The spit and trail are part of the Skwelwil'em Squamish Estuary Wildlife Management Area. (Dogs must be leashed.)

HELM LAKE

Fire and ice in the shadow of The Black Tusk

Distance: 26 km (16.2 mi)
Time: 9.5 hours (out and back)
Elevation gain: 940 m (3,080 ft)
High point: 1,765 m (5,790 ft)

Difficulty: ■
Maps: NTS 92-G/14, 92-J/2; Clark
Geomatics 102 Garibaldi Park
Trailhead: 50°02'31" N, 122°59'22" W

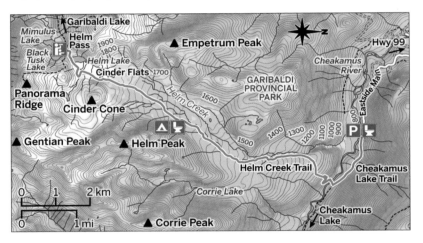

THE HANGING valley of Helm Creek is a delight from forested bottom to subalpine top. Enter centuries-old conifer groves, ascend to varicoloured wildflower meadows, and traverse a volcanic moonscape on the way to Helm Lake in Garibaldi Provincial Park, the Squamish Nation's Kwáyatsut Wild Spirit Place, and Líĺwat Nation territory. A particularly dramatic vantage of The Black Tusk (T'ek̲t'ak̲múy̓in tl'a In7iny̓áx̲a7en to the Squamish, Q'elqámtensa ti Skenknápa to the Líĺwat), an andesite plug, awaits.

GETTING THERE
Vehicle: On Highway 99 (Sea to Sky Highway), turn east onto Cheakamus Lake Road at Whistler's Cheakamus Crossing (opposite Function Junction), 50 km (31 mi) north of Downtown Squamish and 7.5 km (4.7 mi) south of Whistler Village. Quickly go left on Cheakamus Lake Forest Service

The Black Tusk (T'ekt'akmúyin tl'a In7inyáxa7en) from the Helm Creek Trail. Photo by Joan Septembre

Road—instead of straight over the Cheakamus River bridge—and left again for Eastside Main (2WD). Keeping left, continue 7 km (4.3 mi) on gravel to the busy Cheakamus Lake parking lot (toilet available).

THE HIKE

From the trailhead, head east on an old road shared with mountain bikers. Pass the outhouse and enter the woods, leaving behind the whistles of American pikas. The Cheakamus Lake Trail crosses an avalanche path and, in 15 minutes, comes to a grove of towering old-growth Douglas-firs.

A half-hour (1.5 km/0.9 mi) from the parking lot, reach a junction (50°02'04" N, 122°58'11" W). Hikers bound for Cheakamus Lake (Hike 11) go straight through. However, turn right onto the less-trafficked Helm Creek Trail and cross the Cheakamus River (Ch'iyákmesh Stákw to the Squamish, Nsqwítsu to the Lílwat). Bikes are not permitted beyond the steel truss bridge, which replaced a cable car.

Stiff switchbacks immediately follow. A log bench offers a respite and a partial view of Whistler Mountain (Kacwitma to the Lílwat). Big western red cedars lord over the mossy forest floor. Another bench off to the left tempts as the grade eases, a half-hour past the bridge. Helm Creek is audible before

Approaching Helm Lake in autumn snow.

it's visible. Listen for the hooting of the sooty grouse as the terrain opens up. Bridges span feeder streams, and the first heather meadow is encountered. Soon rotten-topped Helm Peak rises above the trees ahead to the left.

After 3 hours (9 km/5.6 mi) of hiking, arrive at Helm Creek campground (49°59′46″ N, 122°59′49″ W) at 1,550 m (5,090 ft) above mean sea level. In addition to meadow tent pads, pit toilets, and a food hang, the site confers a grand perspective of The Black Tusk and Empetrum Peak (named after the crowberry). Push on, crossing bridges over tributaries.

The view blows wide open, revealing the crater-topped Cinder Cone ahead. Part of the Garibaldi Lake Volcanic Field, the Cinder Cone is actually composed of two intersecting tephra cones. They erupted in the late Pleistocene, giving rise to the Helm Creek basalt and Desolation Valley basaltic andesite lava flows that lie beneath your feet. Davidson's penstemon, mountain arnica, silky phacelia, spreading phlox, and western bog-laurel adorn the floral carpet, which is strewn with pyroclastic bombs.

An hour past the campground, a B.C. Parks sign implores visitors to stay off loose slopes of volcanic cinders or moraine gravels, in order to preserve the area's special geomorphological features. Plod south on the otherworldly plain of the Cinder Flats, skirting a lake at the foot of the Cinder Cone. Stakes with orange diamonds show the way. The trail detours upstream to cross braided Helm Creek with the aid of a bridge. Due to climate change, the creek's source, the Helm Glacier, has shrunk by more than 30 per cent in the past 25 years. Arrive at the south shore of swim-worthy Helm Lake.

For an elevated perspective, continue 20 minutes farther to the signed junction at Helm Pass (5 hours up; 49°57'52" N, 123°01'41.0" W). With hoary marmots for company, survey the Helm Creek valley and Fitzsimmons Range to the northeast, and Black Tusk Lake and Panorama Ridge to the southeast. Retrace your steps to the Cheakamus Lake trailhead.

If you can arrange a car shuttle, a crossover hike to the Garibaldi Lake trailhead is an attractive and slightly shorter proposition. From Helm Pass, head west through bustling Black Tusk Meadows, past the Taylor Meadows campground, and down the Garibaldi Lake Trail to reach the parking lot by Rubble Creek (Spú7ets' to the Squamish, Spó7ez to the Líl̓wat) in 11 km (6.8 mi).

Dogs, drones, fires (subject to a $345 fine), hunting, motorized vehicles, and berry, flower, and mushroom picking are prohibited throughout Garibaldi Provincial Park. Camping is allowed at designated sites only, and reservations are required year-round.

STOP OF INTEREST
BRANDYWINE FALLS

While an alcoholic haze surrounds the origin of its name, a visit to Brandywine Falls is guaranteed to clear your cobwebs. The thunderous waterfall sees Brandywine Creek (Stamsh to the Squamish Nation, Cwéscwest to the Líl̓wat Nation) dive 66 m (220 ft) over a volcanic escarpment on its way to Daisy Lake. Stare across the canyon at layer upon layer of basaltic lava flows with columnar jointing. Brandywine Falls Provincial Park is located on the east side of Highway 99 (Sea to Sky Highway), 17 km (10.6 mi) south of Whistler Village. The viewing platforms are an easy 10-minute (one-way) walk or snowshoe from the parking lot. (Dogs must be on leash.)

CHEAKAMUS LAKE

See the forest for the old-growth trees

Distance: 14.5 km (9 mi)
Time: 4 hours (out and back)
Elevation gain: 145 m (480 ft)
High point: 890 m (2,920 ft)

Difficulty: ●
Maps: NTS 92-J/2 Whistler; Clark Geomatics 102 Garibaldi Park
Trailhead: 50°02'31" N, 122°59'22" W

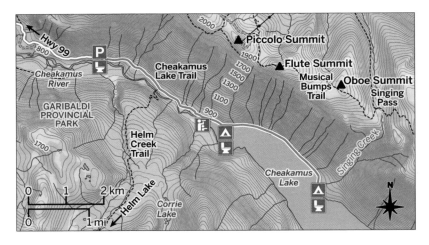

COME FOR the turquoise waters of glacial-floured Cheakamus Lake. Stay for the majestic Douglas-fir and western red cedar giants. Slow down and see the forest for the old-growth trees. Rain or shine, you probably won't be in any hurry to leave these ancient woods, located in Garibaldi Provincial Park, the Squamish Nation's Kwáyatsut Wild Spirit Place, and Lílwat Nation territory.

GETTING THERE

Vehicle: On Highway 99 (Sea to Sky Highway), turn east onto Cheakamus Lake Road at Whistler's Cheakamus Crossing (opposite Function Junction), 50 km (31 mi) north of Downtown Squamish and 7.5 km (4.7 mi) south of Whistler Village. Quickly go left on Cheakamus Lake Forest Service Road—instead of straight over the Cheakamus River bridge—and left again for Eastside Main (2WD). Keeping left, continue 7 km (4.3 mi) on gravel to the busy Cheakamus Lake parking lot (toilet available).

A wet summer day at Cheakamus Lake.

THE HIKE

From the map board, set off east on an old road shared with mountain bikers and portaging canoeists and kayakers. Rock-dwelling American pikas, smaller cousins of rabbits and hares, welcome you to the Cheakamus Lake Trail with whistling alarm calls. Pass the outhouse and enter the woods. Culverts convey water underneath the path.

A sign indicates an area logged in 1963 and reforested in 1975. Crossing an avalanche path, briefly trade shade for sun. In 15 minutes, come to a grove of towering Douglas-firs. (Fun fact: A coastal forest in B.C. is considered old-growth if it has trees older than 250 years.) Stroll the level, muddy path through amabilis fir, western hemlock, and devil's club.

A half-hour (1.5 km/0.9 mi) from the trailhead, reach a junction (50°02′04″ N, 122°58′11″ W). The Helm Creek Trail goes right to cross the Cheakamus River (Ch'iyákmesh Stákw to the Squamish, Nsqwítsu to the Lílwat) en route to Helm Lake (Hike 10) and the Garibaldi Lake area. However, continue straight ahead on the Cheakamus Lake Trail, getting near enough to the milky river to earn a look at the swift current below. Take note of uprooted western red cedar giants and seedlings nourished by nurse logs, as well as orange coral mushroom, pear-shaped puffball, sulphur tuft, woolly pine spike, and other fungi.

Twenty minutes past the junction, detour right for a view of the lake outlet. The trail skirts the base of a boulder field. After little more than an hour of hiking, arrive at the Cheakamus Lake campground (50°01′31″ N, 122°56′50″ W)—with its shoreline tent sites, outhouses, and food caches—at the 3-km (1.9-mi) mark. It's worth pushing on, following the undulating trail east in lush forest, through avalanche paths with edible thistle, and along the base of bluffs.

After 2 hours (7 km/4.3 mi) on foot, a sign marks the end of the maintained trail at the Singing Creek campground (50°00′39″ N, 122°54′42″ W). Facilities include tent sites, an outhouse, and a food cache. Wander down to the mouth of Singing Creek, enjoy lunch on the pebbly beach and perhaps a chilly swim, and survey the second-largest lake in Garibaldi Provincial Park. Historically stocked with rainbow trout, Cheakamus Lake sits in a glacial trough at an elevation of 831 m (2,730 ft) and reaches a maximum depth of 119 m (390 ft). Potential wildlife sightings include black bears (got bear spray?), Canada geese, dark-eyed juncos, and Douglas squirrels. Retrace your steps to the trailhead.

Thanks to the advocacy of the B.C. Mountaineering Club and Alpine Club of Canada, Garibaldi was established in 1927 as B.C.'s fourth provincial park. Garibaldi's 1990 master plan describes the park as the "singularly most significant protected wilderness in the Lower Mainland." In 2014, B.C. Parks amended the plan and nixed the idea of building a hiking trail between the Singing Creek delta and Singing Pass (Hike 12).

Dogs (subject to a $115 fine), drones, fires, hunting, motorized vehicles, and berry, flower, and mushroom picking are prohibited throughout the park. Camping is allowed at designated sites only, and reservations are required year-round. Pack it in, pack it out.

STOP OF INTEREST
ALEXANDER FALLS

With three tiers, Alexander Falls is an eye-catching sight and requires less walking than more popular waterfalls in the Highway 99 (Sea to Sky Highway) corridor between Squamish and Pemberton. Just upstream from its confluence with Callaghan Creek (Sts'áḵ'aýs to the Squamish Nation, Scwálem to the Líl̓wat Nation), Madeley Creek plunges 43 m (141 ft). On Highway 99, 3 km (1.9 mi) north of Brandywine Falls Provincial Park and 14 km (8.7 mi) south of Whistler Village, turn west onto Callaghan Valley Road. (Black bear sightings are common.) In 9 km (5.6 mi), the Alexander Falls Recreation Site, with its wheelchair-accessible viewing platform, is on the left (before the Callaghan Creek Forest Service Road turnoff).

Cheakamus Lake from Whistler Mountain (Kacwitma).

Hiking on the Cheakamus Lake Trail.

12 WHISTLER
SINGING PASS

The hills are alive with a symphony of wildflowers

Distance: 23.5 km (14.6 mi)
Time: 7 hours (out and back)
Elevation gain: 1,040 m (3,410 ft)
High point: 1,730 m (5,680 ft)

Difficulty: ■
Maps: NTS 92-J/2 Whistler; John Baldwin Backcountry Whistler
Trailhead: 50°06'47" N, 122°57'08" W

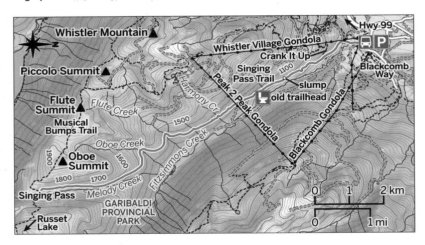

DON'T BE surprised if you're tempted to burst into song at Singing Pass. In summer, the hills are alive with a symphony of wildflowers. Yodelling also helps avoid a face-to-face encounter with a black bear. One of five main entry points to Garibaldi Provincial Park, the well-graded Singing Pass Trail crescendoes between the two ski hills of Whistler Blackcomb and lies in the territories of the Lílwat and Squamish First Nations.

GETTING THERE
Transit: Take Whistler Transit Bus 5, 6, 7, 8, 20, 21, 25, 30, 31, or 32, or Pemberton Valley Transit Bus 99 (Pemberton Commuter) to Gondola Transit Exchange. (Epic Rides offers daily coach service to Whistler's Gateway Loop from Burrard Station in Vancouver.)

Subalpine wildflowers at Singing Pass. Photo by Joan Septembre

Vehicle: On Highway 99 (Sea to Sky Highway) at Whistler Village, 58 km (36 mi) north of Downtown Squamish, turn east onto Village Gate Boulevard. Go left on Blackcomb Way and turn right to enter the Whistler Village day lots. Park in Day Lot 1 (electric vehicle charging station available) or 2, or as close as possible. (Designated overnight parking spots for Garibaldi Provincial Park are located in Day Lot 4. The nearest restrooms are at the Pan Pacific Whistler Mountainside hotel, next to the bus loop.)

THE HIKE

Find the Singing Pass trailhead kiosk at Gondola Transit Exchange (across Blackcomb Way from Day Lot 1). From the gate under the Excalibur Gondola, walk south up the service road on the edge of the Lower Olympic ski run, between the ziplines and Fitzsimmons Express chairlift, forking right at the start. Take note of the downhill action in the Whistler Mountain Bike Park. In 500 m (0.3 mi), go left at the signed turnoff. Continue up the gravel road and the valley of Fitzsimmons Creek (Tsíqten in the Ucwalmícwts dialect of the Lílwat Nation), passing a water reservoir, taking a right fork, and crossing the Crank It Up free-ride trail.

After 45 minutes on foot, bear right at a boulder barrier. Shortly thereafter, reach the Fitzsimmons Creek slump. A form of mass wasting, a slump occurs when part of the ground slips—and often rotates backward—over the surface of underlying material. In the early 1990s, this geotechnical instability cut off

Sitka columbine in summer bloom. Photo by Joan Septembre

vehicular access to the old Singing Pass trailhead, lengthening the hike appreciably. In recent years, the Federation of Mountain Clubs of B.C. has sought a new trailhead and parking lot on the Blackcomb side of the Fitzsimmons Creek hydropower intake to restore public access to Singing Pass.

A series of narrow bridges follow the slump. Arrive at the former trailhead and its weathered outhouses (1 hour up; 50°05′05″ N, 122°55′46″ W), 4 km (2.5 mi) from Whistler Village. Beyond, the Singing Pass Trail rises more steeply, following an old mining road. Pass under Whistler Blackcomb's Peak 2 Peak Gondola, which boasts world records for the highest cable car above ground and the longest unsupported span between two cable car towers. The bridge over Harmony Creek is gone; fording the dramatic debris channel is dangerous in high water.

Encounter the Garibaldi Provincial Park boundary and cross bridges over the plunging waters of Flute and Oboe Creeks, the latter at the 8-km (5-mi) mark and 1,400 m (4,590 ft) high. Lovely conifers are draped in witch's hair lichen, and moss blankets the steep forest floor. Spot a variety of macrofungi: conifer tuft, red-belted polypore, scurfy twiglet, and yellow coral.

The woods open up as you parallel Melody Creek en route to Singing Pass. After 3.5 hours on foot, you've earned the stroll through the subalpine meadows ahead. Flies and mosquitos pollinate the floral ensemble—jazzy with arctic lupine, broad-leaved willowherb, green false hellebore, mountain arnica, leafy aster, leatherleaf saxifrage, and Sitka columbine in summer bloom. Stick to the trail to protect the sensitive vegetation.

March over open terrain to the Singing Pass junction (4 hours up; 50°01'46" N, 122°53'25" W), on the periphery of the Squamish Nation's Kwáyatsut Wild Spirit Place. Amble left to a nearby interpretative panel and pond, and bask in the sumptuous meadows, before retracing your steps back to the village.

From the pass, the left-hand trail continues east to Russet Lake, at the base of Fissile Peak, in 3 km (1.9 mi). A designated camping area and pit toilet are situated by the lake, where the B.C. Mountaineering Club erected the small Himmelsbach Hut in 1968. Opened in 2019, the Kees and Claire Hut is located near the high point of the Russet Lake Trail. The Spearhead Huts Society plans to construct two more donor-funded huts, at Mount Macbeth and Mount Pattison, along the Spearhead ski traverse. A proposal would see the three huts, operated by the Alpine Club of Canada's Whistler section, linked by a hiking trail.

A right turn at the pass points the way to Flute Summit via the Musical Bumps Trail, and beyond to the top of the Whistler Village Gondola on Whistler Mountain (Kacwitma to the Lílwat), 9.5 km (5.9 mi) distant.

Dogs, drones, fires, hunting, motorized vehicles, and flower and mushroom picking are banned throughout Garibaldi Provincial Park. Mountain biking is prohibited in the Singing Pass area. Camping is permitted at designated sites only, and reservations are required year-round. Whistler Blackcomb is smoke-free.

WHISTLER MUSEUM

Once named Summit Lake, the settlement of Whistler sprang up along the Lillooet–Burrard Inlet Trail of 1877. This historic pack route, also known as the Pemberton Trail, followed a First Nations trade route. In 1966, the Garibaldi Lift Company opened the original ski area on Whistler Mountain (Kacwitma to the Lílwat Nation), setting the stage for today's bustling resort municipality. Explore the area's natural and human history at the Whistler Museum (4333 Main Street), located behind the Whistler Public Library. Open daily, the museum houses exhibits about mountain culture, ski racing, and Vancouver's 2010 Olympic and Paralympic Winter Games. Admission is by donation.

DECKER MOUNTAIN

Get off the beaten path in the Spearhead Range

Distance: 12 km (7.5 mi)
Time: 6.5 hours (out and back)
Elevation gain: 600 m (1,970 ft)
High point: 2,421 m (7,943 ft)

Difficulty: ◆◆
Maps: NTS 92-J/2 Whistler; John Baldwin Backcountry Whistler
Trailhead: 50°05'45" N, 122°53'59" W

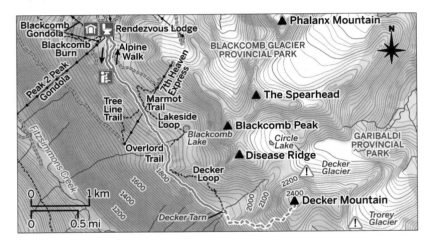

SURVEYING THE grand panorama atop Decker Mountain, Blackcomb Peak rises to the northwest and the rest of the Spearhead Range looms large in the opposite direction. The mollycoddling approach on resort-maintained trails pays off big time too, with the whistles of hoary marmots, oodles of brilliant wildflowers, and a milky tarn to boot. Seeking the seldom-visited summit demands off-trail route-finding, however, and is better left to experienced scramblers. From Whistler Blackcomb's controlled recreation area to Garibaldi Provincial Park, this excursion uses public lands in the territories of the Líl̓wat and Squamish First Nations.

GETTING THERE

Transit: Take Whistler Transit Bus 5, 6, 7, 8, 20, 21, 25, 30, 31, or 32, or Pemberton Valley Transit Bus 99 (Pemberton Commuter) to Gondola Transit

Wildfire smoke obscures the view from Decker Mountain.

Exchange. Walk east on Blackcomb Way for 500 m (0.3 mi) to Blackcomb base in the Upper Village. (Epic Rides offers daily coach service to Whistler's Gateway Loop from Burrard Station in Vancouver.)

Vehicle: On Highway 99 (Sea to Sky Highway) at Whistler Village, 58 km (36 mi) north of Downtown Squamish, turn east onto Village Gate Boulevard. Go left on Blackcomb Way and turn right to enter the Whistler Village day lots. Park in Day Lot 1 (electric vehicle charging station available) or 2, or as close as possible. Walk east on the Fitzsimmons Trail to Blackcomb base. (Restrooms are available at the Blackcomb Daylodge.)

THE HIKE

The trailhead lies near the Rendezvous Lodge at 1,860 m (6,102 ft). So the first order of business is to hoof it up the Blackcomb Burn ascent trails (5.2 km/3.2 mi one-way with 1,175 m/3,855 ft of elevation gain) or cough up for a ride on the new Blackcomb Gondola. Either way, start up the Alpine Walk on the rim of Blackcomb Bowl, and immediately turn right. In 10 minutes, the gravel loop delivers a pleasing view of the Musical Bumps and Whistler Mountain (Kacwitma in the Ucwalmícwts dialect of the Lílwat Nation) from Fitzsimmons Lookout.

At the next right, go southeast on the Overlord Trail (3.7 km/2.3 mi), and leave most of the selfie-obsessed sightseers behind. Stick with mellow

Disease Ridge reflected in Decker Tarn.

Overlord as it ducks under the 7th Heaven Express chairlift, slices across ski runs, drops to 1,820 m (5,970 ft), and enters Garibaldi Provincial Park. Ignore turnoffs for the Marmot Trail (left), Tree Line Trail (right), Lakeside Loop (left twice), and Decker Loop (left). Listen for the drumming wings of the ruffed grouse, and admire the kaleidoscopic sight of arctic lupine, fan-leaved cinquefoil, pink mountain-heather, red paintbrush, and western pasqueflower in the subalpine meadows.

Your alpine objective fills the view ahead as Decker Tarn (1,925 m/ 6,320 ft) nears. Cross the outflow creek, take note of a boot-beaten path leaving to the right, and reach the idyllic pond, 4.3 km (2.7 mi) from the lodge. After an hour and 15 minutes of moderate hiking, you've earned a brief cooling-off period in the shadow of Disease Ridge (north) and Decker Mountain (east). When you're ready to tackle the ascent, return to the afore-mentioned path (50°04′04″ N, 122°52′18″ W); it's distinguished by a Whistler Blackcomb sign warning of "uncontrolled and unmarked hazards" beyond the hiking area boundary. (Inexperienced and ill-equipped hikers should proceed no farther.)

The path quickly dissipates. Traverse a boulder moraine to gain the low end of Decker Mountain's long southwest ridge. Intermittent cairns and tracks point the way through stunted trees and loose boulders, but they are challenging to discern, especially in fog or smoke. The path of least resistance soon swings well right of the ridge crest. A relentless talus plod, broken up by patches of heather and lingering snow in summer, completes the straight-forward ascent. Mountain sorrel flowers amid the rocks of the upper slopes.

Two hours and 1.8 km (1.1 mi) after the tarn, reach the broad, breccia-strewn plateau atop Decker Mountain. A wooden stake denotes the indistinct summit (50°04′08″ N, 122°51′19″ W). The mountaintop sundeck invites wandering, but be sure to stay well back from cliffs and cornices. Lunch and look southeast to rugged Tremor Mountain, Mount Pattison, and Mount Trorey, towering dramatically over the Tremor and Trorey Glaciers. To the south, the Fitzsimmons Range spreads out across the deep valley of Fitzsimmons Creek (Tsíqten to the Líl̓wat). Soaking its toe in a lake, the Decker Glacier abrades the precipitous northern aspect of its namesake mountain. Circle Lake occupies the higher bowl beneath Blackcomb Peak and The Spearhead to the northwest.

Once satiated, reverse your ascent route to return to Decker Tarn. Follow the Overlord Trail back to the Alpine Walk, where you go right to complete the tourist loop en route to the lodge and gondola. (Make sure to check the schedule.)

Dogs, drones, fires, hunting, motorized vehicles, and flower and mush-room picking are banned throughout Garibaldi Provincial Park. Whistler Blackcomb is smoke-free (no tobacco, marijuana, e-cigarettes, or vaporizers). Camping is not permitted in this area. Please use Leave No Trace practices. Mountain goats roam the Spearhead Range.

STOP OF INTEREST
SQUAMISH LÍL'WAT CULTURAL CENTRE

Travelling north on Highway 99 (Sea to Sky Highway) between West Vancouver and Pemberton entails visiting the territories of the Squamish and Líl̓wat peoples. These First Nations have a long history of sharing the land and resources of the Whistler area. In 2008, the Squamish Líl'wat Cultural Centre (4584 Blackcomb Way) opened in the Upper Village. Exhibits spotlight the art, heritage, languages, and stories of both nations. Open daily, the SLCC is the centrepiece of the self-guided Cultural Journey tour, which features interpretive kiosks at stops along the Sea to Sky Highway. SLCC day passes cost $18 for adults and $5 for youths.

WEDGEMOUNT LAKE

An alpine jewel worth the steep price of admission

Distance: 12.5 km (7.8 mi)
Time: 8.5 hours (out and back)
Elevation gain: 1,165 m (3,822 ft)
High point: 1,920 m (6,300 ft)

Difficulty: ◆
Maps: NTS 92-J/2 Whistler
Trailhead: 50°10'24" N, 122°51'46" W

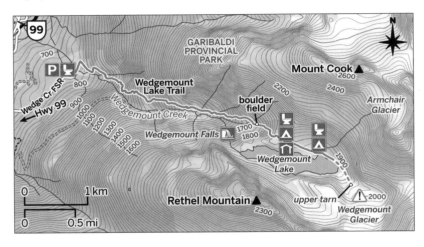

AMONG THE turquoise jewels of the Coast Mountains, Wedgemount Lake's popularity with selfie-seekers perhaps pales only in comparison to Joffre Lakes. It's no mystery why. The prize for undertaking this unrelentingly steep trail is a dramatic tarn fed by melting glaciers and lorded over by the highest peak in Garibaldi Provincial Park. A waterfall and wildflowers add sparkle to the ascent.

GETTING THERE

Vehicle: From Highway 99 (Sea to Sky Highway), 11.5 km (7.1 mi) north of Whistler Village and 1.7 km (1.1 mi) south of the WedgeWoods housing sub-division, go east on Wedge Creek Forest Service Road (2WD). Cross a railroad track and bridge over the Green River, and bear left at the first fork. Keep right at the second fork with a gated road, go left at the third fork, and ascend

The glacial milk of Wedgemount Lake.

an 18 per cent grade. Arrive at the small but busy Wedgemount Lake parking lot (toilet available), 2.5 km (1.6 mi) from the highway. Warning: Vehicle break-ins have been reported here.

THE HIKE

Despite empirical evidence to the contrary, flip-flops are not suitable footwear for the strenuous Wedgemount Lake Trail. However, hiking poles are advisable, especially for the descent. Start by crossing a bridge over Wedgemount Creek, which empties into the Green River (Emhátkwa in the Ucwalmícwts dialect of the Lílwat Nation). After a brief flat stretch, follow orange diamonds uphill through a regenerating clear-cut with blueberries and fireweed. The construction of the bankrupted Wedgemount Creek run-of-river power plant necessitated this re-route.

Enter the shady forest, where devil's club lurks in the understory. Despite its noxious yellow spines, this deciduous shrub tempts bears with its bright red berries and is greatly valued by Indigenous peoples from Alaska to Oregon for its medicinal and other uses. Go back and forth over a dry creek bed using a series of log bridges. In 20 minutes, there's a negligible viewpoint off to the right. A half-hour later, spy a cave to the left through the tall trees, and merge with the old trail. Shortly after, huge boulders on the edge of a rockslide to the left beckon for a rest.

The milky tarn at the toe of the Wedgemount Glacier.

Negotiate talus at 2.9 km (1.8 mi), then cross and recross a small creek. Earn glimpses of lofty Wedgemount Falls through the trees to the right, 2.5 hours in. As you gain elevation, the wildflowers—arctic lupine, pink mountain-heather, Sitka columbine, western pasqueflower, etc.—multiply. From west to east, the trail visits three biogeoclimatic zones: coastal western hemlock, mountain hemlock, and coastal mountain-heather alpine.

At 4 km (2.5 mi), emerge from the trees in a subalpine bowl. An impos-ing boulder field lies before you. Scramble steeply up the exhilarating final chute—with a handline for aid near the top—to the lip of the cirque. Find the pint-sized Wedgemount Lake Hut (3.5 hours up; 1,900 m/6,230 ft; 50°09′45″ N, 122°48′58″ W), built by the B.C. Mountaineering Club in 1970 and now used as an emergency shelter, several minutes away at the 4.8-km (3-mi) mark. Tent pads, a pit toilet, a map board, and hoary marmots are close by. Commanding a sublime prospect of glacial-floured Wedgemount Lake beneath Parkhurst and Rethel Mountains, this viewpoint is a thrilling-enough destination for most hikers.

For a closer look at the receding Wedgemount Glacier, push on for another hour (1.4 km/0.9 mi) toward the foot of Wedge Mountain (2,904 m/ 9,527 ft). A path leads down through the boulders to the shore. More tent pads are sited where meltwater from Mount Weart's Armchair Glacier flows into the lake, and a seasonal toilet is nearby. Spot golden-crowned sparrows and hardy wildflowers—broad-leaved willowherb, moss campion, red paintbrush, and silky phacelia—amid the alpine till. Go for a chilly swim if you dare.

Continue southeast along the shore and past the lakehead. Follow an intermittent path up the rocks and over a riegel (transverse bedrock ridge) to the snowy upper tarn (50°09'22" N, 122°48'05" W) at the toe of the Wedgemount Glacier. A few decades back, the glacier terminated in Wedgemount Lake. Admire the milky water, blue ice, and dicey seracs—from a safe distance. Stay off the glacier and out of the crevasses, and beware of calving ice. Retrace your steps to the trailhead. Make sure to save enough light—natural or artificial—for the tiring descent. Etiquette dictates downhill hikers yield to uphill travellers.

Wedgemount Lake lies in the territories of the Líl̓wat and Squamish First Nations. Dogs, drones, fires, hunting, motorized vehicles, and berry, flower, and mushroom picking are prohibited in Garibaldi Provincial Park. Camping is permitted at designated sites only, and reservations are required year-round. Pack out all trash, take care not to foul the lake water, and use earphones to listen to music (if you must).

STOP OF INTEREST

SHADOW LAKE INTERPRETIVE FOREST

One of three sites in the Sea to Sky Corridor reserved for the demonstration of silviculture, Shadow Lake Interpretive Forest lies at the foot of the Soo River (Sú7a to the Líl̓wat Nation) valley. A small network of trails leads to clear-cut and selectively logged woods, and a grove of old-growth western red cedars. Shadow Lake (Tselel'elh) itself is encircled by a seasonal swamp that provides winter habitat for moose. A place of cultural significance, it's designated as a Líl̓wat A7x7ūlm̓ecw (spirited ground) area. Find the parking lot on the east side of Highway 99 (Sea to Sky Highway), 18 km (11 mi) north of Whistler Village. (Parking is also available along the Soo River Forest Service Road. Dogs must be on leash.)

SEMAPHORE LAKES

A little piece of paradise in the Coast Mountains

Distance: 5.5 km (3.4 mi)
Time: 3 hours (out and back)
Elevation gain: 315 m (1,030 ft)
High point: 1,659 m (5,440 ft)

Difficulty: ■
Maps: NTS 92-J/11 North Creek
Trailhead: 50°35'26" N, 123°01'04" W

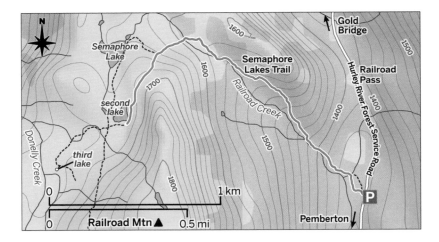

A LAND of rolling meadows, attractive tarns, and intriguing peaks, the Semaphore Lakes area is a little piece of paradise in the Coast Mountains—and it only takes a brief hike to get there. The reward-to-effort ratio is off the charts! Although it's not a park or designated recreation site, this patch of Sťáťimc territory at the headwaters of Railroad Creek and Donelly Creek is an increasingly popular backcountry destination. Its fragile environment and spectacular natural features deserve protection.

GETTING THERE
Vehicle: From Whistler, head north on Highway 99 (Sea to Sky Highway). In Pemberton, turn left onto Portage Road at the traffic lights. Go left at a roundabout, across the train tracks, and onto Birch Street. Turn right onto Pemberton Meadows Road. In 23 km (14 mi), head right on (Upper) Lillooet

Semaphore Lakes and Railroad Mountain from Face Mountain.

River Forest Service Road and keep left on the far side of the Lillooet River bridge. After 8.5 km (5.3 mi) on Lillooet River FSR, make a right onto Hurley River FSR (rough 2WD). In another 14 km (8.7 mi), before the road crests Railroad Pass, find the small parking area on the left.

THE HIKE

Yellow flagging indicates the start of the Semaphore Lakes Trail, though the tapes don't remain colour consistent. Set off northwest on the muddy, braided path and quickly cross a stream. Staying on river left of Railroad Creek, the trail steepens and doesn't let up until the first meadow, a half-hour in. Then the grade relaxes. Arctic lupine, broad-leaved willowherb, green false hellebore, mountain arnica, partridge-foot, pink mountain-heather, Sitka valerian, and subalpine daisy paint a floral rainbow.

After an hour on foot, with Face Mountain imposing ahead, veer left to cross lazy Railroad Creek in a shallow meadow bowl. Follow the main path southwest, over a rise, to a pretty lake (1.5 hours up; 50°35'41" N, 123°02'14" W), upstream of Semaphore Lake itself, bypassed en route. Bouldery meadows, little ponds, clumps of conifers, rocky moraines, and a web of boot paths surround this second lake in the open terrain.

A number of toponyms in the vicinity are a rail fan's (or ferroequinologist's) dream. To the southwest, Locomotive Mountain (2,340 m/7,680 ft), Tender Mountain, and Caboose Mountain rise behind the Train Glacier,

Locomotive Mountain and the Train Glacier from Face Mountain.

Face Mountain at sunrise from the meadows at Semaphore Lakes.

whose meltwater gushes forth in a spectacular waterfall feeding Donelly Creek. Locomotive is a favoured objective via its south ridge. Face Mountain, due west and concealing the Freight Glacier behind it, is a more difficult, Class 3 scramble. Water cascades over Face's eastern cliffs. Railroad Mountain (1,827 m/5,990 ft), just south of the second lake, is the nearest summit.

Semaphore Lake is named for a formerly widespread form of fixed railway signal that has been mostly superseded by coloured lights; the larger lake lies 300 m (0.2 mi) north at a slightly lower elevation. A third lake in the meadows is found by a moraine, 400 m (0.2 mi) southwest; it drains to Donelly Creek, a Hurley River tributary, rather than Railroad Creek. The latter empties into the Lillooet (Lílwat) River—Lilwatátkwa in Ucwalmícwts, the language of the Lílwat Nation—in the Pemberton Valley. When satisfied with this splendid landscape, return the way you came.

The Semaphore Lakes area is in dire need of designated campsites and trails, pit toilets, and food caches. (Be bear aware!) It's certainly magical, but the meadows are trampled, toilet paper flowers are sprinkled here and there, and the proliferation of tent sites, firepits, and boot paths is out of control. Campfires have no place in the alpine and subalpine, where wood is scarce and plant growth is slow. A bug net will help you fend off biting insects. Please stick to the well-established trails and tent sites, so as to prevent further damage to this sensitive environment. This is as good a place as any to put the seven principles of Leave No Trace into practice.

STOP OF INTEREST
PEMBERTON MUSEUM

Port Pemberton sprang up as a stop along the 1858 Harrison-Lillooet Trail, also known as the Douglas Trail, to the Fraser Canyon goldfields. Today, the Pemberton Museum (7455 Prospect Street) highlights the lives of local settlers, the impact of gold fever, and the history of the Sťáťimc people. The Pemberton and District Museum and Archives Society focuses its collections on the region drained by rivers emptying into Anderson Lake and the north end of Harrison Lake. Find the museum in Pemberton's downtown area, just off Highway 99 (Sea to Sky Highway) via Portage Road. It's open May to November, and admission is by donation.

16 PEMBERTON
MARRIOTT BASIN

Fall under the spell of a pair of enchanting lakes

Distance: 10.5 km (6.5 mi)
Time: 5.5 hours (out and back)
Elevation gain: 710 m (2,330 ft)
High point: 2,110 m (6,920 ft)

Difficulty: ◆◆
Maps: NTS 92-J/8 Duffey Lake; John Baldwin Duffey Lake
Trailhead: 50°24'18" N, 122°27'44" W

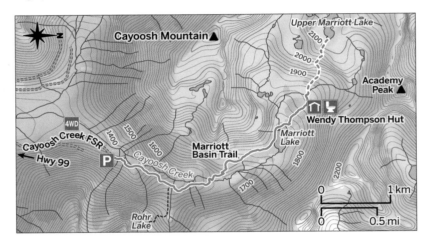

IN WINTER, the alpine basin southeast of Mount Marriott, formerly known as Aspen Peak, is a ski tourer's playground. Marriott Basin is seventh heaven for summer hikers too. This trip leads to rapturous meadows and two enchanting lakes at the headwaters of Cayoosh Creek, in the territory of the Stát̓imc people, including the Líl̓wat and N'Quatqua First Nations. The Wendy Thompson Hut is a suitable destination for most hikers, though, as the upper lake requires off-trail route-finding.

GETTING THERE

Vehicle: From Pemberton, head east on Highway 99 (Sea to Sky Highway). At the Mount Currie intersection, go right and stay on Highway 99 (Duffey Lake Road) for 26 km (16 mi). Past the Cayoosh Creek #1 bridge, turn left onto the unsigned Cayoosh Creek Forest Service Road—before the sand shed. With 4WD and high clearance, drive north as far as 2.3 km (1.4 mi), keeping left, to

Rohr Lake, Marriott Lake, and Mount Marriott from Mount Rohr.

the trailhead at road's end. (Motorists with 2WD or worried about their vehicle's paint should park near the bottom or on the roadside by the sand shed and walk the rest of the way.)

THE HIKE

At the end of Cayoosh Creek FSR (1,390 m/4560 ft), a trailhead map points out the simple, challenging, and complex avalanche terrain awaiting in Marriott Basin during the snow season. Head north under the cover of forest, pursuing orange markers. Within 20 minutes, come to a key junction (50°24′37″ N, 122°27′30″ W). Right leads to Rohr Lake, so take the left fork, signed for "Aspen."

The Marriott Basin Trail steepens, crosses streams, and encounters the first small meadow, blueberries, and mud. Cross Cayoosh Creek to river right on a log with a handline. Watching for tapes of various colours, stay on the main path to protect the meadows. A lovely floodplain is visible through the trees to the right. Travel through heather, passing diminutive ponds and rock fields with pikas.

An hour from the trailhead, Marriott Lake enters the picture as cairns show the way across boulder-strewn meadows. Shaped like a peanut, the beautiful blue lake lies at the base of avalanche slopes. The path stays above the shore until reaching a pretty little delta. Cross the creek on boulders, and continue past the lake to head northwest and upstream alongside another creek. The blooms include leatherleaf saxifrage, partridge-foot, subalpine daisy, and western pasqueflower.

Arrive at the Wendy Thompson Hut (1,820 m/5,970 ft; 50°25'48" N, 122°28'29" W), 2 hours (4.2 km/2.6 mi) from the trailhead. Built by the Alpine Club of Canada's Whistler section in 2000, the rustic gothic-arch cabin sleeps 16 guests and 4 custodians. (Reservations are required. No outside fires.) A creek is out front and an outhouse is close by.

This is the end of the provincially sanctioned recreation trail (difficulty rating: moderate). For experienced hikers, the upper lake beckons 1 hour (1 km/ 0.6 mi) west-northwest. The fading path continues through a bouldery meadow, then heads steeply up through shrubs. Follow intermittent tracks and sparse cairns, with easy scrambling in boulder fields, into gorgeous rocky alpine terrain. Surmount the final rise and gaze upon Upper Marriott Lake (3 hours up; 50°25'59" N, 122°29'11" W), a place at home in a fantasy world. It's an incredible (and cold) swimming hole. Retrace your steps to the trailhead.

Marriott Basin falls within the Líĺwat Nation's Nlháxten Nt'ákmen (Our Way) Area—wherein wilderness is to be maintained, cultural practices sustained, and industrial development and intensive tourism prohibited—in the Cayoosh Creek drainage. The Líĺwat highly value Nlháxten as a site of legends, vision quests, culturally modified trees, and rock art. Pack it in, pack it out, and tread lightly on this land.

East of Pemberton, Highway 99 crosses the Lillooet River (Lilwatátkwa) and passes Lillooet Lake (Lúlwata Tselálh). The Líĺwat Nation has proposed that the anglicized toponyms for these geographical features be formally corrected to Líĺwat River and Líĺwat Lake, respectively.

LÍĹWAT7ÚL CULTURE CENTRE

The Líĺwat7úl Culture Centre celebrates the art, crafts, and language of the Líĺwat Nation. Located at the Tszil Learning Centre (125 Lillooet Lake Road) in Mount Currie, it showcases artifacts, basketry, leatherwork, and contemporary art, and hosts programs aimed at revitalizing Ucwalmícwts, the dialect of Stát̓imcets spoken by the Líĺwat and their neighbours. This language reclamation work is critical; as of 2018, there were 98 fluent Stát̓imcets speakers. (According to the First Peoples' Cultural Council, B.C. is home to 34 living First Nations languages, including no less than 93 dialects, and at least 3 sleeping languages.) Find the Líĺwat7úl Culture Centre immediately east of Highway 99's Mount Currie intersection. It's open weekdays, and admission is free.

Wildfire smoke at Upper Marriott Lake.

BLOWDOWN PASS

Swimming is bliss at Blowdown Lake

Distance: 8.5 km (5.3 mi)
Time: 4 hours (out and back)
Elevation gain: 490 m (1,610 ft)
High point: 2,160 m (7,090 ft)

Difficulty: ■
Maps: NTS 92-J/8; Trail Ventures Stein
to Joffre; John Baldwin Duffey Lake
Trailhead: 50°22'12" N, 122°11'43" W

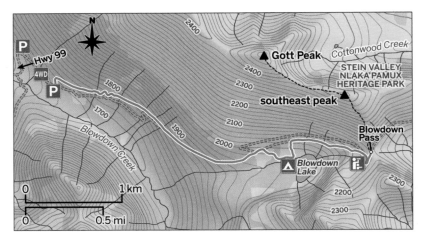

ON THE way to Blowdown Pass, in the territories of the Nlaka'pamux and Státimc peoples, you'll travel through radiant wildflower meadows and go by a blissful swimming lake. The gap between Gott Peak (Hike 19) and Gotcha Peak (Hike 18) is a back door to Stein Valley Nlaka'pamux Heritage Park, which is jointly managed by the Lytton First Nation and B.C. Parks. From the pass, you can peer into the remote valley of the south fork of Cottonwood Creek, a tributary of the storied Stein River (Sti'yen ["hidden place"] in Nlaka'pamuchin).

GETTING THERE

Vehicle: From Highway 99 (Duffey Lake Road), 52 km (32 mi) northeast of Pemberton and 47 km (29 mi) southwest of Lillooet, go east on Blowdown Creek Forest Service Road (high-clearance 2WD). This turnoff is by the

A pond near Blowdown Lake, with Gott Peak in the background.

double avalanche gate north of Duffey Lake Provincial Park. Expect water bars. Continue straight where a branch leaves to the left. At 2.5 km (1.6 mi), take the left fork. Park on the shoulder, 10 km (6.2 mi) from the highway. With 4WD, continue right and up, through bigger water bars, for 600 m (0.4 mi) to a second parking area, where a rough 4×4 road exits to the left.

THE HIKE

From the 4WD parking area (1,670 m/5,480 ft), set off north on the 4×4 road, which quickly swings east. Some rugged vehicles drive this narrow road all the way to Blowdown Pass, so be prepared to get out of the way in a hurry. Bear scat (got bear spray?), a cornucopia of wildflowers (fireweed, fringed grass-of-Parnassus, orange agoseris, and tiger lily), and magical kaleidoscopes of northern blue butterflies may distract you during the steady rise.

After an hour (2.5 km/1.6 mi), the road enters an S-bend and splits into high and low tracks. At a leftward curve, turn right (east) onto the low road. In a moment, look for an easy-to-miss path, marked by a pink tape, in the shrubs on the right (50°21'49" N, 122°09'55" W). The muddy, sometimes faint single-turned-double track traverses wet subalpine meadows with the imposing northwest face of Gotcha Peak ahead. Bracted lousewort, fragrant white rein-orchid, globeflower, partridge-foot, sticky false asphodel, and white mountain marsh-marigold co-star in the lavish flower show. Cross a broad meadow, with a backdrop of Blowdown Pass.

Boulders in Blowdown Lake.

Arrive at the outlet of glorious Blowdown Lake (1,980 m/6,500 ft; 50°21′46″ N, 122°09′40″ W), less than 1.5 hours (3 km/1.9 mi) from the 4WD parking area. Tent sites are found left and right along the lakeshore. The clear water invites swimming, with rainbow trout, to submerged boulders. Clark's nutcrackers and varied thrushes lurk in the trees, and pikas call from the rocks across the lake.

To push on to the pass, 40 minutes (1.2 km/0.7 mi) distant, keep left at the lake outlet. In a grassy patch, steps away, find a steep trail leading north to the low road. Turn right at the junction (50°21′52″ N, 122°09′39″ W), marked with orange tape, and follow the deteriorating double track, which fades to single track in the meadows to the east. Cut across a boulder field, with hoary marmots, to merge with the high road (50°21′47″ N, 122°09′01″ W) en route to the pass. This turnoff is easy to miss on the way down.

From a leftward bend on the high road, the westward view of the Pacific Ranges is incredible, particularly at sunset. Continue several more steps to the summit of Blowdown Pass (2 hours up; 50°21′47″ N, 122°08′57″ W). A sign welcomes you to Stein Valley Nlaka'pamux Heritage Park, which protects many places of cultural significance to the Nlaka'pamux, including an arborglyph and petrographs (never touch these artifacts), spirit caves, and village sites.

The old road continues into the Cottonwood Creek drainage, offering connections to the abandoned Silver Queen mine site and the Stein Heritage Trail. Gott Peak and Gotcha Peak are both fine ridge rambles from the pass, with scrambly Gotcha being slightly more of a challenge than the more popular Gott. It's no fun dodging pickup trucks the whole way back. Take the scenic route down, via the lake, and retrace your steps to the parking area.

The Stein Valley was a major battleground in B.C.'s "war in the woods," wherein conservationists, First Nations, and local communities fought valley by valley in the 1970s, '80s, and '90s to protect old-growth forests from logging. Líĺwat Nation Chief Leonard Andrew and Lytton First Nation Chief Ruby Dunstan signed the Stein Declaration in 1987, affirming their commitment to preserving the Stein watershed as wilderness. In 1989, the First Nations jointly proclaimed the establishment of Stein Valley Tribal Heritage Park. The B.C. government finally created Stein Valley Nlaka'pamux Heritage Park in 1995. In 2018, Canada added the Stein Valley to its tentative list of potential candidates for a United Nations World Heritage Site.

Visitors are asked not to bring dogs into Stein Valley Nlaka'pamux Heritage Park. Bikes, drones, fires, flower picking, motorized vehicles, smoking, and vaping are prohibited in the park. Respect this special place.

STOP OF INTEREST

ONE MILE LAKE

A roadside jewel at the southern gateway to Pemberton, One Mile Lake is a lovely place to take a nature walk, paddle a canoe, hunt for geocaches, or play a round of disc golf. The shallow open-water wetland sits at the base of Signal Hill, known as Speíkúmtn to the Líĺwat Nation. Signal Hill is designated as a A7x7úĺméecw (spirited ground) area by the Líĺwat, who regard it as an important spiritual, cultural, and food gathering site. The Sea to Sky Trail runs through One Mile Lake Park on its way from Squamish to D'Arcy. Access the park from Highway 99 (Sea to Sky Highway), north of Nairn Falls Provincial Park.

GOTCHA PEAK

Scramble above Blowdown Pass for a panoramic payoff

Distance: 10.5 km (6.5 mi)
Time: 6 hours (out and back)
Elevation gain: 780 m (2,560 ft)
High point: 2,450 m (8,040 ft)

Difficulty: ◆◆
Maps: NTS 92-J/8; Trail Ventures Stein to Joffre; John Baldwin Duffey Lake
Trailhead: 50°22'12" N, 122°11'43" W

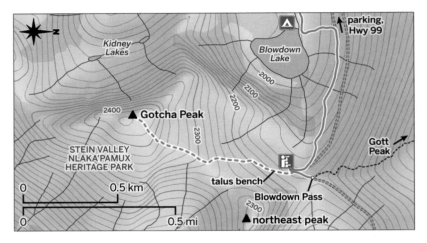

THE UNOFFICIALLY named Gotcha Peak is an enjoyable off-trail scramble from Blowdown Pass (Hike 17), an entry point to Stein Valley Nlaka'pamux Heritage Park. The route is less obvious than Gott Peak (Hike 19), its counterpart across the pass, so more route-finding is required. Once on top, the Coast Mountains panorama is glorious, especially at dusk.

GETTING THERE

Vehicle: From Highway 99 (Duffey Lake Road), 52 km (32 mi) northeast of Pemberton and 47 km (29 mi) southwest of Lillooet, go east on Blowdown Creek Forest Service Road (high-clearance 2WD). This turnoff is by the double avalanche gate north of Duffey Lake Provincial Park. Expect water bars. Continue straight where a branch leaves to the left. At 2.5 km (1.6 mi), take the left fork. Park on the shoulder, 10 km (6.2 mi) from the highway. With

The evening sun shines on the summit of Gotcha Peak.

4WD, continue right and up, through bigger water bars, for 600 m (0.4 mi) to a second parking area, where a rough 4×4 road exits to the left.

THE HIKE

From the 4WD parking area (1,670 m/5,480 ft), set off north then east on the 4×4 road. Some rugged vehicles drive this narrow road all the way to Blowdown Pass. After an hour, the road enters an S-bend and splits into high and low tracks. At a leftward curve, turn right (east) onto the low road. In a moment, look for an easy-to-miss path, marked by a pink tape, in the shrubs on the right (50°21'49" N, 122°09'55" W). The muddy, sometimes faint track traverses wet subalpine meadows.

Arrive at Blowdown Lake (1,980 m/6,500 ft; 50°21'46" N, 122°09'40" W), less than 1.5 hours from the 4WD parking area. Keep left at the outlet to push on to the pass, 40 minutes distant. In a grassy patch, steps away, find a steep trail leading north to the low road. Turn right at the junction (50°21'52" N, 122°09'39" W), marked with orange tape, and follow the deteriorating track through meadows. Merge with the high road (50°21'47" N, 122°09'01" W) en route to the pass. Gain the summit of Blowdown Pass (2,160 m/7,090 ft; 50°21'47"N, 122°08'57" W), after 2 hours (4.2 km/2.6 mi) of hiking. A sign welcomes you to Stein Valley Nlaka'pamux Heritage Park.

Gotcha Peak is an hour or so (1 km/0.6 mi) away. From the park-boundary sign, double back toward the scenic bend in the road right before the pass.

Head up the boulders to the bench just above the road and below the subpeak, Gotcha's northeast summit, adjacent to the pass.

Bypassing the subpeak and pursuing occasional cairns south, ascend the talus bench, which harbours lingering snow (and pesky bugs), to Gotcha's northeast ridge. Beware of drop-offs on both sides. Look east over the valley of the south fork of Cottonwood Creek, a tributary of the Stein River (Sti'yen in Nlaka'pamuchin, the language of the Nlaka'pamux people). Scramble up easy but loose rock to gain the ridgetop. Continue southwest to the summit of Gotcha Peak (3 hours up; 50°21'17" N, 122°09'16" W).

Bask in the tremendous panorama: Mount Matier and Joffre Peak behind Mount Caspar to the west; the steep, verdant meadows of Gott Peak to the north; Siwhe Mountain in the east; Petlushkwohap Mountain and Skihist Mountain to the southeast; and Notgott Peak to the south. At 2,968 m (9,740 ft) above mean sea level, Skihist is the highest peak in southwestern B.C. Peer down at the gleaming Kidney Lakes, towered over by Gotcha's summit cliffs. Retrace your steps back to Blowdown Pass, swim-worthy Blowdown Lake, and the parking area.

Visitors are asked not to bring dogs into Stein Valley Nlaka'pamux Heritage Park, which lies in the territories of the Nlaka'pamux and Státimc peoples, and is jointly managed by the Lytton First Nation and B.C. Parks. Bikes, drones, fires, flower picking, motorized vehicles, smoking, and vaping are prohibited inside the park. The headwaters of Blowdown Creek fall within the Líĺwat Nation's Nlháxten Nt'ákmen (Our Way) Area in the Cayoosh Creek basin. Leave No Trace practices are critical on either side of the park boundary. Be bear aware.

STOP OF INTEREST
NAIRN FALLS

Nairn Falls is known as Yélmícw in Ucwalmícwts, the language of the Líĺwat Nation. For the Líĺwat, Yélmícw is a place of spiritual importance, as well as a fishing hole. Established in 1966, Nairn Falls Provincial Park lies on the east side of Highway 99 (Sea to Sky Highway), just south of Pemberton. From the day-use parking lot, it's a 1.5 km (0.9 mi) walk (one-way) above the steep left bank of the Green River (Emhátkwa), partially following an ancient Líĺwat trail, to the waterfall. A spectacular viewing platform overlooks the falls, potholes, and a natural rock bridge. (Dogs must be leashed.)

The Coast Mountains from Gotcha Peak before sunset.

A Coast Mountains rainbow from the summit of Gotcha Peak.

GOTT PEAK

The ridge walk is going to get you

Distance: 12 km (7.5 mi)
Time: 6.5 hours (out and back)
Elevation gain: 840 m (2,760 ft)
High point: 2,511 m (8,240 ft)

Difficulty: ◆
Maps: NTS 92-J/8; Trail Ventures Stein to Joffre; John Baldwin Duffey Lake
Trailhead: 50°22'12" N, 122°11'43" W

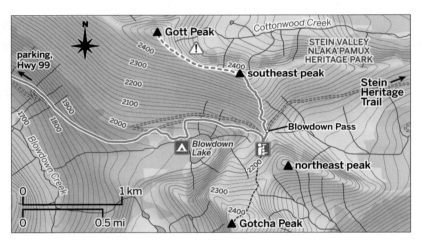

FROM THE stony summit of Gott Peak, the Joffre Group, Cayoosh Mountain, and Mount Marriott are lambent beacons on the western skyline. To get there and back entails a delightful ridge walk on the edge of Stein Valley Nlaka'pamux Heritage Park. Not bad for a day's hike.

GETTING THERE

Vehicle: From Highway 99 (Duffey Lake Road), 52 km (32 mi) northeast of Pemberton and 47 km (29 mi) southwest of Lillooet, go east on Blowdown Creek Forest Service Road (high-clearance 2WD). This turnoff is by the double avalanche gate north of Duffey Lake Provincial Park. Expect water bars. Continue straight where a branch leaves to the left. At 2.5 km (1.6 mi), take the left fork. Park on the shoulder, 10 km (6.2 mi) from the highway. With 4WD, continue right and up, through bigger water bars, for 600 m (0.4 mi) to a second parking area, where a rough 4×4 road exits to the left.

Ridge walking on Gott Peak above Blowdown Lake.

THE HIKE

From the 4WD parking area (1,670 m/5,480 ft), set off north then east on the 4×4 road. Some rugged vehicles drive this narrow road all the way to Blow-down Pass (Hike 17). After an hour, the road enters an S-bend and splits into high and low tracks. At a leftward curve, turn right (east) onto the low road. In a moment, look for an easy-to-miss path, marked by a pink tape, in the shrubs on the right (50°21′49″ N, 122°09′55″ W). The muddy, sometimes faint track traverses wet subalpine meadows.

Arrive at more-than-swimmable Blowdown Lake (1,980 m/6,500 ft; 50°21′46″ N, 122°09′40″ W), less than 1.5 hours from the 4WD parking area. Keep left at the outlet to push on to the pass, 40 minutes distant. In a grassy patch, steps away, find a steep trail leading north to the low road. Turn right at the junction (50°21′52″ N, 122°09′39″ W), marked with orange tape, and follow the deteriorating track through meadows. Merge with the high road (50°21′47″ N, 122°09′01″ W) en route to the pass. Gain the summit of Blow-down Pass (2,160 m/7,090 ft; 50°21′47″N, 122°08′57″ W), after 2 hours (4.2 km/2.6 mi) of hiking. A sign welcomes you to Stein Valley Nlaka'pamux Heritage Park.

Gott Peak is 1.5 hours (1.8 km/1.1 mi) away. From the park-boundary sign, a steep path climbs north on the Cottonwood Creek–Blowdown Creek divide to the nearest subpeak. Chunks of quartz are everywhere, and mica makes

The view from a ridge east of Gott Peak.

the dirt sparkle. Lance-leaved stonecrop, moss campion, spreading phlox, and woolly pussytoes bloom, and juniper and kinnikinnick bear fruit.

A couple of cairns lead to Gott's southeast peak (2,440 m/8,010 ft). As an appetizer, the panorama is far from subpar. Gotcha Peak (Hike 18) rises across the pass and above gleaming Blowdown Lake. Due east, a trio of summits divide the north and south forks of Cottonwood Creek, a tributary of the Stein River (Sti'yen in Nlaka'pamuchin, the language of the Nlaka'pamux people).

Savour the alpine ridge walk ahead. Pursue an intermittent track west through lichen-covered rocks, staying left of the crest and well back from cornices. While the south slope is convex and steep enough, the north aspect is a loose precipice upon which precariously stacked boulders perch. Pass the low point of the ridge, and ascend the main summit of Gott Peak (3.5 hours up; 50°22'22" N, 122°09'53" W).

To the north, Gott Creek drains a U-shaped valley and Elusive Peak can't help but stand out. South of Blowdown Lake, the Kidney Lakes and Notgott Peak are visible. Mount Matier and Joffre Peak are particularly eye-catching in the west. Enjoy spotting high-living hoary marmots and pikas on the return ridge walk. Retrace your steps to the parking area.

This is black and grizzly bear country. Visitors are asked not to bring dogs into Stein Valley Nlaka'pamux Heritage Park, which lies in the territories of the Nlaka'pamux and Sťáťimc peoples, and is jointly managed by the Lytton First Nation and B.C. Parks. Bikes, drones, fires, flower picking, motorized vehicles, smoking, and vaping are prohibited inside the park. The headwaters of Blowdown and Gott creeks fall within the Lílwat Nation's Nlháxten Nt'ákmen (Our Way) Area—wherein wilderness is to be protected, cultural practices sustained, and industrial development banned—in the Cayoosh Creek basin. Leave No Trace practices are essential on either side of the park boundary.

DUFFEY LAKE

Known as Teq to the Lílwat Nation, Duffey Lake is a beautiful sight in the Cayoosh Creek valley and an important hunting, trapping, and gathering area for the First Nation. Watched over by Mount Rohr, the lake is home to rainbow trout and mountain whitefish. Established in 1993, Duffey Lake Provincial Park protects habitat for black and grizzly bears, mountain goats, and other wildlife, and pockets of old-growth Douglas-fir and Engelmann spruce trees. Stop at the boat launch or one of the pullouts along Highway 99 (Duffey Lake Road), halfway between Pemberton and Lillooet. (Dogs must be leashed.)

DIEZ VISTAS TRAIL

The case of the hidden viewpoints

Distance: 13 km (8.1 mi)
Time: 6 hours (loop)
Elevation gain: 460 m (1,510 ft)
High point: 555 m (1,820 ft)

Difficulty: ■
Maps: NTS 92-G/7; Canadian Map Makers Coquitlam; Trail Ventures PoMo
Trailhead: 49°20'10" N, 122°51'31" W

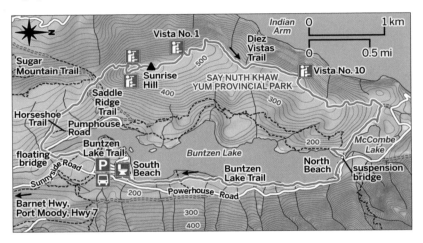

AS ITS Spanish name promises, the Diez Vistas Trail delivers 10 viewpoints. All of the numbered lookouts face the beautiful fjord of Indian Arm (Slilutulh to the Squamish Nation, Tsleil-Wat to the Tsleil-Waututh Nation), but half are easy to miss, overgrown, or view-challenged. No matter—the traverse of forested Buntzen Ridge (Kwe kwe xau to the Tsleil-Waututh) in Anmore is a reliably enjoyable shoulder-season favourite. Our clockwise loop visits the Buntzen Lake Recreation Area, Belcarra Regional Park, and Say Nuth Khaw Yum Provincial Park.

GETTING THERE

Transit: Take TransLink Bus 182 (Belcarra) to Anmore Grocery. Walk north, shortly bearing left onto Pumphouse Road, to meet the Buntzen Lake Trail at the floating bridge, in 1 km (0.6 mi). In summer, Bus 179 (Buntzen Lake) provides service to South Beach.

Indian Arm (Tsleil-Wat) from Buntzen Ridge (Kwe kwe xau). Photo by Bob Hare

Vehicle: From its junction with Highway 7 (Lougheed Highway) in Coquitlam, head west on Barnet Highway (formerly Highway 7A), then quickly north on Johnson Street. Turn left on David Avenue, right on Forest Park Way, and left on Aspenwood Drive, which becomes East Road. Go right on Sunnyside Road. Continue 2.7 km (1.7 mi) to the South Beach parking area (toilet available). Note the posted closing time.

THE HIKE

Go to the southwest corner of Buntzen Lake's main parking area to find the trailhead. Set off south on the Buntzen Lake Trail. Ignore the first path to the right, then keep right to cross the causeway and floating bridge at the south end of the B.C. Hydro reservoir.

Formerly known as Lake Beautiful, Buntzen Lake is the setting of "The Deep Waters," a flood story retold in *Legends of Vancouver*. Mohawk poet E. Pauline Johnson (Tekahionwake) authored the 1911 classic, based on her conversations with Chief Joe Capilano (Sahp-luk) and Mary Capilano (Lixwelut) of the Squamish Nation.

Cross Pumphouse Road and grind up the Diez Vistas Trail. Pass the Horseshoe Trail on the right. In the saddle between Sugar Mountain and Buntzen Ridge, go straight to cross a power-line corridor. (Don't go left on the Sugar Mountain Trail or right on the Saddle Ridge Trail.)

Steep switchbacks lead to a fork, after almost an hour of hiking, with your pick of bonus viewpoints—not included in the official 10. Opt right to see the

The Fannin Range from Buntzen Ridge (Kwe kwe xau). Photo by Bob Hare

South Beach and Eagle Ridge. Choose left for Burrard Inlet and Indian Arm, which Spanish naval officers charted as the Brazo de Floridablanca and the Canal de Sasamat in the 1790s. The paths quickly rejoin to the north, so you can visit both, if you desire. Next, the Sendero Diez Vistas passes Cima Amanecer, the viewless top of Sunrise Hill, the loftiest bump on lowly Buntzen Ridge.

Entering Say Nuth Khaw Yum Provincial Park, the trail drops, passing the first of several ridgetop ponds, then rises to signed Vista No. 1 (49°20′48″ N, 122°52′45″ W). Naturally, as numero uno, the views don't get any better than this. To the southwest, tiny Jug Island and Racoon Island sit in Indian Arm, whose entrance (Kapulpaqua to the Tsleil-Waututh) is flanked by Belcarra Mountain and Deep Cove (Guy-angulton). Behind the main stem of Burrard Inlet, the cuestas of Burnaby Mountain (officially Mount Burnaby, Lhúḵw'lhúḵw'áyten to the Squamish) and Capitol Hill rise in front of the Fraser Lowland.

Continue on the pleasantly undulating trail, pausing at mossy bluffs for more views. Watch your step on slippery inclines and near drop-offs. Vista No. 2 offers a similar but less expansive outlook than the first, and No. 3 is grown in. Spy Mount Seymour across the fjord at No. 6, and a cave by No. 8. An hour after No. 1, reach viewless No. 10 (3 hours up; 49°21′38″ N, 122°52′27″ W). At 6.5 km (4 mi) from South Beach, it's the halfway point, distancewise, of the loop.

Descend the rooty path, bearing right on a dirt road featuring a charming corduroy section. Steep switchbacks spill you out onto Powerhouse Road. Keep right to go south on the Old Buntzen Lake Trail under a power line. Across McCombe Lake (no swimming), the intake pond of the reservoir, eye Swan Falls on Eagle Ridge.

Turn left to take the suspension bridge across the narrows to North Beach, a decent swimming spot. Head up to Powerhouse Road to bypass the century-old tunnel supplying water from Coquitlam Lake. Exit right onto the Buntzen Lake Trail, and dodge joggers and dog walkers all the way down the east shore to South Beach.

Buntzen Lake lies in the territories of the Musqueam, Qayqayt, Squamish, Stó:lō, and Tsleil-Waututh First Nations. Drones, fires, motorized vehicles, smoking, and vaping are prohibited in Say Nuth Khaw Yum Provincial Park, which is co-managed by the Tsleil-Waututh Nation and B.C. Parks. Dogs must be leashed. Say Nuth Khaw Yum means "Serpent's Land," reflecting time-honoured Tsleil-Waututh stories about Indian Arm.

STOP OF INTEREST
PORT MOODY STATION MUSEUM

In 1886, the first scheduled passenger train to travel the Canadian Pacific Railway from east to west arrived at Port Moody. Learn about the area's history at the Port Moody Station Museum (2734 Murray Street). Run by the Port Moody Heritage Society, the museum is housed in a CPR station built in 1908 and relocated in 1978. A restored 1921 CPR sleeping car sits out front. In the back, visitors can descend a ladder into a replica World War I trench, dug in honour of a local soldier killed on the Western Front in 1916. Find the museum south of Rocky Point Park, across the CPR tracks from TransLink's Moody Centre Station, via the Moody Street overpass. It's open daily in summer and Wednesday to Sunday in winter. Admission is by donation.

DENNETT LAKE

Make a splash on Burke Mountain

Distance: 16 km (9.9 mi)
Time: 7.5 hours (lollipop)
Elevation gain: 750 m (2,460 ft)
High point: 1,070 m (3,510 ft)

Difficulty: ◆
Maps: NTS 92-G/7; Canadian Map Makers Coquitlam; Trail Ventures PoMo
Trailhead: 49°18'49" N, 122°44'56" W

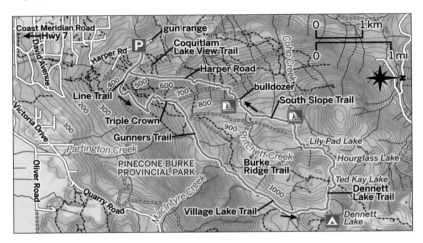

FORMERLY KNOWN as Dollar Mountain, Coquitlam's Burke Mountain is the site of an abandoned ski resort that operated for two seasons in the 1960s. On this hike to Dennett Lake in Pinecone Burke Provincial Park, you'll see intriguing vestiges of the area's skiing and logging past. Backed by a tall cliff, the lake offers excellent swimming and is remarkably quiet for somewhere so close to the city. Make sure to carry a detailed map. You'll need it to navigate the web of roads and trails.

GETTING THERE

Vehicle: From Highway 7 (Lougheed Highway) in Port Coquitlam, 2 km (1.2 mi) west of the Pitt River Bridge, go north on Lougheed-Meridian Connector. Turn left on Coast Meridian Road (which traces a historical Dominion Land Survey line) and enter Coquitlam. In 5 km (3.1 mi), turn right on Harper

Hourglass Lake from the South Slope Trail.

Road. Drive 2 km (1.2 mi) farther, turning left on Upper Harper Road, to find the inconspicuous Pinecone Burke Provincial Park gate on the right, outside of the Port Coquitlam and District Hunting and Fishing Club. Park on the shoulder, but not in the club's driveway.

THE HIKE

From the Harper Road gate and park boundary sign, head east up the gravel road and away from the noisy gun range (closed Tuesdays). Smile and wave at mountain bikers. Ignore the first road on the left (Coquitlam Lake View Trail). Notice bike paths to the right. At the second gravel fork, keep right for the Line Trail to start a counterclockwise loop. (Left is the continuation of Harper Road.) Pass a yellow gate. Go left at the third fork, just before the power lines. Stay left at the fourth fork, in the fireweed-brightened corridor.

Make a sharp right at the fifth tri-junction, 2.4 km (1.5 mi) in, climbing a gravel spur under the high-voltage lines. Facing an electricity pylon at road's end, go right on an unsigned single-track trail, Triple Crown (49°19′00″ N, 122°44′03″ W). Before entering the shady woods, look back to see Burnaby Mountain (Lhúḵw'lhúḵw'áyten to the Squamish Nation) and Vancouver. Follow occasional pink ribbons to Harper. (Bike trail etiquette: Hike in single file, step aside to let bikers pass, and be courteous.) Turn right and up on the gravel road, watching out for 4×4s.

At 3.5 km (2.2 mi) from the trailhead, fork right onto Gunners Trail (770 m/2,530 ft), an old mossy roadbed that gets progressively muddier.

A western toad on Burke Mountain.

After crossing Partington Creek, the road peters out. An orange diamond on a stump marks the path forward. Drop into the MacIntyre Creek (tə'cnəc to the Katzie First Nation) ravine and climb out with a handline. Spot old ski trail signs for Munro Lake on trees.

Hit a three-way junction marked with a cairn and signs, after 2 km (1.2 mi) on Gunners. Go right on the muddy Village Lake Trail toward Munro. Follow varicoloured markers by marshes and over brooks. Admire tiger's eye and violet cort mushrooms. Don't step on western toads, a species of special concern. Toadlets migrate en masse in summer. Be bear aware.

Arrive at another tri-junction, 1.2 km (0.7 mi) past the last, and with the same distance remaining to our destination. Faded signs indicate left for Dennett Lake, right for Munro. Go left on a rough and tricky-to-follow route over deadfall, through wet meadows (with fragrant white rein-orchids, fringed grass-of-Parnassus, and narrow-leaved cotton-grass), and by ponds. Finally, spot a cliff ahead. Make your way to the shore of secluded Dennett Lake by a boulder (3.5 hours up; 955 m/3,130 ft; 49°20′58″ N, 122°41′59″ W). There are tent sites, but no facilities. Pack it in, pack it out.

After an adequate rest at our trip's halfway point, go left (west) along the lakeshore. Boot it up the steep and rooty Dennett Lake Trail to the day's high point. At a junction with decayed signage, hang a left on the Burke Ridge Trail, followed quickly by a right at the next intersection, before Ted Kay Lake. Head west on the South Slope Trail to Hourglass Lake, then south to Lily Pad Lake. (These three smaller lakes also invite you to cool off on a hot day.) Descend wooden steps beside the canyon of Coho Creek. Choose from upper (yellow tapes) and lower (pink tapes) crossings. Situated below a little waterfall and pool, the lower option is only advisable when the rock is dry later in the season.

Continue south onto an old roadbed. Keep right to stick with the South Slope Trail. Old metal logging cables are exposed. Pass a small cascade on Pritchett Creek, a tributary of the Coquitlam River (kwikwetl'em in the hǝṅq̓ǝmiṅǝṁ dialect), and encounter a rusty old bulldozer in the woods. Farther downstream, you have a choice: go left on a path closer to the creek or stay right on the road. The two routes rejoin shortly. Keep left on the road, and cross Pritchett Creek.

Enter Harper Road from the right (below a green gate), 5.5 km (3.4 mi) from Dennett Lake, and with 2.7 km (1.7 mi) left to go. Descend the 4×4 road, going under the power lines and passing several bike trails. At the bottom, follow Harper right and walk the final steps to the trailhead.

Burke Mountain lies in the territories of the Katzie, Kwikwetlem, and Stó:lō First Nations. As Coquitlam Search and Rescue advises, if you can see snow on the North Shore mountains, expect snow on Burke too. Pinecone Burke Provincial Park was legislated into existence in 1995, thanks to the efforts of the Burke Mountain Naturalists, Wilderness Committee, and others. No drones, fires, foraging for mushrooms or plants, smoking, or vaping. Dogs must be leashed.

MACKIN HOUSE MUSEUM

Coquitlam's oldest neighbourhood, Maillardville, was once Canada's largest francophone community west of Manitoba. This demographic feat resulted from the Canadian Western Lumber Company's efforts to displace Chinese, Japanese, and Indian workers at its Fraser River (staləẃ in hǝṅq̓ǝmiṅǝṁ) sawmill with French Canadian migrants, following the 1907 anti-Asian riots in Vancouver. Occupying an Edwardian residence built in 1909, the Coquitlam Heritage Society's Mackin House Museum (1116 Brunette Avenue), is a monument to this local history. Drop in for a guided tour. The museum is open Tuesday to Saturday, and admission is by donation. Remember to visit Fraser Mills Station, built by the Canadian Pacific Railway in 1910, next door. It's right by the yellow caboose.

EAST CANYON TRAIL

A trail of two beaches

Distance: 19.5 km (12.1 mi)
Time: 6 hours (out and back)
Elevation gain: 170 m (560 ft)
High point: 330 m (1,080 ft)

Difficulty: ■
Maps: NTS 92-G/8 Stave Lake; Canadian Map Makers Golden Ears
Trailhead: 49°20'04" N, 122°27'24" W

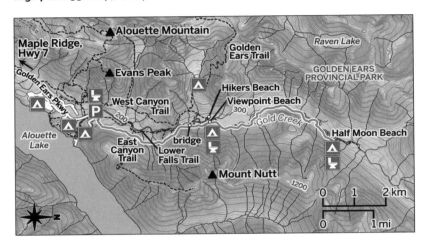

A **LUSH** temperate rainforest beckons in the valley of Gold Creek. Hike the East Canyon Trail to commune with majestic old-growth giants and dawdle at two delightful creekside beaches, in Golden Ears Provincial Park and the territories of the Katzie and Stó:lō First Nations. Keep this one in your back pocket—for kids, rainy days, and shoulder season.

GETTING THERE

Transit: Parkbus offers coach service on summer weekends to the Gold Creek parking lot from Burrard Station in Vancouver.

Vehicle: Heading east on Highway 7 (Lougheed Highway) in Maple Ridge, turn left onto Dewdney Trunk Road, 5 km (3.1 mi) east of the Pitt River Bridge. (On Trans-Canada Highway 1, take Exit 57 in Surrey or Exit 58 in Langley. Follow signs for the Golden Ears Bridge, take the Maple Ridge exit, and

A point bar at Half Moon Beach.

continue onto Dewdney Trunk.) In 6 km (3.7 mi), make a left on 232 Street. At the traffic circle, go right on 132 Avenue/Fern Crescent. Stay on Fern, bear left onto 128 Avenue, and rejoin Fern, which becomes Golden Ears Parkway. Continue to the Gold Creek parking lot (toilet available) at parkway's end. The park gate is closed 11 p.m. to 7 a.m. from April to mid-October, and 5:30 p.m. to 8 a.m. from mid-October to March.

THE HIKE

Shared with horse riders and mountain bikers, the East Canyon Trail starts at the northeast corner of the parking lot. In short order, take the left fork and go left again where the trail merges with an old logging road. After 15 minutes, notice the trail to the Mount Nutt viewpoints (Hike 23) exiting to the right. Keep going north on the gently rising road. Pass a landslide area marked off with red "danger" tape, and go through a rusty gate. Cross a bridge fashioned out of two huge logs.

Forty minutes in, spurn the Lower Falls turnoff on the left (a short loop option). Stick with the road as it descends to Gold Creek and intersects the East-West Canyon Connector (no bikes or horses) at 3.7 km (2.3 mi), after 1 hour on foot. Detour left to take in the pure forest and freshwater views from the Gold Creek bridge, which rests on an old concrete pier that supported a logging bridge until the 1960s.

Continue 10 minutes upstream on river left to an outhouse and the Viewpoint Beach turnoff (49°21'58" N, 122°27'16" W), at 4.4 km (2.7 mi) on the East Canyon Trail. Go left to emerge at a gravel point bar on a lovely zigzag in Gold Creek. If the water's low, it's possible to ford the creek to Hikers Beach on the right bank (also reachable from the East-West Canyon Connector) or take a swim. The dramatic double summits of Edge Peak and Golden Ears (1,716 m/5,630 ft) on the Mount Blanshard massif (xɛ'ɛc'ɛnxʷ in the həńq̓əmińəm̓ language of the Katzie First Nation) loom in the background. Up to this point, the hike merits an "easy" rating; it's "moderate" going forward. Leaving its bustling lower section behind, the East Canyon Trail weaves upstream—crossing bridges, negotiating channels, skirting oxbows, climbing cutbanks, and ducking blowdowns on the floodplain. Occasional orange squares and ribbons denote the rooty, silty path, which can be tricky to follow. Ignore numerous side paths to the water. Any reroutes for deadfall or erosion are fleeting. Go on—hug one of the giant western red cedars along the trail. Devil's club, false lily-of-the-valley, salmonberry, and skunk cabbage (or, more complimentary, swamp lantern) flower in the understory.

Finally, pink tapes at 9.8 km (6.1 mi) indicate the Half Moon Beach turnoff (3 hours up; 49°24'05" N, 122°26'44" W). The East Canyon Trail perseveres north to a ford on Gold Creek for the rough route to distant Hector Ferguson Lake. However, go left now, pass a mossy campsite and an outhouse with a tarp for a door, and explore the secluded rocky bar and sandy bank. Sitka columbine blooms bright with red sepals and yellow stamens. Retrace your steps to the parking lot. (A backcountry camping permit is required to stay overnight at Half Moon Beach or Viewpoint Beach.)

In 1967, the B.C. government created Golden Ears Provincial Park out of the southern portion of Garibaldi Provincial Park. No drones, fires, smoking, or vaping. Be bear aware, and don't leave food scraps behind. Ridge Meadows Outdoor Club volunteers deserve our thanks for their dedication to maintaining these trails.

STOP OF INTEREST
SPIREA NATURE TRAIL

The Spirea Nature Trail welcomes everyone to Golden Ears Provincial Park. Circling a bog and weaving through the mossy forest, this short "universal access" loop is designed for wheelchairs and features interpretive panels about the history, flora, and fauna of the park in Chinese, English, French, and German. According to one panel, the lower Alouette River (sa'anəsaʔɬ to the Katzie First Nation, Sa'nisalh to the Stó:lō people) valley was hand-logged in the 1920s. Logs were sent to the sawmill via a logging railway, whose old rail bed is followed by today's Golden Ears Parkway. Find the Spirea Nature Trail just south of the main Alouette Lake (sa'anəsaʔɬ xa'cɛʔ to the Katzie) day-use area. (Dogs must be leashed.)

An old-growth western red cedar on the East Canyon Trail.

MOUNT NUTT VIEWPOINTS

Admire Golden Ears from afar

Distance: 10.5 km (6.5 mi)
Time: 5.5 hours (out and back)
Elevation gain: 970 m (3,180 ft)
High point: 1,130 m (3,710 ft)

Difficulty: ■
Maps: NTS 92-G/8 Stave Lake; Canadian Map Makers Golden Ears
Trailhead: 49°20'04" N, 122°27'24" W

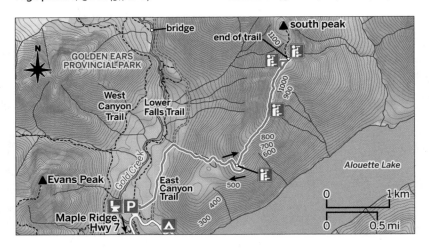

FOR PEAK baggers, the twin summits of the Mount Blanshard massif (xɛ'ɛc'ɛnxʷ in the hәṅ́q̓әmiṅ́әṁ language of the Katzie First Nation) are the star attraction of Golden Ears Provincial Park. However, a very long day's hike and scramble to the top of Golden Ears is not essential to admire their rugged beauty. A shorter option is the trail, built by the Ridge Meadows Outdoor Club, to the ridge south of Mount Nutt. It's a steep grind, for sure, but the payoff—the massif view—isn't exactly peanuts.

GETTING THERE

Transit: Parkbus offers coach service on summer weekends to the Gold Creek parking lot from Burrard Station in Vancouver.

Vehicle: Heading east on Highway 7 (Lougheed Highway) in Maple Ridge, turn left onto Dewdney Trunk Road, 5 km (3.1 mi) east of the Pitt River Bridge.

Mount Crickmer and Alouette Lake (saʼanəsaʔɬ xaʼcɛʔ).

(On Trans-Canada Highway 1, take Exit 57 in Surrey or Exit 58 in Langley. Follow signs for the Golden Ears Bridge, take the Maple Ridge exit, and continue onto Dewdney Trunk.) In 6 km (3.7 mi), make a left on 232 Street. At the traffic circle, go right on 132 Avenue/Fern Crescent. Stay on Fern, bear left onto 128 Avenue, and rejoin Fern, which becomes Golden Ears Parkway. Continue to the Gold Creek parking lot (toilet available) at parkway's end. The park gate is closed 11 p.m. to 7 a.m. from April to mid-October, and 5:30 p.m. to 8 a.m. from mid-October to March.

THE HIKE

A quick warmup on the East Canyon Trail (Hike 22) kicks things off. Find the trailhead at the northeast corner of the parking lot. In short order, take the left fork and go left again where the trail merges with an old logging road. After 15 minutes (1.3 km/0.8 mi), immediately before the road crosses a creek, look right to spot the signed start of the trail to the Mount Nutt viewpoints (49°20′37″ N, 122°26′56″ W).

The rugged path is well marked with orange diamonds. Cross a downed cedar giant and a brook. Zigzag relentlessly uphill in the shady second-growth woods. Aiming for the end of the ridge extending south from Mount Nutt, the path parallels a debris-choked creek, then crosses it. The grade relaxes. Less than an hour after leaving the East Canyon Trail, arrive at a muddy lily-pad lake nestled in a forested bowl (530 m/1,740 ft). The trail turns left in the woods to bypass the lakeshore. Delight in the dappled light and soft single track.

The forest trail to the Mount Nutt viewpoints.

At the next fork, signs present a choice: the "tricky" branch to the left, or the "easy" one to the right. The former is a steeper, scrambly affair—fun on the ascent. The latter offers gentler switchbacks and is recommended for the way down. In any case, the branches soon reunite at the first viewpoint (670 m/2,200 ft; 49°20′25″ N, 122°26′06″ W), 40 minutes from the lake. Having gained the ridge crest, take a breather and enjoy the tree-impeded vistas of Alouette Lake (sa'anəsaʔɬ xa'cɛʔ to the Katzie) and Blanshard Peak.

Plod upward in prettier forest with mossy ground. (Please don't deface trees with graffiti.) Squeeze through a pair of big boulders. An arrow points left for the second viewpoint (1,000 m/3,280 ft) on a rock high above Alouette Lake, 45 minutes after the first. Good news: you're less than a half-hour from trail's end.

Continue steeply up to the open ridgetop, where the trail briefly splits once again. Pick one side of the loop, and save the other for later. To the left, there's a fine perch overlooking Gold Creek, the foot of Alouette Lake, the Fraser Lowland, and the Salish Sea. Go right to score views of the lake's narrows, Mount Crickmer, and Mount Baker (Kwelxá:lxw to the Stó:lō people). Film fact: Alouette Lake played "Alkali Lake"—where Jean Grey kills Cyclops—in 2006's *X-Men: The Last Stand*.

Where the branches rejoin, the day's best viewpoint lies off to the left. To the west, the dramatic pinnacle of Blanshard Peak, the rugged fortress of Edge Peak, and the twin summits of Golden Ears—together composing the Mount Blanshard massif—spectacularly overshadow lowly outliers Evans Peak and Alouette Mountain. Mount Nutt is the wooded double peak due north.

Five minutes farther north, the signed end of the trail (3 hours up; 49°21′23″ N, 122°25′23″ W) awaits just over the high point of the pre-Nutt ridge. From this final viewpoint, the rocky massif of Mount Robie Reid dominates while the jagged double peak of Mount Judge Howay lurks behind. Turn around here.

The Mount Nutt viewpoints lie in the territories of the Katzie and Stó:lō First Nations. Drones, fires, smoking, and vaping are prohibited in the backcountry of Golden Ears Provincial Park.

STOP OF INTEREST

ALOUETTE LAKE

Known as sa'anəsaʔɬ to the Katzie First Nation and Sa'nisalh to the Stó:lō people, the Alouette River was first dammed during the "roaring" 1920s, decimating its salmon runs. With the creation of a reservoir out of a pair of pre-existing Lillooet Lakes, the B.C. Electric Railway Company began diverting water through a tunnel under Mount Crickmer to the hydroelectric plant at Stave Lake (šxʷeẏəqʷs to the Stó:lō). Today, Alouette Lake (sa'anəsaʔɬ xa'cɛʔ to the Katzie) is a popular place to go camping, canoeing, swimming, and windsurfing in Golden Ears Provincial Park. The South Beach day-use area is located at the foot of the lake, by B.C. Hydro's 1984 Alouette Dam, 6 km (3.7 mi) southwest of the Gold Creek parking lot. It's a good spot for barbecues and picnics, and frequented by Canada geese. Bring a blanket if you plan to sit—anywhere. (Dogs must be on leash, but are prohibited on the beach near Parking Lot 2.)

STATLU LAKE

Drink up the sparkling mountain views

Distance: 13 km (8.1 mi)
Time: 6 hours (out and back)
Elevation gain: 300 m (980 ft)
High point: 630 m (2,070 ft)

Difficulty: ◆
Maps: NTS 92-G/9 Stave River; Backroad Mapbooks VCBC 14 Harrison Lake
Trailhead: 49°30'22" N, 122°00'23" W

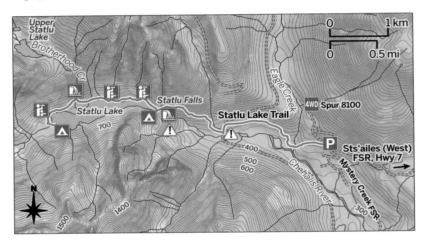

AS A destination, Statlu Lake has much to offer hikers: colossal conifers, wondrous waterfalls, majestic mountains, and superb swimming. The price of admission: a lengthy approach on logging roads, an overgrown trail, and no shortage of deadfall. Early in the season, high water can make for dangerous creek crossings, but summer and fall are excellent times to visit. Statlu Lake lies on the Chehalis River, southeast of Mount Clarke, in the territories of the Kwantlen, Sťáťimc, Stó:lō, and Sts'ailes First Nations.

GETTING THERE
Vehicle: Take Highway 7 (Lougheed Highway) to Harrison Mills in Kent, 15 km (9 mi) west of Highway 9 (Rosedale-Agassiz Bypass Highway) at Agassiz. By the Sasquatch Inn (46001 Lougheed Highway), turn north onto Morris Valley Road. Keep right at the Hemlock Valley Road fork. Hit gravel,

Mount Bardean and Mount Ratney from Statlu Lake.

11 km (7 mi) from the highway. Go straight onto Weaver Creek Road, where Morris Valley goes right. Continue onto bumpy Sts'ailes (West) Forest Service Road. After 30 km (19 mi) on gravel—where the Sts'ailes mainline curves right after a winding descent—turn left (west) onto rougher Mystery Creek FSR (2WD, high clearance recommended). After Mystery's 7-km (4.3-mi) marker, some cars may have difficulty with the steep and loose downhill grade. At the 7.5-km (4.7-mi) sign, Mystery bends left at an intersection with a road on the right (Spur 8100). Find a parking spot on the shoulder, without blocking either road.

THE HIKE

Logging activity has altered the route and may do so further. Locate the trailhead, 150 m (0.1 mi) up Mystery Spur 8100, on the left. The Statlu Lake Trail follows an old road westward, and down to Eagle Creek. Carefully cross the rushing waters on a shaky, high, narrow log bridge with a hand cable for balance—not recommended for acrophobes or young kids! Follow the trail onto an old logging road, which leads to a new road.

Where the new logging road swings sharply right, exit left and take another road to a creek—this one missing a bridge. Pursue pink tapes across this Chehalis River tributary. Crossing here is dangerous in high flow. Find the continuation of the road on the far bank, slightly downstream. Immediately,

The view from a rockslide at Statlu Lake.

turn right (west) on an older road (49°30'30" N, 122°01'48" W). (Do not continue south to a condemned bridge over the Chehalis River.)

Ascend the road until it peters out. Follow tapes right and uphill, clambering over rocks, roots, and deadfall. In one particularly messy patch, duck under a huge downed tree. From high above the Chehalis River, look across the valley at Mount Orrock. Enter a grove of massive old-growth Douglas-firs.

As you near Statlu Falls, an ominous handwritten sign advises against attempting to view the waterfall, warns of a hidden drop-off, and informs you that several people have died at this spot. With this knowledge in mind, cross the smooth, wet gully ahead—don't even think about approaching the edge—and climb up the far bank with the aid of a handline. Stay on the trail to arrive at a small campsite—and your first vista of Mount Clarke—at the outlet of Statlu Lake (49°30'44" N, 122°02'45" W), less than 1.5 hours (3.8 km/ 2.4 mi) from the trailhead.

Follow the overgrown path west along the quiet lakeshore, breaking out of the trees at two rockslides; the boulders' muted tones contrast beautifully with fall foliage. Stay close to the sparkling green water and keep your eyes peeled for ribbons to pick up the trail on the other side. The views of ruggedly handsome Mount Bardean and Mount Ratney from the gigantic boulders are tremendous. A dip in the shallows calls your name. Eventually, the trail bears right and uphill, away from the lake.

A little more than an hour (1.7 km/1.1 mi) from the outlet, engraved letters on a tree trunk mark the start of the Brotherhood Trail on the right. This very steep and rough route leads to Upper Statlu Lake. However, continue straight to ford or rock-hop Brotherhood Creek (49°30′52″ N, 122°03′54″ W), just below an enchanting waterfall. Although you could happily turn around here, it's only a half-hour (1 km/0.6 mi) farther to the head of the lake.

Scramble up the steep bank. Past Brotherhood Creek, the Statlu Lake Trail gets trickier to follow. Orange squares and tapes lead to another rockslide with a superb view, and down to the silty flats at the west end of the lake. Cross a couple of channels, perhaps on sketchy logs. Then bear left under the trees to reach tent sites in the vicinity of where the Chehalis River enters Statlu Lake (3 hours up; 49°30′36″ N, 122°04′13″ W). Please use Leave No Trace techniques to protect water quality.

Watch for spotted sandpipers on the delightful sandspit. This is a glorious spot for a summer swim. Downstream of Statlu Lake, the Chehalis River empties into the Harrison River, below Harrison Lake (Peqwpa:qotel to the Stó:lō) and just above its confluence with the Fraser River (Stó:lō). Head back the way you came.

AGASSIZ-HARRISON MUSEUM

Housed in a Canadian Pacific Railway station built in 1893, the Agassiz-Harrison Museum (7011 Pioneer Avenue) trains a light on local history. The museum collects and displays artifacts from the Fraser Valley communities of Agassiz, Harrison Hot Springs, and Harrison Mills. Run by the Agassiz-Harrison Historical Society, it's open between the Victoria Day and Thanksgiving long weekends. Admission is by donation. Find the museum beside Highway 9 (Rosedale-Agassiz Bypass Highway) in Kent's Agassiz townsite, named after an English family that settled here in the 1880s.

CHADSEY LAKE

Cool off on Sumas Mountain

Distance: 10 km (6.2 mi)
Time: 5 hours (out and back)
Elevation gain: 510 m (1,670 ft)
High point: 660 m (2,170 ft)

Difficulty: ■
Maps: NTS 92-G/1 Mission
Trailhead: 49°07'19" N, 122°11'18" W

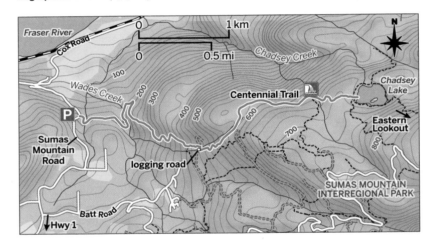

SURROUNDED BY floodplain, Sumas Mountain (see also Hike 26) is a prominent landmark in the Fraser Valley. Known as T'exqé:yl in the Halq'eméylem language of the Stó:lō people, the modest mountain is traversed by the Centennial Trail, a fruitful but fading project of the 1960s. A hike on the pleasant trail to Chadsey Lake is ideal in shoulder season, especially when the fall foliage is at its polychromatic peak. On hot summer days, this swimming hole is a refreshing proposition. It's a quiet and beautiful spot in the winter too—when the lake freezes and everything is covered in snow.

GETTING THERE

Vehicle: On Trans-Canada Highway 1 in Abbotsford, take Exit 95 (numbered by kilometres from Horseshoe Bay). Head north on Whatcom Road. Quickly turn right on North Parallel Road. In 2.3 km (1.4 mi), go left on Sumas

A frozen pond on Sumas Mountain (T'exqé:yl) in winter.

Mountain Road and drive through the Sumas First Nation reserve. Keep left at Atkinson Road and Carlyle Road to stay on Sumas Mountain Road for 9 km (5.6 mi). Hit gravel (2WD) and continue 400 m (0.2 mi) to an S-bend, where the trailhead is on the right. Park on the shoulder, 12 km (7.5 mi) from Exit 95.

THE HIKE

From the western trailhead of the Centennial Trail's Sumas Mountain section, enter the mixed woods and quickly take a bridge over a stream. Head up a ravine, turning downstream just before crossing Wades Creek, which empties into the Fraser River (Stó:lō). Ascend an old roadbed, pursuing red rectangles through deadfall. Reach the 1.5-km (0.9-mi) marker in 30 minutes.

Approach a logged area, and emerge on a gravel road, after 1 hour on foot. Golden Ears (xɛ'ɛc'ɛnxʷ to the Katzie First Nation) is visible to the left. Heed a Chadsey Lake sign pointing to the right. Shortly thereafter, turn left at an entrance indicated by pink flagging (49°07'06" N, 122°10'14" W). Hike up between clear-cuts, following antique Centennial Trail 1966–1967 signs bearing maple leaf and Pacific dogwood logos. From the forest edge, earn southwest views of Sumas Mountain's knolls and the Fraser Lowland. Cross a creek. Pass the 3.5-km (2.2-mi) marker. The trail, marked by orange diamonds, levels out. There are vistas of Fraser Valley farmland through the trees on the left.

The Centennial Trail at Chadsey Lake in winter.

An old Centennial Trail marker on Sumas Mountain (T'exqé:yl).

Sidehill pleasantly across steep wooded slopes to reach trail signs and the 4.5-km (2.8-mi) marker. Cross the tumbling south fork of Chadsey Creek on a log bridge above a waterfall. Head upstream on the Centennial Trail under Douglas-firs. Pass a pond on your right, and descend into the Chadsey Lake basin. Hit the 5-km (3.1-mi) marker and a junction. The Centennial Trail goes left on its way east to Chilliwack Lake (Sx̱óchaqel), the Skagit River, Cathedral Lakes, and beyond. However, opt right to arrive at the shore of Chadsey Lake (2.5 hours up; 49°07'25" N, 122°08'46" W).

With extra time and energy to burn, you might consider circumnavigating the pretty lake—with its little island and water lilies—though the trail on the south shore is rough and littered with blowdowns. On the far side, a trail switchbacks higher up the mountain, providing access to Sumas Peak (910 m/2,990 ft) and the Eastern Lookout, an hour from the lake loop.

Sumas Mountain lies in the territory of the Stó:lō people, including the Sumas First Nation, whose oral history situates the mountaintop as a refuge during a great flood. Part of the former Sumas Mountain Provincial Park, established in 1965, Chadsey Lake was folded into Sumas Mountain Interregional Park in 2002.

STOP OF INTEREST
GUR SIKH TEMPLE AND HERITAGE MUSEUM

Designated a national historic site in 2002, the Gur Sikh Temple and Heritage Museum (33089 South Fraser Way) in Abbotsford is the home of North America's oldest existing gurdwara. Built in 1911 by Punjabi settlers, the temple is a wood-frame building with a false front typical of Old West architecture. Opened in 2011, the ground-floor museum hosts exhibits exploring the history of Sikh migration to Canada, including the federal government's racist rejection of passengers aboard the *Komagata Maru* in 1914. It's run by the Khalsa Diwan Society of Abbotsford and the University of the Fraser Valley's South Asian Studies Institute. The museum is open seven days a week, and admission is free. On Trans-Canada Highway 1, take Exit 90, go north on McCallum Road, and turn left on South Fraser Way.

TAGGART PEAK

Enjoy the silence beyond the Abby Grind

Distance: 10.5 km (6.5 mi)
Time: 4.5 hours (out and back)
Elevation gain: 770 m (2,530 ft)
High point: 796 m (2,610 ft)

Difficulty: ■
Maps: NTS 92-G/1 Mission
Trailhead: 49°04'50" N, 122°09'37" W

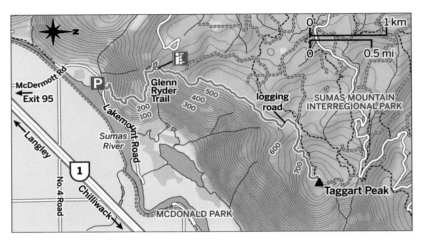

FOR FITNESS-FOCUSED Fraser Valley residents, the Glenn Ryder Trail in Abbotsford is a convenient little version of North Vancouver's Grouse Grind. Popularly known as the Abby Grind, the trail is named after its builder, local naturalist Glenn Ryder (1938–2013), the 2012 recipient of the B.C. Field Ornithologists' Steve Cannings Award. Most folks out for a workout turn back at the Abby Grind lookout. Hikers can escape the hustle and bustle by carrying on to Taggart Peak, a quiet sub-summit of Sumas Mountain (T'exqé:yl in the Halq'eméylem language of the Stó:lō people).

GETTING THERE

Vehicle: On Trans-Canada Highway 1 in Abbotsford, take Exit 95. Head north on Whatcom Road. Quickly turn right on North Parallel Road, and continue onto Eldridge Road. Go right on Atkinson Road, cross the Sumas River,

The view from the Abby Grind lookout at sunset. Photo by Cassie Markham

and continue straight onto North Parallel. Turn left on McDermott Road, recross the river, and follow Lakemount Road to the large parking area, 7 km (4.3 mi) from Exit 95.

THE HIKE

Set off uphill on the Glenn Ryder Trail in the shady mixed woods. Meandering north, the path is steep and eroded—slippery when wet. After 25 minutes, reach a partial viewpoint. Peek through the trees at Cheam Ridge. Watch out for stinging nettle, an edible and medicinal herb whose stem hairs irritate the skin.

Continue to a signed junction, 50 minutes in. Left is for Taggart Peak; go straight to arrive at the Abby Grind lookout (440 m/1,440 ft; 49°05'12" N, 122°09'49" W), 1.7 km (1.1 mi) from the trailhead. Below, the Sumas River (Semá:th Stótelō) snakes across the floodplain. The rich farmland between Sumas Mountain (see also Hike 25) and Vedder Mountain constitutes the Sumas Prairie, but it wasn't always this way. In the 1920s, the B.C. government diked and drained Sumas Lake (Semá:th X̱ótsa), dispossessing the Sumas First Nation of a vital cultural, fishing, and hunting site, and transportation route—without consent or compensation.

Pick up the path on the far side of the lookout. Go right to rejoin the main trail. Taggart Peak is 1.5 hours (3.6 km/2.2 mi) to the northeast. From this point forth, the trail is quiet, pleasant, and bushy, with Oregon grape underfoot and some deadfall to negotiate. Lose some elevation, and pass a pond.

An hour past the lookout, turn left on a logging road, then go right at a signed fork. As the forest opens up, hike steadily uphill, following blue, orange, and pink flagging. Come to a fenced-off bit of communications apparatus. On the other side, turn right. Head up the road to find more technological detritus on the summit of Taggart Peak (2.5 hours up; 49°06′20″ N, 122°08′31″ W), which is also visited by mountain bikers.

Sumas Peak (910 m/2,990 ft), the true summit of Sumas Mountain, is the wooded mound immediately northeast. Rising behind Black Mountain to the southeast, Mount Baker (Kwelxá:lxw), an iconic glaciated stratovolcano in Washington, is the scenic highlight. Retrace your steps to the trailhead.

Taggart Peak lies in Sumas Mountain Interregional Park, which covers 1,470 hectares (3,632 acres) and is jointly managed by the Fraser Valley Regional District and Metro Vancouver. Dogs must be leashed. No camping, fires, hunting, or smoking. Sumas Mountain provides habitat for the coastal giant salamander, mountain beaver, Oregon forestsnail, Pacific water shrew, red-legged frog, snowshoe hare, Townsend's big-eared bat, western screech owl, and other species at risk.

STOP OF INTEREST

MCDONALD PARK

Due to light pollution, city dwellers are accustomed to being deprived of celestial scenery, such as the Milky Way. That's one reason why the International Dark-Sky Association has advocated for the protection of the night sky for more than three decades. In B.C., the Royal Astronomical Society of Canada has designated only one place, Abbotsford's McDonald Park, as a dark-sky preserve. The Fraser Valley Astronomers Society holds public observing nights at the park, which lies along the Sumas River (Semá:th Stótelō to the Stó:lō people) in the shadow of Sumas Mountain (T'exqé:yl) and is devoid of any artificial light. Access McDonald Park at the west end of No. 3 Road via Exit 104 on Trans-Canada Highway 1. (Dogs must be leashed.)

The Sumas River (Semá:th Stótelō) floodplain from the Abby Grind lookout.

PIERCE LAKE

Lupines, thimbleberries, and big trees, oh my!

Distance: 11.5 km (7.1 mi)
Time: 6 hours (out and back)
Elevation gain: 1,080 m (3,540 ft)
High point: 1,400 m (4,590 ft)

Difficulty: ◆
Maps: NTS 92-H/4 Chilliwack; Trail Ventures BC Chilliwack East
Trailhead: 49°05'09" N, 121°40'36" W

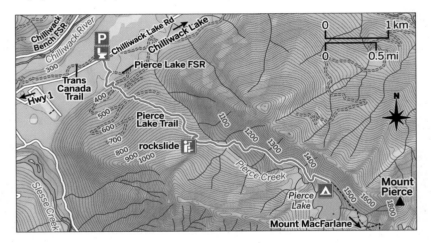

WITH AN average grade of 19 per cent, the hike from the Chilliwack River (Sts'elxwíqw in the Halq'eméylem language of the Stó:lō people) valley floor to Pierce Lake is a terrifically steep but rewarding grind. A provincially designated recreation trail climbs through old-growth forest and thimbleberry thickets to the sizeable tarn, which fills a cirque headed by Mount Pierce (1,957 m/6,420 ft) and Mount MacFarlane (2,090 m/6,860 ft), northwest of iconic Slesse Mountain (Selísi). Watch rainbow trout and Dolly Varden char jumping, enjoy the quiet, and savour the dramatic setting.

GETTING THERE

Vehicle: On Trans-Canada Highway 1 in Chilliwack, take Exit 119. Head south on Vedder Road for 5 km (3 mi). At the roundabout before the Vedder Bridge, take the second exit and go east on Chilliwack Lake Road for 22.5 km

Mount MacFarlane looms across Pierce Lake.

(14 mi). After passing the Department of National Defence's General Vokes Range, turn right into the signed Pierce Lake Trail parking lot (toilet available). Warning: This trailhead is notorious for vehicle break-ins.

THE HIKE

The Pierce Lake trailhead (330 m/1,080 ft) sits on Larsons Bench—in the territory of the Stó:lō people, including the Ts'elxwéyeqw Tribe. (The tribe encompasses the Aitchelitz, Skowkale, Shxwhá:y Village, Soowahlie, Squiala, Tzeachten, and Yakweakwioose First Nations.) Glacial meltwater deposited this late Pleistocene sandur, or outwash plain, circa 11,500 years ago.

From the gate, set off south on the fenced-in Pierce Lake Forest Service Road through a forest assessment plot. A sign posted by Ts'elxwéyeqw Forestry Limited Partnership warns of active log hauling between 4 a.m. and 4 p.m. In a few minutes, spot the wooden signpost marking the old trailhead to the right, beside a large log. Head into the shady timber on an old road and begin the relentless uphill trudge. Keep left of a creek, ascending boulders arranged to form steps. Follow orange squares, ribbons, and paint blotches on single track. Northern maidenhair fern and Oregon grape beautify the forest floor.

Cross a logging road, perhaps noting another active hauling sign. Pass the 500-m (0.3-mi) marker—the distance relative to the old trailhead. Above a revegetating cutblock, peer through the trees at wooded slopes across the

The swimming dock at Pierce Lake.

Chilliwack River valley. After 30 minutes, go across an overgrown road. Encounter the first little wooden bridge, over a steep creek. Bypass a clearcut on your right.

Reach the Pierce Lake Trail's 2-km (1.2-mi) marker after an old boulder patch. An orange arrow points right at a switchback. Enter a big rockslide, and go up and across—earning your first glimpse of Pierce Creek—with a cairn showing the way. A lush forest of majestic old-growth fir and spiny devil's club awaits on the other side. Lose a bit of elevation and resign yourself to muddy boots.

Cross Pierce Creek (960 m/3,150 ft; 49°04′23″ N, 121°39′02″ W) on a tippy plank and mesh-topped log combo, after more than 1.5 hours (3.4 km/ 2.1 mi) on foot. Continue your upward march, in an old-growth management area. Angel wings, bear's-head, fragile russula, pink coral, and rounded earthstar are among the forest's fungi. Pay attention to flagging to stay on the switchbacks. The grade slackens some, and you cross a few creeks. Duck under a big blowdown at a leftward switchback.

More than an hour (2.3 km/1.4 mi) past the Pierce Creek crossing, look for a trail dropping down to the right in the woods. Descend the path through thimbleberries and colourful wildflowers (arctic lupine, cow parsnip, edible thistle, fireweed, mountain arnica, and red paintbrush) to arrive, 5 minutes later, at tent sites on the north shore of beautiful Pierce Lake (3 hours up;

1,360 m/4,460 ft; 49°04'01" N, 121°37'44" W). A swimming dock beckons. Mount MacFarlane looms formidably across the reflecting water. Hiking poles will prove their value as you head back down the way you came. Pack it in, pack it out.

From the junction above the campsite, the main trail continues south— crossing a rocky subalpine meadow, ascending sharply to Upper Pierce Lake, and providing access to the scramble route for Mount MacFarlane. The Trans Canada Trail crosses Chilliwack Lake Road at the Pierce Lake trailhead, which is curiously sandwiched between a military rifle and grenade range and the former site of the Mount Thurston Correctional Centre, closed in 2002.

STOP OF INTEREST

CHILLIWACK MUSEUM

Would it surprise you to learn that Chilliwack was home to not only one but two Chinatowns? Sadly, their architectural legacy was erased by fires in the 1920s and '30s, and institutional racism. Through physical and virtual exhibitions, the Chilliwack Museum (45820 Spadina Avenue) sheds a light on the heritage of local settlers and the Stó:lō people. Run by the Chilliwack Museum and Historical Society, it's housed in Chilliwack's former city hall. The museum is open Monday to Saturday. Admission is $3 for adults and free for kids aged 12 and younger. On Trans-Canada Highway 1, take Exit 119. Head north on Yale Road, and turn left on Spadina.

GREENDROP LAKE

Enter for two chances to swim

Distance: 12 km (7.5 mi)
Time: 5.5 hours (out and back)
Elevation gain: 340 m (1,120 ft)
High point: 970 m (3,180 ft)

Difficulty: ■
Maps: NTS 92-H/3 Skagit River; Trail Ventures BC Chilliwack East
Trailhead: 49°05'56" N, 121°27'30" W

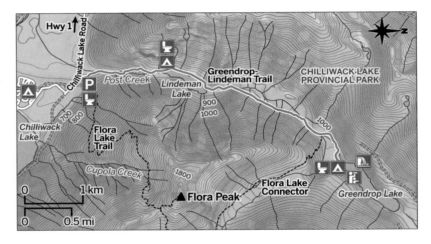

BOASTING TWO lovely lakes and a welcome variety of terrain, the Greendrop-Lindeman Trail in Chilliwack Lake Provincial Park is a crowd-pleaser. It's also ideal for early and late-season hiking, due to its relatively low elevation. B.C. Parks maintains backcountry campgrounds, with pit toilets and bear caches, at bustling Lindeman Lake (Suxwi:ts in the Halq'eméylem language of the Stó:lō) and quieter Greendrop Lake. The family-friendly trail is found in the territories of the Nlaka'pamux and Stó:lō peoples, including the Ts'elxwéyeqw Tribe.

GETTING THERE
Vehicle: On Trans-Canada Highway 1 in Chilliwack, take Exit 119. Head south on Vedder Road for 5 km (3 mi). At the roundabout before the Vedder Bridge, take the second exit and go east on Chilliwack Lake Road for 39 km

Crossing a rockslide at Lindeman Lake (Suxwi:ts).

(24 mi). Before the pavement ends, turn left into the Post Creek parking lot (toilet available). Warning: Vehicle break-ins have been reported here.

THE HIKE

The well-trafficked Greendrop-Lindeman Trail shares its trailhead (630 m/ 2,070 ft) with the Flora Lake Trail (Hike 29). From the kiosk and yellow gate, set off on the gravel road. In 1 minute, pass the signed Flora Lake turnoff. Following Post Creek (Kwôkwelem) upstream, cross a log bridge to river right. (River directions are given from the perspective of looking downstream.) Steadily gain elevation on the rocky, rooty trail in the shady forest. Go by a massive boulder.

Arrive at the Lindeman Lake campground, after 40 minutes (1.7 km/ 1.1 mi) on foot. Round the west shore, traversing sun-baked rockslides with pikas and tremendous views. Unofficially named Flora Peak and The Gargoyles on its northwest ridge loom over the gorgeous lake. The brilliant blue-green water invites swimming—at the risk of chattering teeth and a brain freeze—or stand-up paddleboarding, if you happened to pack a lightweight model.

Descend wooden stairs, and keep going upstream with the help of boardwalks. Cross small tributaries. Rock-hop the main creek. The trail runs through a sequence of woods and boulder fields. Orange squares are bolted to rocks. Cross a wooden bridge. (Trail etiquette tips: Downhill hikers yield to those going uphill. If you absolutely must listen to music, use headphones. Don't litter—carry out all garbage, including food scraps.)

At 5.3 km (3.3 mi), pass the signed turnoff for the Flora Lake Connector in the forest. Soon after, enter the shady Greendrop Lake campground, 6 km (3.7 mi) from the trailhead. Find a path to the right and arrive at a viewpoint on the southeast shore of the quiet lake (3 hours up; 49°08'17" N, 121°26'06" W). Eye a waterfall and talus across the emerald water, and consider a refreshing swim. The route quickly peters out beyond this point. Retrace your steps to the parking lot.

The Greendrop-Lindeman Trail is part of the old Centennial Trail. Nature has reclaimed the unmaintained portions of the 1960s route, which continued east via the northwest side of Greendrop Lake to the valley of Hicks Creek and beyond. Post Creek, Lindeman Lake, and Greendrop Lake lie in an ancient meltwater channel that carried glacial lake outburst floods from the valley of Silverhope Creek (Tl'íkw'elem) to the Chilliwack River (Sts'elxwíqw).

A backcountry camping permit is required to stay overnight at Lindeman Lake or Greendrop Lake. No drones, fires (subject to a $345 fine), mushroom or plant harvesting, off-road vehicles, smoking, or vaping. Dogs must be leashed.

GREAT BLUE HERON NATURE RESERVE

The great blue heron is designated a species of special concern in B.C. At the Great Blue Heron Nature Reserve (5200 Sumas Prairie Road) in Chilliwack, a colony of these wading birds nests in a grove of cottonwoods. Managed by the Great Blue Heron Nature Reserve Society, the site features an interpretative centre, lagoon, salmon spawning channel, and walking trails next to the Vedder River (Lhewálmel to the Stó:lō people). The best time to view the heronry is between March and July. On Trans-Canada Highway 1, take Exit 109 and go east on Yale Road. Turn right on Chadsey Road, left on Keith Wilson Road, and right on Sumas Prairie Road. (Dogs must be on leash and are allowed only on the Centre Trail.)

A boulder field on the Greendrop-Lindeman Trail.

A waterfall in the trees above Greendrop Lake.

29 CHILLIWACK
FLORA PASS

Catch the subalpine flower show above Chilliwack Lake

Distance: 11 km (6.8 mi)
Time: 5.5 hours (out and back)
Elevation gain: 1,110 m (3,640 ft)
High point: 1,740 m (5,710 ft)

Difficulty: ■
Maps: NTS 92-H/3 Skagit River; Trail Ventures BC Chilliwack East
Trailhead: 49°05'56" N, 121°27'30" W

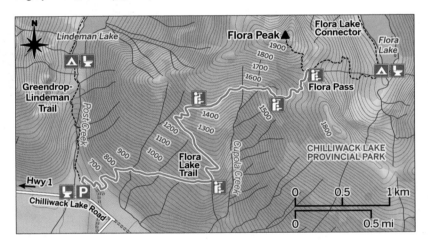

MANY HIKERS do the Flora Lake Trail as part of a clockwise loop over a long day, saving the steepest part for the final descent. However, tackling the stiff climb straight away, turning around at Flora Pass, and heading back down the same way affords the best scenery in almost half the time. The rewards are grand: wildflower meadows bursting with colour and sweeping views of the Cascade Mountains surrounding Chilliwack Lake (Sxóchaqel in the Halq'eméylem language of the Stó:lō people).

GETTING THERE

Vehicle: On Trans-Canada Highway 1 in Chilliwack, take Exit 119. Head south on Vedder Road for 5 km (3 mi). At the roundabout before the Vedder Bridge, take the second exit and go east on Chilliwack Lake Road for 39 km (24 mi). Before the pavement ends, turn left into the Post Creek parking lot (toilet available). Warning: Vehicle break-ins have been reported here.

Chilliwack Lake (Sxóchaqel) from the Flora Lake Trail.

THE HIKE

The Flora Lake Trail shares its trailhead (630 m/2,070 ft) with the Greendrop-Lindeman Trail (Hike 28). From the kiosk and yellow gate, set off on the gravel road. In 1 minute, turn right at the signed Flora Lake turnoff and go through the boulder blockade. Follow the old road and orange squares left at a Please Keep Trail Clean sign, where there's a mossy spur straight ahead. Go left at the next fork.

The well-graded trail curves right and begins climbing steadily in the open woods. Don't add graffiti to a defaced boulder. After a couple of switchbacks—one with an orange arrow keeping you on the right track—make an ascending rightward traverse through mossy outcrops. Earn a vista of Mount Webb, and step over several streams. Bracken fern, bunchberry, Oregon grape, and salal grow on the forest floor and devil's matchstick lichen on rock.

Switchback up to a viewpoint and unsanctioned campsite (1,110 m/ 3,640 ft) at the 2.3-km (1.4-mi) marker. (Backcountry camping permits are required for overnight stays in the park.) Look out over cascading Cupola Creek and Chilliwack Lake, the latter impounded by an end moraine left behind by a valley glacier 11,000 years ago.

Start a leftward traverse. Arctic lupine is abundant. Spy the Chilliwack Lake campground through the trees. Pass the 3-km (1.9-mi) marker. Hit the third set of switchbacks, as the trees give way to shrubs and more frequent vistas. Traverse right, going by the 3.5-km (2.2-mi) marker. Davidson's

Flora Lake from above.

penstemon, a matted perennial, blooms with lavender corollas on an outcrop to the right, watched over by lodgepole pines. Listen for the echoing hoots of the sooty grouse. Just around the corner, another viewpoint and unsanctioned campsite await.

Sidehilling across steep, dry, rocky terrain at the headwaters of Cupola Creek, the subalpine scenery is superb. Coast penstemon, globeflower, mountain arnica, Parry's campion, partridge-foot, red paintbrush, spreading phlox, tiger lily, and western springbeauty star in the flower show. Paleface Mountain, Mount Meroniuk, and Mount Edgar tower above the east shore of Chilliwack Lake, with Mount Webb and Mount Lindeman opposite. Negotiate a muddy section below a boulder field, and step over a clear creek. A viewpoint spur to the right offers a look back at your path across the steep meadow.

Duck back into the trees for the final push. Cross a muddy patch and brook, perhaps encountering lingering snow. Follow orange squares left at a bend, where a boot path leads right. (Let it revegetate.) Arrive at the summit of Flora Pass (3 hours up; 49°06′36″ N, 121°25′33″ W), 5.5 km (3.4 mi) from the parking lot. Keep your eyes peeled for Columbian black-tailed deer. (Never approach or feed wildlife.)

Just over the crest, the Flora Lake Trail forks left en route to eventually reunite with the Greendrop-Lindeman Trail via the Flora Lake Connector. However, wander right along the ridge for a few minutes to score a splendid

Spreading phlox in bloom on the Flora Lake Trail.

lunch spot amid white mountain-heather and a glimpse of gleaming Flora Lake, with its cute little island, far below. Flora Peak rises northwest of the pass, and Mount Wittenberg to the northeast, across the deep basin.

Established in 1973, Chilliwack Lake Provincial Park lies in the territories of the Nlaka'pamux and Stó:lō peoples, including the Ts'elxwéyeqw Tribe. No drones, fires, mushroom or plant harvesting, off-road vehicles, smoking, or vaping. Dogs must be leashed. In 2019, the Wilderness Committee called for the watersheds of Paleface Creek and Depot Creek, which flow into Chilliwack Lake, to be set aside as protected areas.

STOP OF INTEREST
CHILLIWACK RIVER HATCHERY

Adored by anglers, the Chilliwack River (Sts'elxwíqw to the Stó:lō people) is home to several species of salmon, trout, and char. At the Chilliwack River Hatchery (55205 Chilliwack Lake Road), built in 1981, you can view spawning chinook (August to November) and coho salmon (October to December), and steelhead trout (March to April). Operated by Fisheries and Oceans Canada, the facility is located 20 km (12 mi) east of the Vedder Bridge, by the mouth of Slesse Creek (Selísi Stótelō). Fishing is prohibited upstream of the Chilliwack-Slesse confluence. Downstream, at Vedder Crossing, the Chilliwack becomes the Vedder River (Lhewálmel), which flows into the Sumas River (Semá:th Stótelō), a tributary of the Fraser River (Stó:lō).

30 CHILLIWACK
RADIUM LAKE

Old-growth trees are aplenty on this quiet trail

Distance: 17 km (10.6 mi)
Time: 7.5 hours (out and back)
Elevation gain: 920 m (3,020 ft)
High point: 1,510 m (4,950 ft)

Difficulty: ■
Maps: NTS 92-H/3 Skagit River; Trail Ventures BC Chilliwack East
Trailhead: 49°05'17" N, 121°27'06" W

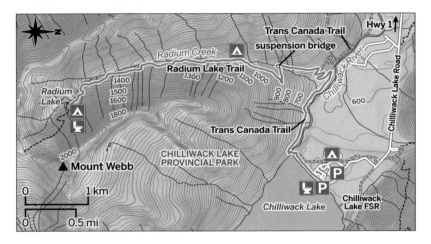

THE CHEMICAL element with the symbol Ra and an atomic number of 88 is described as unstable, radioactive, and toxic. Thankfully, none of these adjectives apply to Radium Lake in Chilliwack Lake Provincial Park. The Radium Lake Trail ascends from the Chilliwack River (Sts'elxwíqw in the Halq'eméylem language of the Stó:lō people) to the subalpine bowl beneath Mount Webb and Macdonald Peak, encountering plenty of old-growth conifers along the way. Despite the easy access, the trail is relatively quiet. The tree cover makes it ideal for both hot and rainy days.

GETTING THERE
Vehicle: On Trans-Canada Highway 1 in Chilliwack, take Exit 119. Head south on Vedder Road for 5 km (3 mi). At the roundabout before the Vedder Bridge, take the second exit and go east on Chilliwack Lake Road for 40 km

Boulder fields at Radium Lake.

(25 mi). Enter Chilliwack Lake Provincial Park, and turn right to go through the main gate (closed 11 p.m. to 8 a.m., and October to May). (If it's shut, park on the shoulder at pavement's end—not in front of the gate.) Follow signs to the day-use area. Pass the upper parking lot, go through another gate (closed at dusk), and turn right before the boat launch to find the lower parking lot (toilet available).

THE HIKE

From the lower parking lot, take the Beach Trail past the outhouses. Chilliwack Lake (Sx̱óchaqel) stays below to the left, and the Paleface Loop campground lies in the trees to the right. Go straight onto the Nature Trail, where the Beach Trail drops left. Go left on a gravel road at an unsigned junction, joining the Trans Canada Trail's Radium Lake Trail section, then turn right, following TCT signage to the bridge over the lake outlet.

Switchback uphill on the TCT (now officially known as the Great Trail), which shares this section with the Centennial Trail and National Hiking Trail, and is also used by horse riders and mountain bikers. Head downstream on an easy double track, and drop to river level momentarily. Cross a bridge over Radium Creek, and follow the TCT left.

Hit a key junction (49°05′15″ N, 121°28′34″ W), 3 km (1.9 mi) from the trailhead. Say bye-bye to the TCT, which switchbacks right onto the Centre Creek Trail. Go left to stay on the Radium Lake Trail. After two more

A long-toed salamander at Radium Lake.

switchbacks, your path points upstream, following orange squares, and gets overgrown and muddy as it nears Radium Creek. Carefully cross to river right on a nifty suspension bridge, with metal cables and wooden decking. Pass a 2-km (1.2-mi) marker—the distance relative to the former trailhead at Post Creek (Kwôkwelem)—then a big Douglas-fir and a landslide area.

Switch to river left via a log crossing (970 m/3,180 ft; 49°04′38″ N, 121°28′46″ W), 5 km (3.1 mi) from the parking lot. Radium Lake is 3.5 km (2.2 mi) away. Encounter tent sites under old-growth Douglas-firs. Take a wooden bridge with a deteriorating handrail back to river right. After the 3.5-km (2.2-mi) marker, enter a disturbed area with a lonely tall tree in the middle. The overgrown path slows progress. Planks and corduroy trail ease your passage in wet spots. Green false hellebore, round-leaved violet, and Sitka valerian bloom, and orange jelly and sulphur tuft fungi grow on wood.

Past the 5-km (3.1-mi) marker, orange tapes identify reroutes around blowdowns. Avalanche paths are visible on the steep slopes of Mount Corriveau, across the Radium Creek valley. Cross tributary creeks on your way upstream. Keep left at a switchback, where a muddy path goes right through a wet meadow. (Leave the latter to revegetate.) Stick with the orange squares to the 6-km (3.7-mi) marker and a signpost indicating your arrival at Radium Lake Camp (4 hours up; 49°03′09″ N, 121°28′14″ W).

Next to the remains of an old log cabin, the sign points the way to tent pads (backcountry camping permit required), a bear cache, a pit toilet, and the scramble route to Mount Webb (2,163 m/7,097 ft) and Macdonald Peak (2,247 m/7,370 ft). The shore of Radium Lake itself is steps away. Eye the cliffs and boulder fields at the head of the basin. Admire elephant's-head lousewort, fan-leaved cinquefoil, leatherleaf saxifrage, sweet coltsfoot, and white mountain marsh-marigold flowers, and perhaps even a long-toed salamander in a lakeside meadow. Head back the way you came. A dip in Chilliwack Lake is a fine way to end the hike.

Bordering Washington's North Cascades National Park, Chilliwack Lake Provincial Park lies in the territories of the Nlaka'pamux and Stó:lō peoples, including the Ts'elxwéyeqw Tribe. No drones, fires, mushroom or plant harvesting, off-road vehicles, smoking, or vaping. Dogs must be leashed.

STOP OF INTEREST
TAMIHI RAPIDS

The Chilliwack River (Sts'elxwíqw to the Stó:lō people) is a hub of whitewater kayaking and rafting. Why not check out the chilling action at the Tamihi Rapids? Every year, the Chilliwack Centre of Excellence Paddling Club hosts the Rich Weiss Memorial kayak and Tamihi 5-0 canoe races at this very place. Spot the slalom gates from the Tamihi Bridge on Chilliwack Lake Road, 10 km (6 mi) east of the Vedder Bridge, and stop at the Tamihi Rapids Recreation Site. Ten campsites are located riverside. Stretch your legs, explore the rocky bank, and watch people fishing for salmon.

EATON LAKE

Conifers, cliffs, and boulder fields ring a remote bowl

Distance: 8.5 km (5.3 mi)
Time: 5.5 hours (out and back)
Elevation gain: 920 m (3,020 ft)
High point: 1,350 m (4,430 ft)

Difficulty: ■
Maps: NTS 92-H/3 Skagit River, 92-H/6 Hope
Trailhead: 49°14'46" N, 121°23'28" W

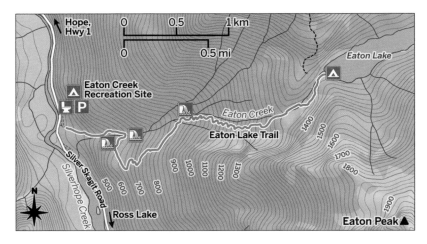

ALSO KNOWN as Crescent Lake for its shape, Eaton Lake fills a large mountain bowl in the Skagit Range, on the east side of the Silverhope Creek (Tl'íkw'elem in the Halq'eméylem language of the Stó:lō people) valley. It's a wonderful spot to float on your back and gaze at the sky. Although the Eaton Lake Trail is demanding, it repays your exertion by visiting old-growth trees and waterfalls en route to the ultimate prize.

GETTING THERE

Vehicle: On Trans-Canada Highway 1 in Hope, take Exit 168, and head southeast on Flood Hope Road. Turn right on Silver Skagit Road, which turns to gravel (2WD). Stay left at the Silver Lake Provincial Park turnoff (just after passing a pretty waterfall on the right). After 16 km (10 mi) on Silver Skagit, turn left and enter the Eaton Creek Recreation Site (dilapidated toilet

A horsetail waterfall on Eaton Creek.

available). The trailhead is 200 m (0.1 mi) up the Eaton Forest Service Road. If there's no room, park on the Silver Skagit shoulder.

THE HIKE

From the trailhead, start up the steep road. Within several minutes, follow a path left and up, marked by orange squares and flagging. Meet a couple of big old-growth firs. A rough, eroded spur leads right to the first (optional) waterfall, 15 minutes in. Five minutes later, cross Eaton Creek to river left on a sturdy log bridge with a handrail. This is a worthy destination on its own. A splendid horsetail plunges upstream—detour left to get a closer look from the signed falls lookout—and a cascade flows over tilted strata downstream.

Contour away from the creek, earning a brief respite from the sweaty climb. In a minute, a path joins from the right where a sign (Old Timers Trail 1960–1990) is nailed to a tree trunk. Pass the 1-km (0.6-mi) and 1.5-km (0.9-mi) markers as you rise in the mossy forest. After less than 1.5 hours, cross a wooden bridge to arrive at a broken bench. Whimsical eyes, a nose, and a mouth decorate a tree trunk at the Eaton Lake Trail's signed halfway point (820 m/2,690 ft; 49°14′48″ N, 121°22′34″ W), as you pull back alongside Eaton Creek.

A few minutes later, a leftward spur offers looks at two waterfalls. Back on the main trail, follow tapes right, continue up the rooty trail, and pass the 2-km (1.2-mi) marker. Red-belted polypores and crested coral fungi produce

Mount Grant stands over Eaton Lake.

spores in these woods. You might mistake a varied thrush for an American robin; the former is a year-round resident in these parts, eats insects and berries, and lays pale blue, lightly brown-dotted eggs. The sound of the creek fades away, and you see a boulder slope through the trees to the right.

Swing back to Eaton Creek and cross to river right below a logjam. In 2019, volunteers with the Hope Mountain Centre for Outdoor Learning replaced a damaged span with this log bridge. They nailed galvanized staples and sawed a criss-cross pattern into the wood to enhance the grip, and used copolymer fibre crab rope for the handrail. (The Hope Mountain Centre also deserves much credit for restoring the Hudson's Bay Company [1849] Heritage Trail, between Hope and Tulameen, and the Tikwalus Heritage Trail in the Fraser Canyon.)

Pass the 3.5-km (2.2-mi) marker and a few big boulders. After several minutes on river right, recross the creek—this time on a slippery log bridge, with a sketchy handrail, that's gone askew. Head round the base of a boulder field to return to the trees. Go under, around, and over deadfall. Crest the final rise and descend, amid blueberries, to the logjam at the outlet and, beyond, a few tent sites by the shore of Eaton Lake (3 hours up; 49°15′02″ N, 121°21′24″ W).

Mount Grant rises to the north, and Eaton Peak (2,117 m/6,950 ft) to the south. Conifers, cliffs, and boulder fields ring the remote bowl. Watch jumping rainbow trout and the wind send ripples across the green-tinted water. It's a fantastic swimming hole and lunch spot, though access to the lakeshore is at a premium. A rough path continues east along the shore but dissipates quickly; unfortunately, it's fouled with rotten scraps of toilet paper. (In many places where toilets are unavailable, the Leave No Trace Center for Outdoor Ethics advises burying poop and toilet tissue in a cat hole 15–20 cm [6–8 inches] deep and 70 adult paces away from water, trails, and campsites.)

The Eaton Lake Trail lies in the territories of the Nlaka'pamux and Stó:lō peoples. The upper Silverhope Creek valley provides habitat for the Red-Listed spotted owl, which is considered endangered in Canada and critically imperilled in B.C. In 2019, the Wilderness Committee called for the upper Silverhope watershed, including Eaton Lake, to be made a protected area.

STOP OF INTEREST
FLOOD FALLS

While some roadside waterfalls, such as Bridal Veil Falls near Chilliwack and Shannon Falls in Squamish, are routinely mobbed, others tumble in relative obscurity. Sure, Flood Falls in Hope (Ts'qó:ls to the Stó:lō people) isn't drawing tourists by the busload, but it's impressive in its own right. Plunging over a towering cliff, the falls are especially awe-inspiring during spring runoff and after heavy rains. On Trans-Canada Highway 1, take the Exit 165 off-ramp and go right. At the south side of the overpass, turn left. In 150 m (0.1 mi), spot the Flood Falls Trail sign at a pullout on the right. It's a brief walk up to the base of the waterfall.

HOZOMEEN LAKE

Tread water beneath the twin towers of Hozomeen Mountain

Distance: 12.5 km (7.8 mi)
Time: 3.5 hours (out and back)
Elevation gain: 330 m (1,080 ft)
High point: 880 m (2,890 ft)

Difficulty: ●
Maps: USGS Hozomeen Mountain;
Green Trails 16 Ross Lake
Trailhead: 48°59'07" N, 121°04'11" W

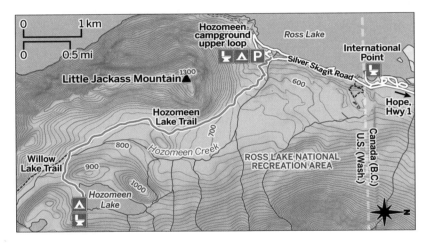

WITH ITS jagged twin peaks, Hozomeen Mountain (Hoz-o-méen in the Halq'eméylem language of the Stó:lō people) in Washington is an eye-catcher from many vantage points in E.C. Manning Provincial Park, including the Poland Lake Trail (Hike 38). Stateside, the greenstone towers are no less awe-inspiring. Take a swim in Hozomeen Lake, and tread water beneath the "most mournful" mountain that captivated Jack Kerouac, author of the 1958 novel *The Dharma Bums*, at his fire lookout post on Desolation Peak. Access is from Canada, though the Hozomeen Lake Trail lies across the international boundary in Ross Lake National Recreation Area, part of the North Cascades National Park Service Complex.

GETTING THERE

Vehicle: On Trans-Canada Highway 1 in Hope, take Exit 168, and head southeast on Flood Hope Road. Turn right on Silver Skagit Road, which turns

Hozomeen Mountain (Hoz-o-méen) towers over Hozomeen Lake.

to gravel (2WD). Stay left at the Silver Lake Provincial Park turnoff. Enter Skagit Valley Provincial Park. After 60 km (37 mi) on Silver Skagit, keep left to bypass the International Point day-use area. Cross the Canada-U.S. border (no checkpoint but carry your passport anyway!), and enter Ross Lake National Recreation Area. In 2 km (1.2 mi), turn left to find the Hozomeen Lake trailhead at the north end of the Hozomeen campground's upper loop (toilet available).

THE HIKE

The trailhead is situated by a historical log cabin built next to Hozomeen Creek. From the kiosk, set off southeast on the gently graded Hozomeen Lake Trail, which doubles as the northernmost section of the horse-friendly East Bank Trail. A 50-km (31-mi) backpacking or stock trip, the East Bank extends south along Ross Lake to State Route 20 (North Cascades Highway) at Ruby Creek, providing access to Desolation Peak on the way.

Blueberries, Oregon grape, and ursine poop (be bear aware!) await in the woods. After travelling through pines dripping with witch's hair, go over a puncheon and into a darker forest of tall fir and cedar trees. Devil's club, huge nurse logs, and boulders are all around. Continue southeast on a lovely old roadbed, going round Little Jackass Mountain (1,337 m/4,387 ft), and crossing a few wooden bridges.

You're now in the Stephen Mather Wilderness, congressionally designated in 1988 and named for the first director of the National Park Service.

The backcountry campground at Hozomeen Lake.

The historic log cabin at Hozomeen Lake trailhead.

Regulations stipulate a maximum party size of 12. (Consider this a general rule for all backcountry areas!) In 5 km (3.1 mi), reach a signposted fork (48°57′15″ N, 121°02′55″ W). The Willow Lake Trail (and East Bank Trail) head right. However, go left to stick with the Hozomeen Lake Trail. Your destination is just around the corner.

Step over shallow Hozomeen Creek, which is fed by Ridley Lake to the southeast and empties into Ross Lake, one of three hydroelectric reservoirs on the Skagit River. Soon Hozomeen Lake is visible through the trees. Rightward turnoffs lead to tent sites (backcountry camping permit required), communal firepits, and a Wallowa-style pit toilet with a wooden box for a seat. Keep going straight to arrive at the group campsite and day-use area on the south shore of Hozomeen Lake (1.5 hours up; 860 m/2,823 ft; 48°57′22″ N, 121°02′17″ W), 1.3 km (0.8 mi) from the fork.

From the rocky peninsula, the formidable towers of Hozomeen Mountain (2,459 m/8,066 ft) dominate the landscape. Little Jackass Mountain sheepishly peeks over the trees to the northwest. Listen to the clear water lapping against the shore, and contemplate cooling off with a dip. When sated with the tranquil scene, retrace your steps to the trailhead.

Hozomeen Lake lies in the territories of the Nlaka'pamux and Syilx peoples. The lake is closed from April 1 to May 31 to protect nesting loons. Grey wolves have been sighted in this area. Bikes, drones, motorized vehicles, feeding wildlife, and plant and mushroom harvesting are prohibited. Dogs must be leashed.

STOP OF INTEREST
SILVER LAKE

Watched over by Hope Mountain (St'ámiya to the Stó:lō people) and Wells Peak, Silver Lake (Pap-loshe-ka) is the jewel of the Silverhope Creek (Tl'íkw'elem) valley. Established in 1964, Silver Lake Provincial Park offers opportunities for boating, camping (May to October), fishing, picnicking, and swimming. South of the park, the Nature Trust of B.C.'s Silverhope Creek property protects habitat for harlequin ducks. The lake and creek are home to coho, chum, pink, and sockeye salmon; cutthroat and steelhead trout; and Dolly Varden char. Access the park via Silver Skagit Road, 6 km (4 mi) south of Flood Hope Road. (Dogs must be on leash and are not permitted on beaches.)

MOUNT LINCOLN

History and heights in the Fraser Canyon

Distance: 3 km (1.9 mi)
Time: 3.5 hours (out and back)
Elevation gain: 595 m (1,950 ft)
High point: 660 m (2,170 ft)

Difficulty: ■
Maps: NTS 92-H/11 Spuzzum
Trailhead: 49°33'50" N, 121°25'19" W

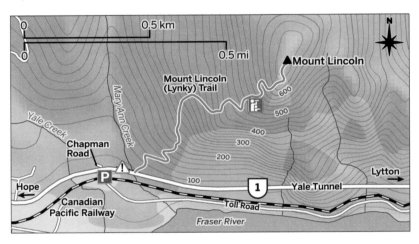

KNOWN LOCALLY as Lynky, Mount Lincoln offers commanding views of historic Yale (X̱wox̱welá:lhp in the Halq'eméylem language of the Stó:lō people) and the foot of the Fraser Canyon. Steep and fun—with an average grade of 37 per cent—the trail to the top makes for a satisfying little outing that's off the beaten path. Mount Lincoln lies in the territories of the Nlaka'pamux, Stó:lō, and Yale First Nations.

GETTING THERE

Vehicle: From its junction with Highway 7 (Lougheed Highway) in Hope, go eastbound on Trans-Canada Highway 1 for 21 km (13 mi) to Yale. Just past the Yale Creek bridge (and before the Yale Tunnel), park in the large gravel pullout on the right—by the entrance to Toll Road (opposite Chapman Road) and across the railroad track from a Yale First Nation reserve.

The Fraser River (Stó:lō) at Yale (X̱wox̱welá:lhp) from Mount Lincoln.

THE HIKE

Spot the Mount Lincoln (Lynky) Trail sign on the north side of Highway 1, 150 m (0.1 mi) east of Chapman Road. Look both ways before carefully crossing the highway. The narrow, rocky path is steep right off the bat and hardly lets up. Switchback between fir trees and mossy outcrops. Pearly everlasting, pink corydalis, and red paintbrush bloom on these slopes. Green spleenwort, a rock fern, and Oregon grape, a berry-producing shrub, grow here as well.

Soon you can look down at Yale (and the suggested parking spot). Traffic noise from the highway intrudes, but the sound of trains on the Canadian Pacific and Canadian National Railway lines adds to the historical flavour of the hike. Pass under an old cable, and cross a boulder field below a cliff. Knotted ropes tied around a fir trunk assist with a fun fall-line section.

Continue up through mossy ground, sticking to the main trail, which is well defined but scarcely marked. Pink flagging indicates a leftward bend in the open woods. Sticks and rocks block side paths. Take care not to trundle loose rocks onto hikers below. Pass beneath an overhang. A rope helps with the next bit.

Reach a viewpoint (500 m/1,640 ft) at a bend in the trail. The cliffs of Mount Allard (Qualark Mountain to the Yale First Nation) lie across the turbid Fraser River (Stó:lō in Halq'eméylem, Quoo.ooy in Nlaka'pamuchin). The mountain's namesake is Ovid "Chatelain" Allard (1817–1874), who ran Fort Yale and Fort Langley as a Hudson's Bay Company clerk. Mount

Oppenheimer lurks behind Yale, which is named for "Little" James Murray Yale (1798–1871), a chief trader for the HBC. The next part of the trail is not for acrophobes—and probably foolhardy when wet. Traverse precariously below a cliff with aging ropes, bolted down, for aid. Scramble up through a gap in the rock. Follow pink tapes through living pines and deadfall to the granodiorite summit (1.5 hours up; 49°34'04" N, 121°24'48" W), passing the remains of an old television rebroadcasting transmitter.

An open bluff facing southeast offers the best vantages. Mount Allard, cradling a colluvial fan at its base, dominates the scene. Lady Franklin Rock (X̱éyl̠x̱elamós in Halq'eméylem, Lawrence Hope Rock to the Yale First Nation), a sacred transformer site, is the narrow outcrop poking out of the Fraser River. You're standing in the Lillooet Ranges of the Coast Mountains; the Cascade Mountains rise across the great salmon river. As for the Fraser Canyon, it runs from Lytton to Yale. The portion between Spuzzum (Shpupz-m in Nlaka'pamuchin) and Yale is known as the Little Canyon. Beneath your feet, Highway 1's Yale Tunnel cuts through the mountain.

Retrace your steps to return to the trailhead and Yale. The Fraser Canyon gold rush of 1858 turned Yale into a boomtown. It even had its own Chinatown. Today, the On Lee property, part of the Yale Historic Site, commemorates the history of early Chinese settlers in the Fraser Canyon. Sadly, the On Lee House, dating back to the 1880s, burned down in the 1980s.

STOP OF INTEREST
ALEXANDRA BRIDGE

At Alexandra Bridge, you can stroll across the Fraser River (Stó:lō in Halq'eméylem, Quoo.ooy in Nlaka'pamuchin) like it was 1926. That's the year the historic suspension bridge was completed as part of the Fraser Canyon Highway—using the abutments of an 1863 span built for the Cariboo Wagon Road, which in turn replaced a cable ferry at Spuzzum (Shpupz-m in Nlaka'pamuchin) dating back to 1858. Alexandra Bridge Provincial Park also highlights the construction of two transcontinental railways through the Fraser Canyon. Access the park via Trans-Canada Highway 1, north of Yale (X̱wox̱welá:lhp in Halq'eméylem) and just upstream of the 1962 bridge currently in use. It's a 10-minute walk to the historic bridge via remnants of the 1926 road. In 1985, the Fraser Canyon transportation corridor was federally designated as a "national historic event." (Yes, such a thing exists.)

A fixed rope on the Mount Lincoln (Lynky) Trail.

Lady Franklin Rock (X̱éylx̱elamós) in the Fraser Canyon.

YAK PEAK

A scrambly affair on Zopkios Ridge

Distance: 5.5 km (3.4 mi)
Time: 6 hours (out and back)
Elevation gain: 840 m (2,755 ft)
High point: 2,039 m (6,690 ft)

Difficulty: ◆
Maps: NTS 92-H/11 Spuzzum; John Baldwin Coquihalla Summit
Trailhead: 49°35'44" N, 121°07'10" W

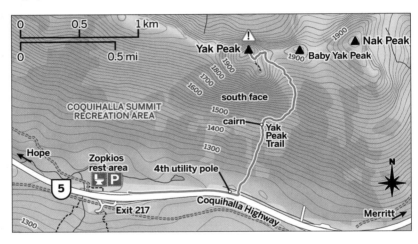

EVER SINCE the opening of the Coquihalla Highway in 1986, the dramatic scoured south face of Yak Peak has tantalized scores of travellers on the high road between Hope and Merritt. Towering above Coquihalla Pass, the wall of 39-million-year-old granite is noted for classic rock climbs such as Yak Crack. For hikers, Yak's summit is attainable via an ultra-steep and scrambly climbers' path (not for newbies or rainy days) in the Coquihalla Summit Recreation Area. From the highest point on Zopkios Ridge, the panorama of the surrounding North Cascades is simply divine.

GETTING THERE

Vehicle: From its junction with Crowsnest Highway 3 (Hope-Princeton Highway) near Hope, head north on Yellowhead Highway 5 (Coquihalla Highway) for 38 km (24 mi). Past the Great Bear Snowshed, take Exit 217 (unsigned

Alpaca Peak, Vicuña Peak, and Guanaco Peak from Yak Peak's summit.

northbound) on the right, before the summit of Coquihalla Pass. Turn left to go under the highway via a one-lane tunnel. Park at the Zopkios rest and brake-check area (toilet available) on the other side. (If you miss Exit 217, turn around at Exit 221 and use the southbound Zopkios off-ramp.)

THE HIKE

At the Zopkios rest area, the onion-skin slabs of Yak Peak—and the avalanche swathes below—dominate the northern scene. The hiking route heads up through trees to the base of the south face, then outflanks it on the right. Find the Do Not Enter road sign at the east end of the gravel parking area; this is our nominal trailhead.

Walk east for 900 m (0.6 mi)—less than 15 minutes—along the north shoulder (stay off the roadway), starting with the southbound off-ramp. From the Exit 217 and Brake Check signs, where the concrete barrier begins alongside the highway, identify the fourth wooden utility pole to the east—with three transformers. Just past this pole, orange flagging on a tree signals the start of the Yak Peak Trail (49°35′43″ N, 121°06′25″ W) to the left.

Drop down through trees to a clear creek, crossed on a log, and a muddy clearing. Enter the woods and begin the stiff ascent—stepping over deadfall and up boulders. Soon, from open terrain, you can look down at the highway and rest area, and over to Needle Peak, another sought-after scramble. Yak and Needle share the magnificent Eocene granite (of countertop dreams)

A subalpine meadow on the Yak Peak Trail.

of the Needle Peak Pluton. Pursue cairns among the boulders. Slip through the shrubs to the base of Yak's south face, close to the start of the 14-pitch Yak Crack, 45 minutes from the highway. A cairn distinguishes the spot (1,470 m/4,820 ft; 49°36′04″ N, 121°06′13″ W).

Go right, following the scarcely marked route along the rubble at the bottom of the slabs. Then scramble up the boulders hugging the bushes on the right side of the wall. Water running down the rock makes for slippery surfaces. Blueberries and salmonberries bear fruit, and leafy aster, mountain arnica, and Sitka columbine show off their flowers. Rocket uphill through trees and shrubs, skirting slabs on both sides. A doubled rope assists with one tricky section. Scramble up a rocky gully to hit heather meadows.

Zigzag up a few ledges to pick up the path through the gorgeous subalpine meadow in the windswept bowl headed by Yak Peak and Baby Yak Peak, the minor summit between Yak and neighbouring Nak Peak. Admire the blossoms of Davidson's penstemon and partridge-foot. The path aims for a point on the ridge, left of the Yak–Baby Yak col, 1.5 hours from the base of the south face.

With 20 minutes to the destination, follow cairns up the ridge crest (stay back from the precipice to the right) and over to the saddle between Yak's true summit and its southeast sub-summit (an optional quick dash to the left). Early in the season, hard snow may call for an ice axe. Turn right for the boot-beaten path to the rock and krummholz summit (3 hours up; 49°36'24" N, 121°06'19" W).

Behold the Cascade Mountains panorama—a setting worthy of primeval supernatural battles. Across the highway, Needle Peak is flanked by Markhor Peak (The Thimble) and The Flatiron. To the southeast, Illal Mountain and Coquihalla Mountain rise in the Bedded Range, east of the Coquihalla River (Kw'ikw'iyá:la to the Stó:lō people). However, it's Alpaca Peak, Vicuña Peak, and Guanaco Peak, looming in the northwest, that really catch the eye. Take care with loose footing on the descent.

The Coquihalla Summit Recreation Area lies in the territories of the Nlaka'pamux, Stó:lō, and Syilx peoples, including the Coldwater Band. Drones, fires, and tree cutting are banned. Dogs must be leashed, but this route is probably unsuitable for most. In 2017, John Baldwin, author of *Exploring the Coast Mountains on Skis*, proposed the expansion of the recreation area into the Bedded Range to protect its natural features.

STOP OF INTEREST

OTHELLO TUNNELS

Comparisons to the Great Wall of China may be slightly off the rails, but the Othello Tunnels would be right at the roundhouse on any list of the Seven Wonders of Historic B.C. Built by the Canadian Pacific Railway in 1914 as part of the Kettle Valley Railway's route along the Coquihalla River (Kw'ikw'iyá:la to the Stó:lō people), the five tunnels remain an astonishing feat of civil engineering. Today, these underground passages might be the coolest historic site in the province to explore on a hot day. Make tracks to Coquihalla Canyon Provincial Park on the outskirts of Hope, via Exit 183 on Yellowhead Highway 5 (Coquihalla Highway), Othello Road, and Tunnel Road. (Dogs must be leashed. The tunnels are closed in winter.)

ZOA PEAK

Marvel at these meadows

Distance: 8 km (5 mi)
Time: 4 hours (out and back)
Elevation gain: 620 m (2,030 ft)
High point: 1,869 m (6,130 ft)

Difficulty: ■
Maps: NTS 92-H/11 Spuzzum; John Baldwin Coquihalla Summit
Trailhead: 49°36'45" N, 121°03'54" W

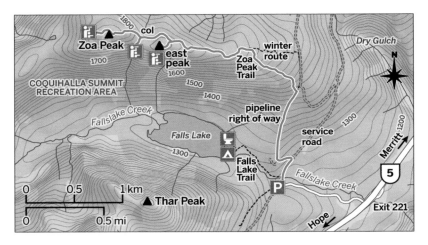

THE FRIENDLY ridge of Zoa Peak rewards hikers with easily gotten views of its dramatic neighbours in the Cascade Mountains. In summertime, many-hued wildflowers light up the path from almost start to finish. Found on the edge of the Coquihalla Summit Recreation Area, Zoa Peak is a deservedly popular destination in all seasons.

GETTING THERE

Vehicle: From its junction with Crowsnest Highway 3 (Hope-Princeton Highway) near Hope, head north on Yellowhead Highway 5 (Coquihalla Highway) for 44 km (27 mi). After cresting the summit of Coquihalla Pass (1,244 m/4,080 ft), take Exit 221 (Falls Lake). Turn left to go under the highway via a one-lane tunnel. Go left on the other side. Immediately turn right (before the on-ramp) onto the park access road, and drive 2 km (1.2 mi) to the

The north face of Yak Peak from Zoa Peak's east col.

Falls Lake and Zoa Peak parking lot. Warning: Vehicle break-ins have been reported here.

THE HIKE

Set off north on a gravel service road, which immediately goes over Fallslake Creek. Keep right at the turnoff for Falls Lake. Cross a livestock guard. (Try to imagine it's for the cattle-yak hybrids that are Zoa Peak's namesake.) Within 5 minutes, heeding signage, turn left on the eroded remains of an old road to Falls Lake. Bear right to head up the right-of-way for Enbridge's Transmission South gas pipeline.

After a half-hour (1.2 km/0.7 mi) on foot, look for a sign and cairn on the left. This is the start of the Zoa Peak Trail proper (49°37′16″ N, 121°03′46″ W). Leaving the pipeline corridor, clamber up the steep cut slope—the crux of the hike, you might say—and take the rocky single track into the trees. Encounter small clearings populated with green false hellebore, leafy aster, and mountain arnica, and follow cairns across rocky, open meadows.

The grade eases as the pleasant trail swings west to ascend the gentle ridge, amid a bounty of blueberries. Save some superfood for the bears. Indeed, purple-stained bear and bird poop is a common find. Ignore side paths to the left and right; better vistas lie ahead. Continue through marvellous heather meadows with stunted conifers.

Leafy aster blooming on Zoa Peak.

With Zoa's subpeak in sight, reach an unsigned junction (49°37′34″ N, 121°04′49″ W), 1.7 km (1.1 mi) from the pipeline corridor. Detour left on an intermittent path (200 m/0.1 mi) over rock and heather that veers right to visit the east peak (1,820 m/5,970 ft) and a precipitous south-facing viewpoint just beyond. Falls Lake, a gleaming blue jewel in the glacier-carved valley between Zoa Peak and Thar Peak, reflects the sky.

Back on the main trail, traverse a steep slope below the east peak. Survey the valley of the Coldwater River (Ntstlatko in Nlaka'pamuchin, the language of the Nlaka'pamux people), a tributary of the Nicola River, to the north. Descend to the lush col between the east and main peaks, 400 m (0.2 mi) from the previous junction. Before continuing right, go left on a brief path through Sitka columbine and western pasqueflower to the boulder field on the south side of the col. With pikas calling, stare at the terrifying north face of Yak Peak (Hike 34), the highest of the summits on Zopkios Ridge.

Continue up the main trail for 500 m (0.3 mi), passing by Zoa Peak's treed and true summit. Ignore a path on the left and arrive at a sign indicating the end of the marked trail (2 hours up; 49°37′38″ N, 121°05′26″ W). The final viewpoint, facing northwest, is steps away. A glorious montane landscape spreads out before you. Alpaca Peak, Vicuña Peak, and Guanaco Peak—all officially named for camelids in the 1970s as suggested by a Vancouver mountaineer—display their granite slabs. Closer but overshadowed is Zum Peak. Head back the way you came.

However, before you depart the area, it's worth considering a side quest to Falls Lake, a fabulous swimming hole. The easy Falls Lake Trail adds 900 m (0.6 mi) each way, and leads to a campground with a pit toilet and bear cache.

In winter, snowshoers can avoid challenging avalanche terrain by exiting the pipeline corridor higher up, sticking to the ridge crest, and turning around at the east peak. Make sure everyone in your party is carrying a transceiver, probe, and shovel (and knows how to use them), and consult Avalanche Canada's South Coast Inland forecast before heading out.

Established in 1986, the Coquihalla Summit Recreation Area lies in the territories of the Nlaka'pamux, Stó:lō, and Syilx peoples, including the Coldwater Band. The recreation area's 1990 master plan identifies a goal of Class A provincial park designation, but this status upgrade has not yet occurred. Drones, fires, and tree cutting are banned, and motorized vehicles are restricted to designated roads. Dogs must be leashed.

STOP OF INTEREST
THACKER MARSH

Home to evening grosbeaks, pileated woodpeckers, and red-tailed hawks, Thacker Marsh is a reliable birding spot in Hope. In autumn, the spawning channels are a great place to view chum, coho, and pink salmon. The Trans Canada Trail runs through Thacker Regional Park (20840 Union Bar Road), which lies between Kawkawa Lake (Q'éwq'ewe to the Stó:lō people) and the Coquihalla River (Kw'ikw'iyá:la). On Crowsnest Highway 3 (Hope-Princeton Highway), take Exit 173 and go west on Old Hope Princeton Way. Turn right on 7th Avenue, right on Kawkawa Lake Road, and left on Union Bar Road. (Dogs must be leashed.)

GHOSTPASS LAKE

Explore an ancient forest and historical horse route

Distance: 17 km (10.6 mi)
Time: 10 hours (out and back)
Elevation gain: 810 m (2,660 ft)
High point: 1,465 m (4,810 ft)

Difficulty: ◆◆
Maps: NTS 92-H/6 Hope; Clark Geomatics 104 Manning Park
Trailhead: 49°14'54" N, 121°10'07" W

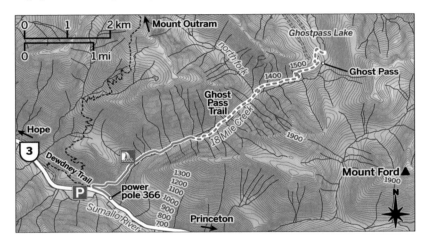

UNRAVELLING THE mystery of the Ghost Pass Trail entails penetrating a lush ancient forest, retracing a historical horse route, and seeking out a remote lake. This solitudinous quest isn't for the faint of heart. Although it begins in the panhandle of E.C. Manning Provincial Park, the Ghost Pass Trail is not maintained by B.C. Parks. It's dreadfully overgrown, beset by deadfall, and all too easy to lose. Only experienced hikers adept at wilderness navigation should attempt this wander in the creaking woods.

GETTING THERE

Vehicle: From Trans-Canada Highway 1 in Hope, head east on Crowsnest Highway 3 (Hope-Princeton Highway). Keep right and take Exit 177 in 6 km (3.7 mi) to stay on Highway 3 at its junction with Yellowhead Highway 5 (Coquihalla Highway). Look for a big gravel pullout on the south side of the

Ghostpass Lake is found on a historical horse trail.

highway, 1 km (0.6 mi) east of Manning Provincial Park's west gate. Park here, immediately before the 18-km (11-mi) marker and across the road from power pole 356 (49°15′00″ N, 121°10′39″ W).

THE HIKE

Find power pole 366 on the north shoulder of Highway 3, 700 m (0.4 mi) east of the pullout and across the road from the Sumallo River (Smalexw in the Halq'eméylem language of the Stó:lō people). Watch out for traffic when crossing. Enter the woods on the remains of a gold-rush wagon road built in 1861. You're treading northwest on a portion of a 40-km (25-mi) section of the 1860 Dewdney Trail (see also Hike 37), upgraded by sappers with the Columbia Detachment of the British Army's Corps of Royal Engineers.

After several minutes (400 m/0.2 mi) on the old road, orange squares and pink tapes indicate the start of the Ghost Pass Trail on the right (49°15′01″ N, 121°10′24″ W). Deceivingly well-defined at first, the trail switchbacks uphill in the forest with Oregon grape underfoot. As the path leads eastward, wooded mountains on the far side of the Sumallo River are glimpsed through the trees. After less than an hour of hiking, the trail turns northeast to enter the valley of 18 Mile Creek. As you begin dropping to the valley floor, the highway noise is drowned out by the burble of freshwater. Blackened axe scars on trees indicate where the trail remains loyal to the historical route.

Cross a creek with pretty cascades above and below the trail (49°15′20″ N, 121°09′36″ W), 2 km (1.2 mi) from the highway. Soon 18 Mile Creek is visible,

The Ghost Pass Trail leads through deadfall to the remote lake.

here and there, through the old-growth Douglas-fir trees. Treading on luxuriously soft ground in dappled light, head up the valley, crossing a small creek on logs. The moist understory teems with devil's club, which is highly valued by Indigenous peoples of the Pacific Northwest for its medicinal and other uses. A relative of American ginseng, this perennial shrub is recognizable by its large, prickly leaves; tall, spiny stems; and inedible red berries.

An hour beyond the cascades, burst into the sunlight on a debris fan with fireweed. The trail drops to 18 Mile Creek (995 m/3,260 ft; 49°15'38" N, 121°08'28" W), 3.7 km (2.3 mi) in. If the water is not dangerously high, cross to river left. Yellow flagging on the steep bank indicates the continuation of the trail, which henceforth proves extremely tricky to follow. Head upslope then upstream for 40 minutes, stubbornly enduring the revenge of the deadfall with the aid of occasional orange tapes.

At the 4.6-km (2.9-mi) mark, a giant cedar lies across 18 Mile Creek (1,081 m/3,550 ft; 49°15'47" N, 121°07'59" W). Recross in this spot. Look for yellow flagging to pick up the route on the right bank. An hour later and 5.9 km (3.7 mi) in, use a log crossing to pass over 18 Mile Creek's north fork (49°16'10" N, 121°07'15" W), which funnels snowmelt and runoff from the eastern slopes of Mount Outram. Switchback up to the left before traversing an avalanche path with stinging nettle.

Chunks of the trail are obliterated by blowdowns and will tax your route-finding savvy. Switchback leftward again and hike north up a wooded ridge, avoiding Ghost Pass itself, to the day's high point on the divide between the Fraser (Stó:lō) and Skagit (Nuch-hái-cheen) river basins. It's 20 minutes to the lakeshore. Flagging points the way down the messy slope. A clear-cut to the left presents a jarring contrast to the unlogged valley of 18 Mile Creek. Finally, the trail veers right to reach lonely Ghostpass Lake (5.5 hours up; 49°16'42" N, 121°05'53" W) at 1,370 m (4,495 ft). Go ahead and feel a sense of accomplishment. Although the shore of the peanut-shaped lake is muddy, you've more than earned a secluded dip in the pristine water before making the retreat through the deadfall. Make sure to carry a headlamp; it gets dark early in these woods.

Built by C.E. Devereux in 1929, the Ghost Pass Trail linked the Dewdney Trail and Hudson's Bay Company (1849) Heritage Trail, bypassing the latter's difficult Manson's Ridge section. In 2007, Wilderness Committee volunteers restored the fading trail, with funding from the Skagit Environmental Endowment Commission, in hopes of seeing 18 Mile Creek added to E.C. Manning Provincial Park as endangered spotted owl habitat.

Manning lies in the territories of the Nlaka'pamux, Stó:lō, and Syilx peoples. Dogs must be leashed, but B.C. Parks discourages taking pets into the backcountry.

STOP OF INTEREST
HOPE SLIDE

On January 9, 1965, the southwest flank of Johnson Peak disintegrated, burying Outram Lake and Crowsnest Highway 3 (Hope-Princeton Highway) under 47 million cubic metres (61 million cubic yards) of rock, mud, and debris. Four people died in the Hope Slide, one of the largest landslides in Canadian history. A viewpoint on the north side of the new section of Highway 3, 17 km (10.6 mi) east of Trans-Canada Highway 1 in Hope (Ts'qó:ls to the Stó:lō), rests on a 55-m (180-ft) thick layer of rubble and offers interpretative displays.

37 E.C. MANNING PROVINCIAL PARK
PUNCH BOWL PASS

Hike into history and the headwaters of the Tulameen River

Distance: 17 km (10.6 mi)
Time: 6.5 hours (out and back)
Elevation gain: 1,020 m (3,350 ft)
High point: 1,770 m (5,810 ft)

Difficulty: ■
Maps: NTS 92-H/3, 92-H/6, 92-H/7;
Clark Geomatics 104 Manning Park
Trailhead: 49°13'51" N, 121°03'22" W

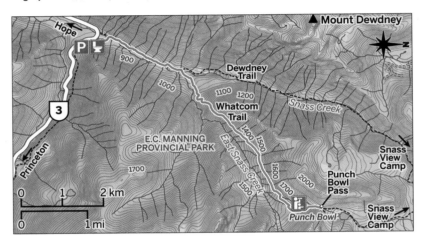

TRACING ANCIENT Indigenous pathways, the Whatcom Trail and Dewdney Trail materialized in the mid-1800s as a result of the Fraser Canyon and Rock Creek gold rushes. Today, the pleasant hike to Punch Bowl Pass traverses sections of both historical trails in E.C. Manning Provincial Park and the territories of the Nlaka'pamux, Stó:lō, and Syilx peoples. The often steep route heads up the valleys of Snass Creek (Slas in the Halq'eméylem language of the Stó:lō) and its east fork, visiting old-growth trees and subalpine meadows, on the way to the high pass overlooking Punch Bowl, the pretty lake at the headwaters of the Tulameen River.

GETTING THERE

Vehicle: From Trans-Canada Highway 1 in Hope, head east on Crowsnest Highway 3 (Hope-Princeton Highway). Keep right and take Exit 177 in

A subalpine meadow on the Whatcom Trail.

6 km (3.7 mi) to stay on Highway 3 at its junction with Yellowhead Highway 5 (Coquihalla Highway). Turn left into the Cascade Recreation Area parking lot (toilet available), 12.5 km (7.8 mi) east of the marmot carving at Manning Provincial Park's west gate.

THE HIKE

American miners travelled the Whatcom Trail, built in 1858, from Whatcom (now Bellingham, Washington) to goldfields north of the 49th parallel, circumventing the British colonial authorities at Fort Victoria. In 1860, Edgar Dewdney (1835–1916), who went on to become lieutenant-governor of B.C. and the Northwest Territories, led the construction of a pack route to the Vermilion Forks (now Princeton) area. The Dewdney Trail (see also Hike 36) helped the British Empire retain control of the new Colony of British Columbia.

From the historical marker at the trailhead (750 m/2,460 ft), embark on the easygoing Dewdney Trail for 2.4 km (1.5 mi) northeast in mature forest. Cross a bridge to the right bank of Snass Creek, and swing right with the main trail, ignoring side paths. In 5 minutes, make a 90-degree turn where steps lead down to the right. Look left to see a collapsed wooden bridge.

At 30 minutes, reached a signed junction at Snass Forks (49°14'50" N, 121°02'42" W). Leaving the Dewdney Trail, turn right and drop down the Whatcom Trail (no horses) to carefully recross Snass Creek on an old slippery

Punch Bowl from above, with Warburton Peak in the background.

bridge. Although markers are few and far behind, the path is well defined, staying on river right of East Snass Creek. Big Douglas-firs stand sentinel around a fallen giant. Several minutes from the junction, hit the first steep switchbacks and start breathing hard.

After an hour on the Whatcom Trail, the path becomes overgrown—be prepared to get drenched by wet vegetation after a rainfall—and, in some parts, badly eroded. Angel wings, Cascade russula, dyer's conk, fragile russula, rosy russula, and yellow-tipped coral fungi are found on the forest floor. Oregon grape, snowberry, and thimbleberry bear fruit. Varied thrushes flit among trees positively dripping with witch's hair. Your first partial views are gained—down-valley and across East Snass Creek, now far below. Cross a few streams en route to a good vantage of Snass Mountain (2,309 m/7,575 ft) at the head of the valley, as the terrain opens up. (Beware of avalanches in snow.)

Two hours from the junction, the path slices across a dry, rocky slope bearing spreading stonecrop, a succulent plant. Then it's up a meadow and over a couple of creeks. Punch Bowl Pass is now visible ahead—up and to the left. Higher, in an open meadow beneath Snass Mountain's west ridge, the wildflowers bloom in technicolour: edible thistle, green false hellebore, heart-leaved arnica, leafy aster, red paintbrush, tiger lily, and western pasqueflower. Don't trample the sensitive environment; keep to the main trail.

The best southwest-facing viewpoint comes 20 minutes before the destination. Spot Marmot Mountain, Silvertip Mountain, and the Skagit Range, across the Sumallo River (Smalexw) valley. Duck back into the trees momentarily. Pikas populate a boulder slope to the right. Run along a mossy brook and into a heather meadow with bog blueberries and mountain chickadees. Tread the gentle path to a fork at the summit of Punch Bowl Pass (3.5 hours up; 49°16′37″ N, 120°59′43″ W), 6.2 km (3.9 mi) from the Dewdney-Whatcom junction. Take several steps farther to the right to peer down at gleaming Punch Bowl (1,650 m/5,410 ft), encircled by lush meadows and verdant conifers, and beyond to distinctive Warburton Peak. Head back the way you came.

Punch Bowl Pass lies on the divide between the Columbia River and Skagit River (Nuch-hái-cheen above Klesilkwa Creek to the Stó:lō) drainage basins. The Whatcom Trail takes the left fork, descends to Punch Bowl, and continues north to reunite with the Dewdney Trail at Snass View Camp (backcountry permit required) in Paradise Valley. Scramblers may set their sights on Snass Mountain, east of the pass. Be prepared for bear encounters.

Dogs must be leashed in E.C. Manning Provincial Park, and fires are discouraged in the backcountry. No bikes, drones, smoking, or vaping.

STOP OF INTEREST
CASCADE LOOKOUT

The Cascade Range extends all the way from northern California to southern B.C., where the chain is officially known as the Cascade Mountains. Stop by the Cascade Lookout in E.C. Manning Provincial Park to survey a bunch of the peaks straddling the Canada-U.S. border. Arrows point out Sheep Mountain, Mount Winthrop, Frosty Mountain, Hozomeen Mountain, and Mox Peaks. From Crowsnest Highway 3 (Hope-Princeton Highway), at the Manning Park Resort, go north on Owl Way. Immediately turn left on Blackwall Road and continue up to the lookout.

POLAND LAKE

A floral rainbow from start to finish

Distance: 16.5 km (10.3 mi)
Time: 5.5 hours (out and back)
Elevation gain: 480 m (1,575 ft)
High point: 1,840 m (6,040 ft)

Difficulty: ●
Maps: NTS 92-H/2 Manning Park; Clark Geomatics 104 Manning Park
Trailhead: 49°04'01" N, 120°53'05" W

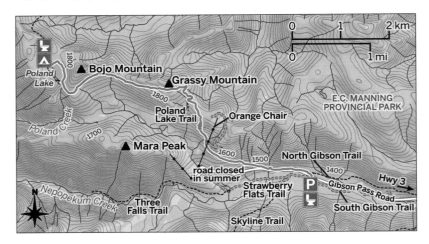

LINED WITH a floral rainbow from start to finish and offering gorgeous views of the North Cascades, the Poland Lake Trail is sure easy on the eyes. It's also a breeze compared to many other hikes in E.C. Manning Provincial Park, as it largely follows a fire-access road. Surrounded by woods and meadows, Poland Lake is a lovely spot for a swim or a nap, not to mention an ideal over-night destination for beginner backpackers.

GETTING THERE

Vehicle: From Trans-Canada Highway 1 in Hope, head east on Crows-nest Highway 3 (Hope-Princeton Highway) for 66 km (41 mi). At the Manning Park Resort, turn right on Gibson Pass Road. Keep right at the Lightning Lake turnoff in 3 km (1.9 mi). Reach the Strawberry Flats parking lot (toilet avail-able), where the road is gated in summer, 8 km (5 mi) from the highway.

Looking across Poland Lake to Bojo Mountain.

THE HIKE

Find the trailhead on the north side of the road, opposite Strawberry Flats (Hike 39). (Don't feed the whisky-jacks!) Spurning the North Gibson Trail, set off west on the multi-use Poland Lake Trail. The flat path parallels Gibson Pass Road. In several minutes, head right on a gravel road, which goes over a few streams as it rises amid lodgepole pines and wild strawberries to enter the downhill ski area. Watch out for black bears.

Forty minutes of hiking earns a big view of the striking greenstone towers of Hozomeen Mountain (Hoz-o-méen in the Halq'eméylem language of the Stó:lō people) in Washington peeking over the ridge traced by the Skyline Trail. Fork right and duck under the Orange Chair. Where the road curves right (49°04′28″ N, 120°54′50″ W), 2.6 km (1.6 mi) from your start, bear left on a path through meadows of green false hellebore, red paintbrush, and western pasqueflower. (Horse riders and mountain bikers stick with the road.) Switchback up the ski area with alacrity and follow a double track to rejoin the bike and horse route (49°04′49″ N, 120°54′58″ W) after 1 km (0.6 mi).

In short order, the mellow road reaches a map and signpost and heads into the woods. The road curves left to peak near the top of Grassy Mountain, almost 2 hours in. (The minor summit [1,889 m/6,200 ft; 49°05′08″ N, 20°55′27″ W] is a quick and easy scramble.) A gentle descent reveals a succession of meadows bearing cow parsnip, heart-leaved arnica, and subalpine

The backcountry campground at Poland Lake.

Poland Lake in E.C. Manning Provincial Park.

daisy, and vantages of Snow Camp, Lone Goat, and Red Mountains across the valley of Nepopekum Creek (Lexwpopeqwem). The road rises to traverse the south slopes of Bojo Mountain. Pass a 3-km (1.9-mi) marker en route to the hitching post at road's end (no bikes or horses beyond this point).

Follow the path up Poland Creek to arrive at the logjammed outlet of Poland Lake (1,750 m/5,740 ft), just over 2.5 hours from the trailhead. Round the eastern shore and turn left at a signpost to find Poland Lake Camp in a broad, inviting meadow. This is a popular winter snowshoeing destination. Facilities include six tent sites (backcountry camping permit required), a pit toilet, a food cache, and a deteriorating log shelter with a designated fire ring out front (3 hours up; 49°05′24″ N, 120°57′25″ W). Return from whence you came.

Formerly known as Paddy Pond, Poland Lake is named after a surveyor for a Great Northern Railway line once proposed to run through the park. Prior to 1956, the lake was stocked with rainbow trout. It tends to stay frozen until early summer. The Memaloose Trail is an alternative approach from Allison Pass. In winter, backcountry skiers access the Poland Lake Trail by skinning up the Horseshoe ski run (on skier's right).

E.C. Manning Provincial Park is located in the territories of the Nla-ka'pamux, Stó:lō, and Syilx peoples. The park was named in honour of B.C.'s fourth chief forester, Ernest C. Manning (1890–1941), who died in a plane crash. Flower and mushroom picking, and motorized vehicles are prohibited. Dogs must be on-leash at all times. Please heed any fire or smoking bans. Mountain bikers yield the right-of-way to hikers, and both give way to horse riders. Nevertheless, it's courteous to step aside for cyclists too.

STOP OF INTEREST

TASHME

Sunshine Valley, 4 km (2.5 mi) east of E.C. Manning Provincial Park's west gate, is the former site of Tashme, the country's largest Japanese Canadian internment camp during World War II. After Japan's 1941 attack on the U.S. naval base at Pearl Harbor, Hawaii, the Canadian government forcibly removed Japanese Canadians from the B.C. coast and seized their property. Opened in 1942 and closed in 1946, the camp at 14 Mile Ranch housed up to 2,644 people in tarpaper shacks. Visit the Sunshine Valley Tashme Museum (14781 Alpine Boulevard) and a historical marker, erected by the B.C. government in 2017, to learn more.

DEREK FALLS

One trail, three waterfalls

Distance: 9 km (5.6 mi)
Time: 3 hours (out and back)
Elevation gain: 170 m (560 ft)
High point: 1,385 m (4,540 ft)

Difficulty: ●
Maps: NTS 92-H/2 Manning Park; Clark
Geomatics 104 Manning Park
Trailhead: 49°03'59" N, 120°53'05" W

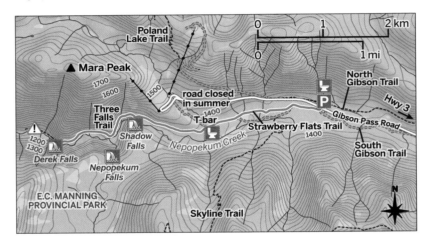

BEGIN WITH a leisurely stroll through vibrant meadows of strawberries and wildflowers on a fire-access road. Follow the Three Falls Trail into the steep-sided valley of Nepopekum Creek (Lexwpopeqwem in the Halq'eméylem language of the Stó:lō people), where witch's hair hangs from the trees and water tumbles over cliffs. With its triple payoff, this short outing is perfect for families, rainy days, or the final morning of a camping trip in E.C. Manning Provincial Park.

GETTING THERE

Vehicle: From Trans-Canada Highway 1 in Hope, head east on Crowsnest Highway 3 (Hope-Princeton Highway) for 66 km (41 mi). At the Manning Park Resort, turn right on Gibson Pass Road. Keep right at the Lightning Lake turnoff in 3 km (1.9 mi). Reach the Strawberry Flats parking lot (toilet available), where the road is gated in summer, 8 km (5 mi) from the highway.

Crossing a boulder field on the Three Falls Trail.

THE HIKE

Locate the Strawberry Flats trailhead on the south side of the road at Gibson Pass, across from the start of the Poland Lake Trail (Hike 38). (Don't feed the whisky-jacks.) An immediate right turn takes you west on a double track into a stand of lodgepole pine, with a middle story of Engelmann spruce and subalpine fir, broken up by meadows. An interpretive panel starring B.C. Parks mascot Jerry the Moose advises everyone to keep their boots on trails, as plants may take up to 25 years to bloom in this subalpine environment.

Meet the Skyline Trail junction in 450 m (0.3 mi). Stay right to stick with the tourist-grade Strawberry Flats Trail, which sees winter use by cross-country skiers. Often achieving peak bloom in July, the varicoloured flower show includes cow parsnip, edible thistle, fireweed, leafy aster, orange agoseris, pink mountain-heather, and Sitka valerian. Keep your eyes peeled for birds (barred owls, pine siskins, red-naped sapsuckers, spruce grouses, and western tanagers) and mammals (black bears, Cascade golden-mantled ground squirrels, and mule deer) too.

After less than 30 minutes on foot, take the right fork where a wooden sign denotes the start of the Three Falls Trail (49°03′53″ N, 120°54′29″ W), almost 2 km (1.2 mi) from the parking lot. Pass the bottom terminal of a T-bar lift and an outhouse, cross a ski run, and re-enter the woods. Blueberries, huckleberries, and thimbleberries grow in the understory.

The first waterfall viewpoint is off to the left at the 3.1-km (1.9-mi) mark. A log fence keeps visitors back from the edge at segmented Shadow Falls, which seemingly springs forth from the forest. Gaze south to see Red Mountain rising above the Nepopekum Creek valley.

It'd be easy to miss slender Nepopekum Falls, at 3.2 km (2 mi), if a sign didn't imply that you stop and look. Across the valley, a tributary dives over a high cliff. As you continue downstream, a break in the trees affords a view of talus below a rock wall. With downcast eyes, you might spot a western toad camouflaged on the forest floor. (A thin, cream-coloured stripe running down the centre of the back helps identify these warty amphibians, which hibernate in winter.) Cross a boulder field.

Soon enough, Derek Falls announces itself with a rumble. (From the Derek Falls sign, a steep and loose path zigzags down to the base of the waterfall.) Stay on the main trail, traversing a large boulder slope to the final viewpoint (49°03′47″ N, 120°56′21″ W), at 4.5 km (2.8 mi). Find a stable rock to sit on and observe Nepopekum Creek pouring over tilted strata amid sheer cliffs and lofty conifers. A sign warns against proceeding any farther west due to a slide area. Retrace your steps on the uphill return.

From its headwaters at Gibson Pass, Nepopekum Creek flows into the Skagit River (Nuch-hái-cheen above Klesilkwa Creek to the Stó:lō), which empties into Puget Sound near Mount Vernon, Washington. Historically, the creek was viewed as a potential route for a road or railway line.

Established in 1941, E.C. Manning Provincial Park is located in the territories of the Nlaka'pamux, Stó:lō, and Syilx peoples. Flower and mushroom picking, and motorized vehicles are prohibited. Dogs must be on-leash at all times. No bikes or horses are allowed at Strawberry Flats. Please heed any fire or smoking bans.

STOP OF INTEREST
RHODODENDRON FLATS

How about stopping to smell more flowers? Follow your nose to Rhododendron Flats, 11 km (6.8 mi) east of the west gate of E.C. Manning Provincial Park on Crowsnest Highway 3 (Hope-Princeton Highway). Situated northeast of the confluence of the Skagit (Nuch-hái-cheen to the Stó:lō) and Sumallo (Smalexw) Rivers, the flats are toured via a 500-m (0.3-mi) walking loop. The star of the show is the Pacific rhododendron, which blooms bigtime in June, but the flats are a pleasant stroll in any season. (Dogs must be leashed.) Another large stand is protected by Skagit River Rhododendrons Ecological Reserve, encircled by neighbouring Skagit Valley Provincial Park. Picking this red flower was once a crime punishable by a $25 fine under B.C.'s Dogwood, Rhododendron and Trillium Protection Act, repealed in 2002.

The Three Falls Trail leads to Derek Falls.

MOUNT KILLAM

Get away to Gambier Island

Distance: 13.5 km (8.4 mi)
Time: 5.5 hours (out and back)
Elevation gain: 840 m (2,760 ft)
High point: 844 m (2,770 ft)

Difficulty: ■
Maps: NTS 92-G/6 North Vancouver
Trailhead: 49°27'00" N, 123°26'21" W

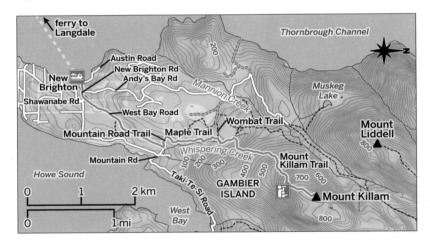

A DAY hike involving a ferry ride can be as refreshing as a long weekend getaway. Coming from Vancouver, this all-season jaunt to one of the tops of Gambier Island (Cha7élḵnech in the S̲ḵwx̲wú7mesh language), in Squamish Nation territory, requires the use of two ferry routes. It's worth the inconvenience. Enjoy the quiet and the views on Mount Killam—a world away from the busier trails of neighbouring Bowen Island (Nex̲wlélex̲wem) in Howe Sound (Atl'ḵa7tsem).

GETTING THERE

Transit: Take TransLink Bus 250, 257, or 262 to the Horseshoe Bay ferry terminal, or Sunshine Coast Regional Transit Bus 1 or 90 to the Langdale ferry terminal.

Bowen Island (Ne̱xwlélé̱xwem) from the Mount Killam viewpoint.

Vehicle: From Vancouver, take Trans-Canada Highway 1 west to the B.C. Ferries terminal at Horseshoe Bay (Exit 3) in West Vancouver. Park in the long-term parking lot. (On the Sunshine Coast, go south on Highway 101 [Sunshine Coast Highway] to Langdale and park at the ferry terminal.)

THE HIKE

Arriving on the Sunshine Coast as a Horseshoe Bay–Langdale ferry foot passenger, you'll see a dock to the right as you disembark. Take the gangway to board the next sailing of the privately operated pedestrian ferry to New Brighton. Verify the schedule for later with the crew. As the *Stormaway* speeds toward Gambier Island, Mount Killam is the right of the pair of wooded peaks ahead.

From the dock, start up the gravel of New Brighton Road, ignoring leftward turnoffs for Austin Road and Andy's Bay Road. In 5 minutes, go left on West Bay Road. Twenty minutes later, the gravel road bends right and descends as Mountain Road. Here, 2.1 km (1.3 mi) from the dock, a signpost on the left marks the start of the Mountain Road Trail (49°27′49″ N, 123°25′21″ W). (Smoking is prohibited on trails, and dogs must be leashed.)

Take the winding path, featuring wooden boardwalks and steps, into the second-growth woods. Keep right, following leaf pictographs, for the Maple Trail, spurning left-leading mountain and wombat symbols. The lovely path pulls alongside a verdant ravine under tall western red cedars and

The final stretch of the Mount Killam Trail.

Douglas-firs. Meet the Wombat Trail again, and turn right to cross salmon-bearing Whispering Creek. Go left on an old roadbed, sticking with the maple symbols.

Forty minutes (1.9 km/1.2 mi) after leaving West Bay Road, signs indicate the bottom of the Mount Killam Trail on the right (49°28'32" N, 123°25'29" W). Follow orange and grey diamonds up the mountainside, your heart pumping as the trail steepens. Moss blankets the forest floor. Cut across a debris flow channel, go over a mossy outcrop, pass through a windblown area, and cross a creek. Admire old-growth survivors, and climb over large logs. Scamper uphill between outcrops. As you gain elevation, the trees get smaller and the woods more open.

Reach a signed fork after 1.5 hours (2.1 km/1.3 mi) on the Mount Killam Trail. Left is for the summit, but go right for the instant gratification of the day's only viewpoint. From this righteous lunch spot atop a lofty bluff (watch your step), spy bald eagles and turkey vultures. Divided by the sparkling waters of Port Graves, Centre Bay, and West Bay, Gambier's southern appendages reach out toward Bowen and Keats Islands. Beyond lie the Gulf Islands in the Strait of Georgia, which combines with the Juan de Fuca Strait and Puget Sound to form the Salish Sea. Spot the Twin Sisters (Ch'ich'iyúy, Hike 5) and Mount Elphinstone (Hike 41) on opposite shores of Howe Sound.

Summit seekers will want to push on to the top, just 20 minutes (600 m/ 0.4 mi) away and 100 m (330 ft) higher. From the fork, go over a mossy bump.

Follow metal arrows, and negotiate deadfall. The cairn hides a soggy summit register, but trees obscure any views (3 hours up; 49°29′20″ N, 123°24′35″ W). Head back to the viewpoint for another look, then retrace your steps to New Brighton, where you might consider cooling off with a swim.

Gambier, the largest island in Howe Sound, is part of the Sunshine Coast Regional District and the Islands Trust. Founded in 1995, the Gambier Island Conservancy supports habitat restoration and trail maintenance. Bring enough water for the day, and take your trash with you. If you have time to kill at Langdale on the way back, there's a sandy beach, immediately north of the ferry terminal, offering a glacial erratic, sea stars, and a view of Mount Killam.

STOP OF INTEREST
GIBSONS PUBLIC MARKET

Opened in 2017, the Gibsons Public Market (473 Gower Point Road) is a gathering place to enjoy the local food and art of the Sunshine Coast. At the main entrance, eagle and salmon carvings by Richard Baker (Ghaslas), a Squamish Nation artist, welcome visitors. On the main level, the Nicholas Sonntag Marine Education Centre exhibits wildlife plucked from the waters of Howe Sound (Atl'ka7tsem in Skwx̱wú7mesh sníchim) under a collect-hold-release model. Featured species include the decorated warbonnet, giant Pacific octopus, and spot prawn. Find the market (open Tuesday to Sunday, 10 a.m. to 6 p.m.) in Gibsons, 5 km (3.1 mi) southwest of the Langdale ferry terminal, via Marine Drive.

MOUNT ELPHINSTONE

Magical views on the Sunshine Coast

Distance: 13 km (8.1 mi)
Time: 6 hours (out and back)
Elevation gain: 1,060 m (3,480 ft)
High point: 1,266 m (4,150 ft)

Difficulty: ■
Maps: NTS 92-G/5 Sechelt
Trailhead: 49°25'44" N, 123°30'30" W

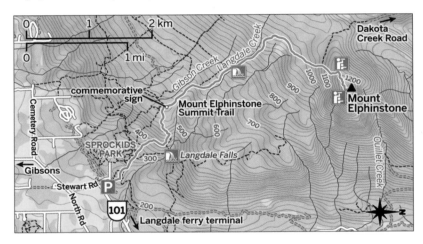

AS THE *Queen of Surrey* sails from Horseshoe Bay (Ch'ax̱áy in S̱ḵwx̱wú7mesh sníchim, the language of the Squamish Nation) to Langdale, Mount Elphinstone rises behind the approaching ferry terminal. It's the wooded hill with a summit knob that resembles the dorsal fin of a chinook salmon. A hike on the Mount Elphinstone Summit Trail is a very agreeable affair, featuring old-growth trees, a waterfall, and grand views of the Tantalus Range (Tsewílx̱) and Howe Sound (Atl'ḵa7tsem).

GETTING THERE

Transit: Take TransLink Bus 250, 257, or 262 to the Horseshoe Bay ferry terminal, or Sunshine Coast Regional Transit Bus 1 or 90 to the Langdale ferry terminal. At Langdale, walk across the ferry parking lot to find a pathway leading to Smith Road. Go right on Smith, passing the No Thru Road sign, to find a pathway on the left to Port Mellon Highway. Carefully cross the highway, and walk west to pick up the trail at the end of Wharf Road. Continue west to meet the Mount Elphinstone Summit Trail.

Vehicle: B.C. Ferries offers daily service between West Vancouver and the Sunshine Coast via the Horseshoe Bay–Langdale route. From the Langdale ferry terminal, go straight onto northbound Highway 101 (Sunshine Coast Highway) for 2.3 km (1.4 mi). At the top of the hill, make a right on Stewart Road. Turn right to find the small parking area outside the yellow gate for Sprockids Park (1235 Stewart Road). (Alternatively, park at the Horseshoe Bay terminal in the long-term parking lot and approach on foot.)

A waterfall on Langdale Creek.

THE HIKE

"No two people climb the same mountain!" Thus, mountaineer Dick Culbert (1940–2017) began the introduction of his 1974 book *Alpine Guide to Southwestern British Columbia.* Consider these words as you explore the Mount Elphinstone Summit Trail, built by Culbert and Peter Cave, and opened in 2010.

The hike begins at the entrance to Sprockids Park. Find the trailhead (210 m/690 ft) on the left of the road to the white private-property gate that's just past the parking area. A sign advises the summit route may take 8 hours return. It's impeccably marked with yellow diamonds and directional triangles; ignore different coloured plates as you navigate the web of mountain-bike trails and old logging roadbeds. Make sure to bring plenty of water.

Head north into the open woods, quickly keeping right twice. Within 5 minutes, meet the trail from the ferry terminal, and turn left (49°25′49″ N, 123°30′33″ W). Fork right, go left at the next map post, and take another right fork. Abandoned cars corrode in the shrubs. At 10 minutes, the trail to Langdale Falls exits right. However, keep left on an old roadbed, admiring big old Douglas-firs and western red cedars. The summit route steepens.

Howe Sound (Atl'ḵa7tsem) from Mount Elphinstone.

Follow the yellow-blazed road up to a four-way junction (49°26′12″ N, 123°31′33″ W) with wooden signs for Langdale and the Sidewinder Loop, 45 minutes (2.2 km/1.4 mi) from the trailhead. Turn right to find a sign commemorating Culbert. Walk a mesh-topped log viaduct and up the pleasant divide between Gibson Creek and Langdale Creek, enjoying the well-sited trail. Huge fire-scarred stumps are pocked with springboard notches. Spot the fruiting bodies of crested and pink coral, and lilac conifer and violet cort fungi on the forest floor. Notice bear claw marks on tree trunks. (Got bear spray?)

A half-hour (1.4 km/0.9 mi) later, cross an old logging grade. In winter and spring, a sign warns, deep snow and ice may render the upper trail "difficult and dangerous." A few steps up the path, a pretty cascade lies off to the right (750 m/2,460 ft; 49°26′46″ N, 123°32′06″ W).

Upstream, cross Langdale Creek to river left. Take the single track up the rim of the ravine to a muddy section with skunk cabbage. Cross several streams. Lose a bit of elevation en route to an overgrown viewpoint that overlooks Keats Island. Bear left where a Wrong Way sign on the ground blocks the path ahead. Spy the treed summit knob ahead, and tread a couple of boardwalks, the latter running between two raised ponds in a wetland.

Go straight through a junction (49°27′33″ N, 123°32′07″ W), 1 hour (2.1 km/ 1.3 mi) past the waterfall. The red-diamond trail on the left links to Dakota

Creek Road (Sechelt Dakota Forest Service Road). Pursue yellow markers and flagging up the steep, rooty, and slippery summit route. It's 30 minutes (900 m/0.6 mi) to the top!

Where the trail splits, take the left fork to go by an optional pre-viewpoint. After the branches rejoin, dirty climbing ropes help with a scrambly bit. Head over rock and through heather to a stunner of a perch on the summit plateau. Bask in the glorious view: Steep Bluff at Gibsons, Bowen Island (Nex̱wlélex̱wem), Whytecliff Park (St'éx̱w't'ekw's), Point Grey (Elḵsn), the Gulf Islands, and Mount Baker (Xwsa7k to the Squamish).

Wait—there's more. Keep going north to the summit of Mount Elphinstone (3 hours up; 49°27′47″ N, 123°31′47″ W), with its survey monument, radio repeater, and helipad. (Pro tip: Never camp on a *helicopter landing* pad.) Pick out Mount Steele, Panther Peak, Ashlu Mountain, Mount Tantalus, Mount Garibaldi (Nch'ḵay̓), and Woolridge Island (Wáḵw'waḵw'). Retrace your steps down.

The path to the top is stewarded by the Friends of Mount Elphinstone Summit Trail, with the support of the Sunshine Coast Trails Society, and doesn't enter Mount Elphinstone Provincial Park, a small protected area on the mountain's southwest slopes. ATVs, fires, horses, and smoking are banned in Sprockids Park, and dogs must be leashed.

STOP OF INTEREST
SOAMES HILL

One of the sights from atop Mount Elphinstone is Soames Hill (250 m/ 820 ft), between Gibsons and Langdale. Take the Yellow Trail and Green Trail, and climb hundreds of stairs to earn sweet views of Gambier Island (Cha7élḵnech in the Sḵwx̱wú7mesh language), Bowen Island (Nex̱wlélex̱w-em), Keats Island, and Howe Sound (Atl'ḵa7tsem). Budget around 1 hour for the round trip. From Sprockids Park, go south on Stewart Road, left on North Road, right on Chamberlin Road, and left on Bridgeman Road to find Soames Hill Park's northeast entrance (639 Bridgeman Road). (Dogs must be leashed.)

MOUNT HALLOWELL

Survey the Salish Sea from an old fire lookout

Distance: 16.5 km (10.3 mi)
Time: 7 hours (out and back)
Elevation gain: 1,050 m (3,445 ft)
High point: 1,231 m (4,040 ft)

Difficulty: ■
Maps: NTS 92-G/12 Sechelt Inlet
Trailhead: 49°39'36" N, 123°57'24" W

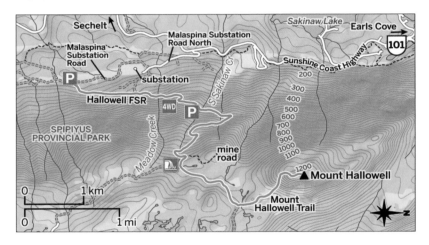

AS THE site of an old fire lookout, Mount Hallowell is an exceptional vantage point from which to survey the Coast Mountains and the Salish Sea. Sadly, the historical tower is in ramshackle condition and in dire need of preservation, with shattered glass lying outside its missing windows. Nevertheless, it's still a sight to behold, and well worth the logging road approach. Located in shíshálh Nation territory, Mount Hallowell belongs to the Caren Range (spipiyus swiya in sháshíshálem) and rises at the north end of Spipiyus Provincial Park on the Sechelt Peninsula.

GETTING THERE

Vehicle: B.C. Ferries offers daily service between West Vancouver and the Sunshine Coast via the Horseshoe Bay–Langdale route. From the Langdale terminal, head north on Highway 101 (Sunshine Coast Highway). In Sechelt,

Jervis Inlet (lékw'émin) from the summit of Mount Hallowell.

turn left at the Wharf Road intersection to stay on the highway. Continue north for 43 km (27 mi). Turn east on gravel Malaspina Substation Road North. In 1 km (0.6 mi), make a right and go past the substation. Follow the bumpy road south to a three-way junction, 2.6 km (1.6 mi) from the highway. 2WD vehicles park here. (High-clearance 4WD vehicles may turn left and go up to 2.6 km [1.6 mi] farther.)

THE HIKE

At the three-way junction, a Suncoaster Trail map displays your position. Set off northeast and uphill on the Hallowell Forest Service Road (Branch 1). Stay right in a clear-cut, with Mount Daniel (shélkém) visible to the left. Follow the mainline through an S-bend, keeping left at a fork. Continue north, pursuing ribbons of various colours. Ignore a steep spur to the right, then curve right to where a washout cuts off the 4×4 road (510 m/1,670 ft; 49°40'46" N, 123°57'03" W), after an hour (2.6 km/1.6 mi) on foot.

Go across the creek, and follow the aging, fern-lined road—better for hiking—through a few bends. An hour beyond the 4×4 trailhead, check out a waterfall just behind the trees on the right. Then go right at a key tri-junction. (Left leads to an old copper mine site.) Turn left at a fork crossed by a creek, and quickly left again, to earn a level stretch with blueberries after a largely steady climb.

A historical fire lookout stands on the summit of Mount Hallowell.

The Malaspina Strait (sínkwu) from the summit of Mount Hallowell.

Orange tapes herald the start of the 1.6-km (1-mi) Mount Hallowell Trail proper on the left (980 m/3,215 ft; 49°41′06″ N, 123°55′41″ W), 1.5 hours (4 km/2.5 mi) past the 4×4 trailhead. Finally, a soft trailbed! The path, overgrown here and there, undulates through lovely firs and cedars standing tall above the mossy forest floor. Look for the burnt orange breast of the varied thrush (common but considered "climate endangered" by the National Audubon Society), or listen for its metallic song. After 20 minutes, fork left twice, the second time heeding a blue arrow painted on rock. With the top 40 minutes away, set about the steepening trail.

Finally, go through shore pines to the impressive summit (3.5 hours up; 49°41′44″ N, 123°56′05″ W). From a granitic bench, bask in layer upon layer of mountains and islands. To the west, Cecil Hill (wah-wey-we'-lath) and Mount Daniel stand guard over Pender Harbour (ḵálpilín); the Malaspina Strait (sínkwu) keeps Texada Island (spílḵsen) at bay; and Mount Troubridge looms behind Nelson Island and Jervis Inlet (lékw'émin).

Spipiyus Provincial Park protects some of Canada's oldest trees, including yellow cedars, and habitat for the threatened marbled murrelet. (*Spipiyus* is the shíshálh word for the seabird.) The Friends of Caren considered its establishment in 1999 a partial victory, having called for the creation of a park double the size and stretching from Pender Harbour to Sechelt Inlet (ʔálhtulich). Since then, the shíshálh Nation has designated the park and surrounding lands as the Caren Range Conservation Area (spipiyus swiya lil ẖemit tems swiya).

Dogs must be leashed, but B.C. Parks does not recommend pets in the backcountry due to potential conflicts with bears. Bikes and motorized vehicles are permitted on logging roads only.

STOP OF INTEREST

HOMESITE CAVES

It's not exactly spelunking, but a walk on the Homesite Creek Cave Trail leads to curious limestone hollows. At the Homesite Creek Falls Recreation Site, a 1.3-km (0.8-mi) counterclockwise loop visits big trees, small caves, a couple of cascades, and a campground. On Highway 101 (Sunshine Coast Highway), 3 km (1.9 mi) north of Halfmoon Bay, turn east onto Homesite Creek Forest Service Road (Branch 1). The trailhead is on the right, 1.4 km (0.9 mi) up the road. For more waterfalls, check out Homesite Creek Park, 400 m (0.2 mi) south, on the highway's west side.

MOUNT GALIANO

Top-notch West Coast scenery on Galiano Island

Distance: 13.5 km (8.4 mi)
Time: 4.5 hours (circuit)
Elevation gain: 300 m (980 ft)
High point: 300 m (980 ft)

Difficulty: ■
Maps: NTS 92-B/14 Mayne Island
Trailhead: 48°52'47" N, 123°19'30" W

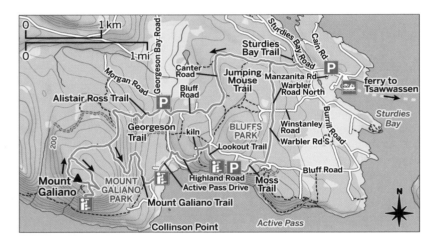

A **HIKE** to the highest knoll on Galiano Island begins with a delightful ferry ride to Sturdies Bay. But there's no need to shell out for transporting a land vehicle across the water. Foot passengers can make it to Mount Galiano and back in a day trip. Our itinerary also includes stops at a swimming beach and a Japanese Canadian historic site, in the territories of the Hul'qumi'num Treaty Group, and the Hwlitsum, Stz'uminus, Tsawwassen, and W̱SÁNEĆ First Nations. How's that for an all-season Gulf Islands getaway?

GETTING THERE

Transit: Take TransLink Bus 620 (Tsawwassen Ferry) to the Tsawwassen ferry terminal.

Vehicle: On Highway 99 (Vancouver-Blaine Highway) in Delta, take Exit 26 for Highway 17 (South Fraser Perimeter Road) or Exit 28 for Highway 17A

A ferry enters Active Pass (Sqthaqa'lh); another departs from Mayne Island.

(Tsawwassen Highway), and head south. Highway 17 and 17A merge en route to the B.C. Ferries terminal at Tsawwassen (toilet available). Park in the long-term parking lot. (If you do ferry a vehicle over, shoulder parking is available along Sturdies Bay Road at Manzanita Road.)

THE HIKE

From the ferry dock, walk (10 minutes) or cycle west on Sturdies Bay Road, passing Burrill Road, to find the trailhead on the left in 700 m (0.4 mi). Set off on the Sturdies Bay Trail, quickly turning left to cross the island. Go right at a signed junction (left goes to Warbler Road North), enter Bluffs Park, and right again (left is the Jumping Mouse Trail) at the next fork. Follow Canter Road, and turn left where a private gate bars the right. Spot several car wrecks and a rusty oven in the woods. Ignore a mossy spur on the left, fork right (left is the Owl Tree Trail), and pass an old gate.

Turn right (downhill) on the gravel Bluff Road, 40 minutes (2.2 km/1.4 mi) from the trailhead. Go through the red gate. Hang a right on Georgeson Bay Road, which is paved and divided by a single yellow line. After 10 minutes (700 m/0.4 mi) of quiet road walking, spot a kiosk and parking area on the left (48°52′30″ N, 123°21′00″ W).

Climb the Alistair Ross Trail, built by the Galiano Trails Society, into the mossy forest. Turn right (uphill) on the Georgeson Trail. Follow this back-road left at the next junction, then keep left to enter Mount Galiano Park

Mayne Island and Active Pass (Sqthaqa'lh) from Bluffs Park.

and intersect the Mount Galiano Trail. Step over logs and go right, noting this junction for the return. Fork left to stay on the main double track, which passes the high point and makes a hard right. At the water tank, go left. Take the final steps to the near-summit viewpoint (48°51′49″ N, 123°21′45″ W), 2 hours (5.9 km/3.7 mi) from Sturdies Bay Road. Burst into the open atop a spectacular conglomerate cliff. Stop yourself (and kids) before the edge. Belonging to the Upper Cretaceous Geoffrey Formation, the sedimentary bedrock dates back to the age of the dinosaurs.

The Garry oak meadow to the right is a so-satisfying perch to lunch and survey the Salish Sea. Watch ferries sail in and out of Active Pass (Sqthaqa'lh in Hul'qumi'num, S,ḴȾAK in SENĆOŦEN) and bald eagles soar. Mount Parke caps Mayne Island to the southeast. North Pender (S,DÁYES), Moresby (ȽO,LE,ĆEN), Saltspring (Klaathem in Hul'qumi'num, ĆUÁN in SENĆOŦEN), and Prevost (W̱ÁS W̱EN) Islands surround Swanson Channel due south.

It's 2 hours back to Sturdies Bay Road via the 7.4-km (4.6-mi) scenic route described as follows. On the way down, keep left at the water tank for an alternate descent path. Rejoin the main trail, and follow it right at the signed junction where you entered from the left earlier. At the bottom of the Mount Galiano Trail (2.7 km/1.7 mi), turn left for the parking lot. (Right goes to Collinson Point Provincial Park.)

Bear left onto Active Pass Drive, and walk the paved road to a signed beach turnoff (shore access 17). Take the Zuker Road stairs down to the water's edge. (How about a swim?) Continue northeast on Active Pass Drive. Go left on Georgeson Bay Road, and immediately right on Highland Road.

Just before the dead end, 1.3 km (0.8 mi) from the Mount Galiano trailhead, spot a sign on the right indicating the way to a Japanese charcoal pit kiln (48°52'06" N, 123°20'38" W). Re-entering Bluffs Park, detour left for the historic site. The remains of earthen ovens are scattered around the Gulf and San Juan Islands, reminders of communities uprooted by the internment of Japanese Canadians and Japanese Americans during World War II.

Continue on the trail to a cedar grove and steeply up to a dirt roundabout on Bluff Road. Just before the road, go right on an easy-to-miss path. Hike southeast over the grassy bluffs, minding the precipice, to the remains of a three-sided log shelter built in 1950. The waters of Active Pass swirl below, and the snow-capped Olympic Mountains are visible in the distance. Follow the bluff-top single track 5 minutes beyond a parking lot, looking left for a faint trail dropping into the woods.

At the bottom, turn right on Bluff Road, 1.3 km (0.8 mi) from the roundabout and with 2.1 km (1.3 mi) to go. Go left onto Warbler Road South, which becomes a forest trail, then cross Winstanley Road and walk to the end of Warbler Road North. Pass the ranch gate, and make two right turns in the woods to return to the trailhead on Sturdies Bay Road.

Mount Galiano Park and Bluffs Park are managed by the Galiano Club. No bikes, camping, fires, smoking, or motorized vehicles.

STOP OF INTEREST
MONTAGUE HARBOUR

Known as Sum'nuw' ("inside place") in Hul'qumi'num, Montague Harbour on Galiano Island is an ancestral Coast Salish village site. A white shell beach is one of several middens in Montague Harbour Marine Provincial Park. Protected by B.C.'s Heritage Conservation Act, these archaeological deposits contain animal remains, charcoal, fire-cracked rocks, and stone artifacts. Spot birds at saltwater marshes and a tidal lagoon, and sea anemones and stars on a glacier-carved rock ledge. Don't feed the raccoons. For kayakers and canoeists, the park is a stop on the Salish Sea Marine Trail. By bicycle or car, the park is 8 km (5 mi) west of the ferry dock via Sturdies Bay Road, Georgeson Bay Road (left), and Montague Road (right). From June to September, a free shuttle offers daily evening service between the Hummingbird Pub (47 Sturdies Bay Road) and the park. (Dogs must be leashed and are not allowed on beaches.)

44 GULF ISLANDS
BODEGA RIDGE

Arbutus trees and endless views of the Salish Sea

Distance: 8 km (5 mi)
Time: 3.5 hours (out and back)
Elevation gain: 130 m (430 ft)
High point: 250 m (820 ft)

Difficulty: ●
Maps: NTS 92-B/13 Duncan
Trailhead: 48°56'58" N, 123°30'45" W

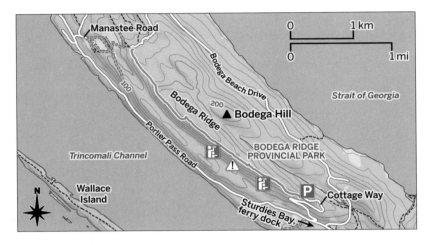

THE EXPANSIVE views from Bodega Ridge, the highest spot on northern Galiano Island, are as stunning as they are effortlessly gained. The sandstone cuesta looks out over Trincomali Channel, across Saltspring Island (Klaathem in the Hul'qumi'num language) and Penelakut Island (Puneluxutth'), and beyond to Vancouver Island. The southwest-facing escarpment provides nesting habitat for the peregrine falcon, a species of special concern. Arbutus trees and their relatives, hairy manzanita shrubs, add to the blissful scene. The ridge rises in the territories of the Hul'qumi'num Treaty Group, and the Hwlitsum, Stz'uminus, and Tsawwassen First Nations.

GETTING THERE
Vehicle: B.C. Ferries offers daily service between Tsawwassen and Galiano Island. From the Sturdies Bay ferry dock, head northwest on Sturdies Bay

Looking out at Trincomali Channel from Bodega Ridge.

Road. Turn right on Porlier Pass Road. Keep left at the Galiano Way intersection to stay on Porlier Pass. Make a hard right on Cottage Way, 17 km (11 mi) from Sturdies Bay. Drive 1.6 km (1 mi) to the top, and park on the shoulder. Don't block driveways.

THE HIKE

Find the Bodega Ridge Provincial Park sign at road's end, and set off northwest. Douglas-fir trees tower over the gently rising path. Within 10 minutes, detour left for the first viewpoint, featuring a small wooden bench. Follow the undulating trail, noticing plenty of yellow-flowered Scotch broom. Introduced to B.C. in the mid-1800s, this invasive European shrub is a threat to the biodiversity of the Gulf Islands.

A sign advises you are entering a "hazardous area." Stay on the trail. Endless views are just around the corner atop sun-soaked bluffs. You're treading on northeast-dipping sedimentary bedrock of the Gabriola Formation. Mind the cliff edge to the left. Be especially careful with kids.

Take your time. This is one of the finest ridge walks in the Salish Sea archipelago. Admire Garry oak trees, so emblematic of the Gulf Islands and southeastern Vancouver Island, and bald eagles. Wallace Island (smím'kwetses), the Secretary Islands (shemétsen), and the Trincomali Channel Rockfish Conservation Area lie offshore. Penelakut Island, due west, was the site of the Catholic-run Kuper Island residential school (1890–c. 1975), where Coast

Salish children were subjected to deplorable experiments, sexual abuse, and other atrocities.

Reach a park regulations sign (48°57'35" N, 123°32'06" W), 1.9 km (1.2 mi) from the trailhead. The best views are behind you—but so is the crowd. It's worth tracing the ridge for another 2.1 km (1.3 mi) to enjoy the quiet and further vistas. Now a bit rougher, the trail cuts left through a hollow with deadfall to transfer to another series of ledges. Pass a pond. Gradually descend to a dirt road, where a wooden sign for Bodega Ridge points back the way you came. Turn around here (1.5 hours one-way; 48°58'17" N, 123°32'55" W).

Located southwest of lower Bodega Hill, Bodega Ridge is also named for Captain Juan Francisco de la Bodega y Quadra (1743–1794). A Spanish naval commander, Quadra befriended his British counterpart, Captain George Vancouver (1757–1798), at Nootka Sound. The latter went on to bestow the toponym "Quadra and Vancouver's Island" on what is now known as just Vancouver Island.

Established in 2001, Bodega Ridge Provincial Park protects a small patch of the coastal Douglas-fir biogeoclimatic zone and is home to Gray's desert-parsley, a threatened species. No camping, fires, horses, smoking, or vaping. Dogs must be leashed. Please practice Leave No Trace techniques, and don't scar arbutus trees with your initials.

STOP OF INTEREST
PEBBLE BEACH

If exploring tide pools and finding colourful rocks in the surf appeal to you, get thee to Pebble Beach on the east side of Galiano Island. Look farther, and pick out Howe Sound (Atl'ḵa7tsem to the Squamish Nation), Vancouver, and Golden Ears across the Strait of Georgia. Access is via the 1.5-km (0.9-mi) Pebble Beach Trail. Owned by the Galiano Conservancy Association, the Pebble Beach Nature Reserve also has trail connections to Laughlin Lake and the Great Beaver Swamp. It's located up McCoskrie Road, off Porlier Pass Road, 1.5 km (0.9 mi) southeast of Cottage Way.

An arbutus tree on Bodega Ridge.

This way to Bodega Ridge.

EXTENSION RIDGE

Step up to The Abyss, an intriguing rock fissure

Distance: 13.5 km (8.4 mi)
Time: 4 hours (out and back)
Elevation gain: 185 m (610 ft)
High point: 255 m (840 ft)

Difficulty: ●
Maps: NTS 92-G/4 Nanaimo
Trailhead: 49°09'03" N, 123°57'42" W

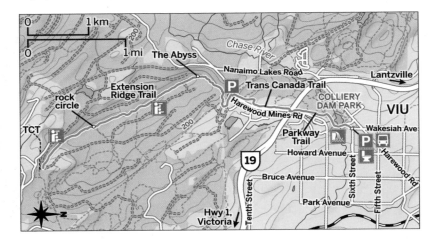

THE ABYSS is the undisputed star of the otherwise low-key Extension Ridge Trail in Snuneymuxw First Nation territory. Ascribed to an earthquake, the narrow and deep rock cleft is cool enough to transform many adults into excited little kids. The ridge itself is a pleasant jaunt through arbutus, Douglas-fir, and Garry oak trees, with views of the Salish Sea, Sunshine Coast, and Lower Mainland. Starting and finishing at Colliery Dam Park places this four-season, family-friendly hike in the context of Nanaimo's coal-mining history and offers easy access to a swimming hole.

GETTING THERE

Transit: Take Regional District of Nanaimo Transit Bus 6 (Harewood) or 40 (VIU Express) to Fifth Street at Hillcrest Avenue. Walk 500 m (0.3 mi) south via Hillcrest, Harewood Road, and Wakesiah Avenue.

The Trans Canada Trail traverses Extension Ridge.

Vehicle: B.C. Ferries offers daily service between Metro Vancouver and Nanaimo via two routes: Horseshoe Bay–Departure Bay and Tsawwassen–Duke Point. From Departure Bay, head south on Trans-Canada Highway 1 for 2.5 km (1.6 mi). Turn right on Comox Road, and continue onto Bowen Road. Make a left on Howard Avenue, right on Harewood Road, and left on Wakesiah Avenue. (From Duke Point, go west on Highway 19 [Duke Point Highway] for 8 km [5 mi]. Keep right to momentarily merge with Highway 1 northbound, and right again to stay on Highway 19 [Nanaimo Parkway] for 6.5 km [4 mi]. Turn right on Fifth Street, and right on Wakesiah.) Arrive at Colliery Dam Park (635 Wakesiah Avenue). Use the parking lot at the corner of Wakesiah and Sixth Street (toilet available).

THE HIKE

Starting at the map board, stroll south on the paved Parkway Trail, part of the multi-use Trans Canada Trail (now known as the Great Trail). Go by interpretative panels, washrooms, and a picnic shelter en route to the lower lake. (Smoking is prohibited, and dogs must be leashed.) Before crossing the Lower Colliery Dam, detour left to see the double-tiered cascade at the end of the old spillway. Built by the Western Fuel Company in the early 1910s, the park's two earth-fill dams supplied water from the Chase River for coal washing and are now listed in the Canadian Register of Historic Places. In 600 m (0.4 mi), turn right to stay on the paved Parkway Trail.

The Abyss slices through a conglomerate outcrop.

At 1.1 km (0.7 mi), split with the Parkway Trail, and follow the TCT under the noisy Nanaimo Parkway overpass, using the shoulder of Harewood Mines Road. On the far side, re-enter the woods on the right. Stick with the main trail as it parallels the road, ignoring side paths on the right and left. At 2 km (1.2 mi), descend wooden stairs to a boardwalk. Fork left, and emerge at a power-line corridor. Pass a gate and cross Harewood Mines Road to find the start of the TCT's Extension Ridge Trail (no camping or fires) and an alternative parking area (49°07′59″ N, 123°58′09″ W), after 35 minutes (2.4 km/ 1.5 mi) on foot.

Head east in the right-of-way, merging with a service road. Shortly thereafter, turn right at a signed junction and climb the steps under the power lines. Go right twice, then left at the base of a pylon to enter a clear-cut. Keep right on the main trail, treading on exposed conglomerate. The path forks but quickly reunites on the way to the top of the clear-cut. Twenty minutes from the Extension Ridge trailhead, ascend a conglomerate outcrop to discover The Abyss (49°07′43″ N, 123°58′23″ W). The enigmatic fissure is narrow enough to step across but wide enough to fall in, and its far side is upthrown.

The TCT continues south in the woods, following the mellow crest. Sitting at the edge of the mined-out Nanaimo Coalfield, Extension Ridge is a cuesta whose steep western escarpment contrasts with its gentler eastern aspect. At times, the persistent clear-cut on the left and gunfire from the nearby Nanaimo Military Rifle Range intrude on the serenity.

Twenty minutes (1 km/0.6 mi) from The Abyss, pass the high point of the ridge and come to a wide-angle viewpoint with two seats carved into stumps at the top of the clear-cut. Beyond the logging slash and power lines, spot Newcastle Island (Saysutshun in the Hul'qumi'num language), Snake Island (xw'ulhquyum), and Gabriola Island around Nanaimo Harbour (Snuneymuxw), and Panther Peak, Sky Pilot Mountain, and the Twin Sisters (Hike 5) beyond the Strait of Georgia. Ravens and turkey vultures patrol the air.

Keep going for 45 minutes (2.4 km/1.5 mi) to enjoy more of the friendly ridge. Go under a power line. Gradually descend to a clearing occupied by an esoteric quartered circle of rocks strewn with miscellaneous trinkets. Stay right, and reach a bluff viewpoint featuring a bench and a canine memorial plaque. Finally, steps lead down to a gravel road, where an Extension Ridge Trail signpost points back the way you came. Turn around here (2 hours up; 49°06'20" N, 123°57'06" W). The TCT goes on to the hamlet of Extension and continues south as the Pipeline Trail, en route to Victoria. Back at Colliery Dam Park, the lower lake may entice you to conclude the day's outing with a swim.

STOP OF INTEREST
PETROGLYPH PROVINCIAL PARK

Ancient rock art is found up and down the Pacific Northwest coast. Established in 1948, Petroglyph Provincial Park (th67thxwem in Hul'qumi'num) in Nanaimo preserves a cluster of Snuneymuxw rock carvings more than 1,000 years old. Engraved in sandstone, the sacred designs include depictions of humans and other animals of the ordinary (bottom fish) and supernatural (sea-wolves) variety. Find the small park on the east side of Trans-Canada Highway 1, 6 km (3.7 mi) south of Departure Bay (stl'etl'iínep). Stick to the trail to protect the petroglyphs. (Dogs must be leashed.)

MOUNT BENSON

This local favourite pays off with coast and mountain views

Distance: 6.5 km (4 mi)
Time: 4.5 hours (out and back)
Elevation gain: 730 m (2,395 ft)
High point: 1,019 m (3,340 ft)

Difficulty: ■
Maps: NTS 92-F/1 Nanaimo Lakes
Trailhead: 49°09'52" N, 124°02'20" W

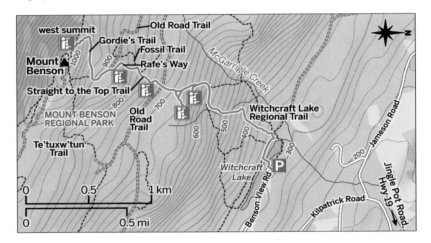

VANCOUVERITES BOOT it up the infamous Grouse Grind (Hike 4) for a steep workout. Nanaimoites hustle it up Mount Benson—and then, without the luxury of an aerial tramway, hike back down. Along with the remains of a fire lookout, the mountaintop prize is panoramic views of the Vancouver Island Ranges, Gulf Islands, Salish Sea, and Coast Mountains. To the Snuneymuxw First Nation, Mount Benson is a sacred site known as Te'tuxw'tun in the Hul'qumi'num language. Another toponym for the local landmark is Wake Siah ("not far") in Chinuk Wawa, the intertribal trade language of the Pacific Northwest.

GETTING THERE

Vehicle: B.C. Ferries offers daily service between Metro Vancouver and Nanaimo via two routes: Horseshoe Bay–Departure Bay and Tsawwassen–

A whisky-jack on Mount Benson (Te'tuxw'tun).

Duke Point. West of Downtown Nanaimo, Highway 19 (Nanaimo Parkway) intersects Jingle Pot Road twice. In either case, head east on Jingle Pot. Continue to Kilpatrick Road, where you go east again. In 1.7 km (1.1 mi), turn right on Benson View Road. Find the parking area for Mount Benson Regional Park on the left in 1.4 km (0.9 mi), just before the dead end.

THE HIKE

From the trailhead kiosk, head through the yellow gate and take the floating bridge over narrow Witchcraft Lake. In the woods on the other side, go right on the Witchcraft Lake Regional Trail, with numbered orange markers leading the way. Ignore two paths on the left, then turn left at a Mount Benson sign on a tree.

Ascend south on the rocky, rooty, braided, and often water-bearing trail, encountering streamlets here and there and entering a Vancouver Island University–licenced woodlot. At a three-way junction with blue flagging, go right. The grade mellows a bit, and the trail outflanks a band of mossy bluffs. Within an hour, a sign at marker 30 indicates a spur on the left to the first, partial viewpoint. Spot Brannen Lake to the north.

At marker 34, fork left for a scenic byway to the second, better viewpoint. Nanaimo fills the foreground, while Newcastle Island (Saysutshun to the Snuneymuxw), Protection Island, and Gabriola Island sit offshore. Back on the main trail, blow straight through a signed junction with the yellow-blazed

The Vancouver Island Ranges from the west summit.

Old Road Trail and onto the aptly named Straight to the Top Trail. Keep chasing the orange markers, now in Mount Benson Regional Park proper. A third viewpoint on the trail offers an even wider outlook. Below marker 113, go left on Rafe's Way, an old road, and keep left at the Fossil Trail junction.

Two hours in, clamber up open rock—slippery when wet—to the fourth viewpoint, gaining the most expansive perspective yet. Take a breather, and enjoy the Steller's jays and whisky-jacks; now's not the time to return phone calls. (If you're listening to music, headphones please!) Some folks turn around here, but it's worth pushing on for another 30 minutes. Beyond marker 119, the route bears right to re-enter the woods. Go left on Gordie's Trail, pursuing orange and red squares up the steep summit route.

Finally, scamper up bare rock to the west summit (2.5 hours up; 49°09'01" N, 124°03'08" W). Although cutblocks and urban sprawl blight the landscape, the 360-degree view is outstanding and far-reaching. Admire Mount Arrowsmith (kał-ka-č'ałḥ ["jagged points pointing up"] to the Hupačasath First Nation of the Alberni Valley), the highest point on southern Vancouver Island, to the west. Peer across the Strait of Georgia at Mount Garibaldi, Sky Pilot Mountain, the Twin Sisters (Hike 5), and Mount Baker. Mount Benson was the site of two fire towers between 1925 and 1967, the first having burned down in 1938. The concrete foundations still stand on the west summit.

The east summit, separated by a gap, is actually slightly higher. However, it's cluttered with transmission antennas and only coveted by committed peak baggers. On the descent, avoid getting lost in the maze of trails by reversing your ascent route, bypassing the lower viewpoints. A dip in charming Witchcraft Lake may be tempting during a hot spell.

Mount Benson Regional Park was established in 2008 thanks to the fundraising efforts of the Coalition to Save Mount Benson and the Nanaimo and Area Land Trust. No camping, fires, harvesting, hunting, or motorized vehicles. The Island Mountain Ramblers spearheaded recent upgrades to the Witchcraft Lake Regional Trail.

STOP OF INTEREST

ENGLISHMAN RIVER FALLS

From its headwaters on Mount Arrowsmith, the Englishman River (k̲éẃx̱eṁolh in Hul'qumi'num) flows east to Parksville, where it empties into the Salish Sea. At Englishman River Falls Provincial Park, in the territories of the K'ómoks and Snaw-Naw-As First Nations, the watercourse plummets more than 20 m (70 ft) into a narrow canyon. A lovely 1.4-km (0.9-mi) walking loop visits old-growth Douglas firs, and the upper and lower falls. The river basin is part of the Mount Arrowsmith Biosphere Region, designated in 2000 by the United Nations Educational, Scientific and Cultural Organisation. From Parksville, head east on Highway 4A (Alberni Highway) to Errington, then south on Errington Road. (Dogs must be on leash.)

47 BELLINGHAM
LOOKOUT MOUNTAIN

A waterfall and woodland wander

Distance: 18.5 km (11.5 mi)
Time: 5.5 hours (out and back)
Elevation gain: 660 m (2,165 ft)
High point: 816 m (2,677 ft)

Difficulty: ●
Maps: USGS Lake Whatcom
Trailhead: 48°43'08" N, 122°21'19" W

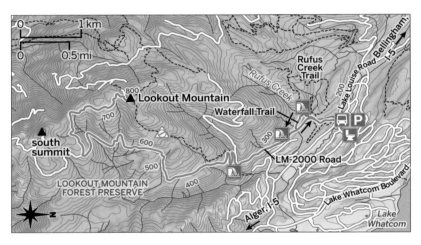

WITH ITS growing network of trails, Lookout Mountain is a pleasant spot for a shoulder-season or rainy-day jaunt in the woods. Why not go for the summit? Sandwiched between Lake Whatcom and Lake Samish, Lookout Mountain Forest Preserve is accessed from the community of Sudden Valley, east of Bellingham.

GETTING THERE

Transit: Take Whatcom Transportation Authority Bus 512 (Downtown) to Lake Louise Road at Gate 9.

Vehicle: On Interstate 5 in Bellingham, take Exit 253. Head east on Lakeway Drive. Continue straight onto North Terrace Avenue and then onto Cable Street. Go right on Austin Street, which becomes Lake Louise Road. Turn right into the Lookout Mountain Forest Preserve parking lot (2537 Lake

Following LM-2000 Road up Lookout Mountain.

Louise Road, toilet available), opposite Sudden Valley Gate 9, 10 km (6.2 mi) from I-5.

THE HIKE

From the Lookout Mountain trailhead, head south up the gated LM-2000 Road, which is shared with mountain bikers. In 500 m (0.3 mi), the gravel road intersects the Rufus Creek Trail at a four-way junction.

Turn right, then immediately left on the hiking-only Waterfall Trail (600 m/0.4 mi). The winding path rises in the mixed woods. Halfway up the trail, visit the viewpoint on the right. Log fencing keeps you back from the drop-off at the falls. A sign asks hikers to stay on the designated trail to protect plants, soil, and water quality. Continue up the Waterfall Trail, and go left at a three-way junction.

At a stop sign, turn right on LM-2000 Road, after 20 minutes on foot. Just up the gravel road, lined by tall western red cedars and Douglas-firs, look right to see a small cascade. Ignore a gated road, on the left, leading to houses whose backyards you are seeing. Follow LM-2000 Road across a slope failure zone. Stick with the mainline, where a vegetated branch goes right.

LM-2000 Road curves right. Spot a waterfall, obscured by trees, in the ravine to the left, 45 minutes in. The road makes three 180-degree bends. A Do Not Enter sign blocks a closed trail on the right. Continue plodding up the road in the charming woods, enjoying the calming sound of creeks, which flow under the road in culverts. Keep right where an old spur goes left.

A waterfall in Lookout Mountain Forest Preserve.

The mainline descends a bit before coming to a fork with high-voltage utility boxes (48°40'53" N, 122°20'51" W), more than 2 hours in. Left leads to the south summit, a former fire lookout site. However, bear right for the north summit, which is a titch higher. To the right, Twin Sisters Mountain (Kwetl'kwítl' Smánit in Lhéchelesem, the language of the Nooksack Tribe) teases you with dramatic glimpses through the trees. Spot communications towers ahead. Bear right at a junction below the top, and shortly thereafter arrive on the north summit of Lookout Mountain (3 hours up; 48°41'19" N, 122°21'39" W).

A U.S. Geological Survey benchmark and a 1925 U.S. Coast and Geodetic Survey triangulation station are embedded in the summit rocks. The mountaintop is home to three communications towers, a few buildings, and propane tanks, and a portion is fenced off with barbed wire. Although the technology tries its best to get in the way, scenic views of Anacortes, Fidalgo Bay (dəgʷalč in Lushootseed, the language of the Tulalip Tribes), Chuckanut Mountain (Hike 49), the San Juan Islands, and the Salish Sea reward your efforts. Retrace your steps to the utility box fork, and follow LM-2000 Road all the way back down to the trailhead.

Lookout Mountain Forest Preserve provides habitat for bald eagles and threatened marbled murrelets. Managed by Whatcom County and incorporating land reconveyed by the Washington State Department of Natural Resources, the preserve is open sunrise to sunset. Camping, fires, fireworks, motorized vehicles, and overnight parking are prohibited. Dogs must be leashed.

STOP OF INTEREST
POINT WHITEHORN MARINE RESERVE

Standing atop the bluff at Point Whitehorn Marine Reserve, try to identify the summits of the Gulf and San Juan Islands on view: Lummi Peak on Lummi Island (Smemiekw to the Lummi Nation), Mount Constitution on Orcas Island (Swalex), Mount Warburton Pike on Saturna Island, and Bruce Peak on Saltspring Island. A path switchbacks down to a cobble beach. The reserve is home to native plants such as coastal black gooseberry, eel-grass, enchanter's-nightshade, and Nootka rose. On Interstate 5, south of Blaine and north of Ferndale, take Exit 266. Head west on northbound State Route 548 (Grandview Road), stay straight on Grandview at a roundabout (SR 548 leaves right), and continue onto Koehn Road. (No dogs allowed.)

LOST LAKE

Find the heart of Chuckanut Mountain

Distance: 15 km (9.3 mi)
Time: 5 hours (out and back)
Elevation gain: 405 m (1,330 ft)
High point: 430 m (1,410 ft)

Difficulty: ●
Maps: USGS Bellingham South; Square One Chuckanut Recreation Area
Trailhead: 48°42'08" N, 122°28'53" W

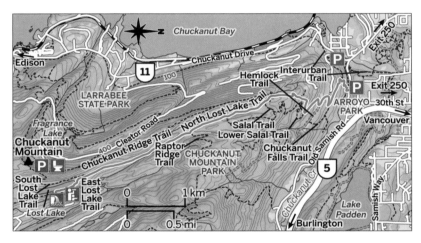

IF YOU find yourself pining for a walk in the woods, an easygoing excursion to Lost Lake might be just the ticket. Starting within Bellingham's city limit and traversing county and state parklands, this hike goes straight to the heart of Chuckanut Mountain. It's ideal for kids, rainy days, and shoulder season—or cooling off on a hot summer's day.

GETTING THERE

Transit: Take Whatcom Transportation Authority Bus 105 (Fairhaven) to Old Fairhaven Parkway at 24th Street. Walk south on 24th, and turn right on Lindsay Avenue. Go left on the Interurban Trail, and follow it 1.5 km (0.9 mi) to Arroyo Park, 20 minutes from the bus stop.

Vehicle: On Interstate 5 in Bellingham, take Exit 250. Head west on State Route 11 (Old Fairhaven Parkway) for 230 m (0.1 mi). Turn left on 30th Street,

Chuckanut Ridge rises behind Lost Lake.

which turns into 32nd Street. Turn right on Old Samish Road, 1.5 km (0.9 mi) from SR 11. Find a small parking area for Arroyo Park on the left in 450 m (0.3 mi). (If it's full, try the next parking area to the west or the large lot at the North Chuckanut Mountain trailhead, off Chuckanut Drive. Both provide access to the Interurban Trail.)

THE HIKE

From Old Samish Road, enter the City of Bellingham's Arroyo Park and drop down a gravel path. Bear right, then left, joining the Interurban Trail as it crosses Chuckanut Creek (Chúkwenet in Xws7ámeshqen, the language of the Samish Nation) on a wooden bridge. The Interurban Trail traces a portion of the historical route of the Bellingham and Skagit Railway, which provided passenger service between Bellingham and Mount Vernon from 1912 to 1928. Pacific Northwest Traction Company, a subsidiary of Puget Sound Power and Light Company, operated the electric rail line, shuttered by the rise of cars and buses.

Marvel at the urban pocket of big ol' Douglas-firs as you ascend the other side of the ravine. Go left at two forks, and pass a glacial erratic. Enter Whatcom County's Chuckanut Mountain Park, and turn right on the Hemlock Trail. (Left leads to Chuckanut Falls.) Bear left on a gravel road to stay with Hemlock until a three-way junction (EMS checkpoint A), 1.6 km (1 mi) from the trailhead. Go right to set off on the North Lost Lake Trail, which is

Autumn leaf litter on the North Lost Lake Trail.

popular with trail runners and also travelled by mountain bikers and horse riders. Keep right at two junctions with the Lower Salal Trail.

Reach the turnoff (checkpoint B; 48°41′24″ N, 122°28′47″ W) for the Chuckanut Ridge Trail (Hike 49) in Larrabee State Park, after 1 hour (3.2 km/ 2 mi) of hiking. Continue straight ahead on the North Lost Lake Trail, immediately spurning the Salal Trail on the left. Follow the undulating gravel road south, ignoring leftward turnoffs for the Madrone Crest Viewpoint and Raptor Ridge Trail (checkpoint D). The road narrows, becoming more trail-like. A series of cliffs, revealing the Eocene sandstone of the Chuckanut Formation, loom to the right. The muddy trail loses elevation as it passes big cedars and parallels a ravine on your left.

With your destination just around the corner, bear left on the East Lost Lake Trail (checkpoint F). (Right is the South Lost Lake Trail, which leads to the Rock Trail and Fragrance Lake Road.) This muddy, rooty, and rocky path is trickier to follow. Use logs to negotiate a wet patch. Pass a huge blowdown, which exposes a massive root system. Head south through the cedars on the east side of the lake to a sandstone ledge. Gaze across the water and up at Chuckanut Ridge.

Continue south momentarily to find the outlet of Lost Lake (2.5 hours up; 48°39′28″ N, 122°27′27″ W), 7.5 km (4.7 mi) from your start. Here, water flows over the sandstone ridge impounding the pretty, narrow lake, creating a waterfall that may be dry—and, therefore, easy to miss—when you visit. Nevertheless, it's a fine spot to get wet and cool off in summer. For the hike out, avoid getting lost by retracing your steps to Arroyo Park.

Dogs must be on leash in Chuckanut Mountain Park and Larrabee State Park. No feeding wildlife, fires, hunting, shooting, smoking, or vaping.

In 1903, the city of Bellingham emerged out of the incremental amalgamation of four towns on Bellingham Bay: Bellingham, Fairhaven, Sehome, and Whatcom. Sehome and Whatcom had merged in 1891 to form New Whatcom, which was connected to the Canada-U.S. border at Sumas via the Bellingham Bay and British Columbia Railroad the same year.

STOP OF INTEREST
SEHOME HILL ARBORETUM

An urban forest lying adjacent to the Western Washington University campus, the Sehome Hill Arboretum covers 71 ha (175 ac) in Bellingham. It's home to native trees (such as big-leaf maple, Douglas-fir, western hemlock, western red cedar) and shrubs (including elderberry, oceanspray, and salal). Established in 1893 and jointly managed by the City of Bellingham and WWU, the arboretum features an observation tower, an outdoor learning centre, a tunnel built in 1923, and the site of a 1935 landslide. Take Exit 252 on Interstate 5, and head west on Bill McDonald Parkway to find the arboretum entrance. (Dogs must be leashed on primary trails, and are prohibited on secondary trails.)

CHUCKANUT RIDGE

Sandstone and Salish Sea scenery

Distance: 16.5 km (10.3 mi)
Time: 6 hours (lollipop)
Elevation gain: 565 m (1,850 ft)
High point: 590 m (1,940 ft)

Difficulty: ■
Maps: USGS Bellingham South; Square One Chuckanut Recreation Area
Trailhead: 48°42'08" N, 122°28'53" W

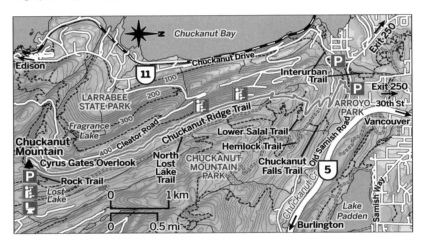

TRACE THE route of an early 1900s interurban railway. Feel the bark of an old-growth Douglas-fir tree. Pursue a forested sandstone ridge to the summit of Chuckanut Mountain. Soak up views of Mount Baker (Kwelshán in Xwlemi'chosen, the language of the Lummi Nation) and the islands of the Salish Sea. Not too shabby for a hike in the "City of Subdued Excitement," as Bellingham is endearingly known.

GETTING THERE
Transit: Take Whatcom Transportation Authority Bus 105 (Fairhaven) to Old Fairhaven Parkway at 24th Street. Walk south on 24th, and turn right on Lindsay Avenue. Go left on the Interurban Trail, and follow it 1.5 km (0.9 mi) to Arroyo Park, 20 minutes from the bus stop.

The woods of Chuckanut Ridge.

Vehicle: On Interstate 5 in Bellingham, take Exit 250. Head west on State Route 11 (Old Fairhaven Parkway) for 230 m (0.1 mi). Turn left on 30th Street, which turns into 32nd Street. Turn right on Old Samish Road, 1.5 km (0.9 mi) from SR 11. Find a small parking area for Arroyo Park on the left in 450 m (0.3 mi). (If it's full, try the next parking area to the west or the large lot at the North Chuckanut Mountain trailhead, off Chuckanut Drive. Both provide access to the Interurban Trail.)

THE HIKE

From Old Samish Road, enter the City of Bellingham's Arroyo Park and drop down a gravel path. Bear right, then left, joining the Interurban Trail as it crosses Chuckanut Creek (Chúkwenet in Xws7ámeshqen, the dialect of the Samish Nation) on a wooden bridge. In addition to tracing a historical electric rail line, the Interurban Trail is a link in the Coast Millennium Trail, a cross-border project connecting White Rock, B.C., and Skagit County, Washington.

Marvel at the urban pocket of big ol' Douglas-firs as you ascend the other side of the ravine. Go left at two forks, and pass a glacial erratic. Enter Whatcom County's Chuckanut Mountain Park, and turn right on the Hemlock Trail. (Left leads to Chuckanut Falls.) Bear left on a gravel road to stay with Hemlock until a three-way junction (EMS checkpoint A), 1.6 km (1 mi) from

Chuckanut Formation sandstone along the trail.

the trailhead. Go right to set off on the North Lost Lake Trail (Hike 48). Keep right at two junctions with the Lower Salal Trail.

Reach the turnoff for the Chuckanut Ridge Trail (checkpoint B; 48°41′24″ N, 122°28′47″ W) in Larrabee State Park, after 1 hour (3.2 km/2 mi) of hiking. Head right, passing below mossy boulders and cliffs. The eroded path U-turns to gain the crest, and the delightfully undulating ridge walk begins. Exposed roots and slippery rocks may challenge your footing as you rise in the woods. In several minutes, earn the first in a succession of east-facing viewpoints atop sheer drops. (Be careful with kids. Stay well back from the edge.)

Keep left at the lower Chuckanut Ridge junction. Come to a particularly striking viewpoint featuring a sharp ridge of Chuckanut Formation sandstone. The lovely path strolls southeast through viewless woods for a bit, then ruggedly rises along the escarpment with abrupt ups and downs. Stay left at the junction between the middle and upper sections of the Chuckanut Ridge Trail.

Bypass a fenced bend in Cleator Road, which you've been paralleling, and steeply ascend the final incline. Ignore a trail entering from the right. Steps away, just left of the path straight ahead, lies the summit of Chuckanut Mountain (48°39′10″ N, 122°27′53″ W). Sadly, the sandstone outcrop is defaced by carved letters. Continue forth on the trail, turning right at the next unmarked junction.

Emerge from the trees at the vehicle-accessible Cyrus Gates Overlook (3 hours up), at the top of Cleator Road. There's a map (checkpoint H), picnic tables, and a pit toilet. An Eagle Scout's interpretative panel helpfully points out Orcas Island (Sx'wálex'), Matia Island (Penáxweng), Sucia Island (Lhéwqemeng), Patos Island (Tl'x'óy7ten), Chuckanut Bay (dxʷšišəlčəb to the Tulalip Tribes), Sandy Point (čəčɫqs), and "Canada."

When you're ready to head back, briefly stroll down Cleator Road to rejoin the Chuckanut Ridge Trail at the fence. Retrace your steps to Arroyo Park.

Dogs must be on leash in Chuckanut Mountain Park and Larrabee State Park. No feeding wildlife, fires, hunting, shooting, smoking, or vaping. These trails are multi-use. Mountain bikers yield to hikers; both give way to horse riders. Nevertheless, it's courteous to step aside for bikers too.

STOP OF INTEREST

WHATCOM FALLS PARK

What better place to view a timeless waterfall than a stone bridge dating back to 1939? There's much more history to see at present-day Whatcom Falls Park (1401 Electric Avenue) in Bellingham. Established in 1908, the park features the Lake Whatcom control dam (1906); a Chicago, Milwaukee, St. Paul and Pacific Railroad trestle (1916); a fish hatchery (1936); and the burn site of a gasoline pipeline fire (1999). It's also a stop on the Cascade Loop of the National Audubon Society's Great Washington State Birding Trail; look out for cedar waxwings, lesser scaups, ospreys, and rufous hummingbirds. Take Exit 253 on Interstate 5, and go east on Lakeway Drive to find the park.

NORTH BUTTE

Searching for solitude on Blanchard Mountain

Distance: 10 km (6.2 mi)
Time: 4.5 hours (loop)
Elevation gain: 405 m (1,330 ft)
High point: 670 m (2,200 ft)

Difficulty: ■
Maps: USGS Bellingham South, Bow; Square One Chuckanut Recreation Area
Trailhead: 48°37'02" N, 122°23'08" W

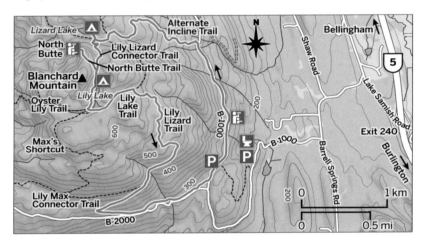

WITH ITS breathtaking cliff edge and Salish Sea perspective, Oyster Dome is the precious gemstone of viewpoints on Blanchard Mountain in Skagit County. While the views are a little less dramatic at neighbouring North Butte, it more than makes up for it with solitude—something in short supply at the popular "pearl" of the Chuckanut Mountains. Both scenic destinations are located in Harriet A. Spanel–Blanchard State Forest. After years of campaigning, Conservation Northwest and other advocates celebrated the permanent protection of Blanchard's core from logging in 2019.

GETTING THERE

Vehicle: On Interstate 5, south of Bellingham and north of Burlington, take Exit 240 (Alger). From the southbound off-ramp, turn right onto Lake Samish Road and head northwest. In 1.1 km (0.7 mi), make a left on Barrell Springs

A glacial erratic on the Lily Lizard Connector Trail.

Road. After 2.6 km (1.6 mi) on Barrell Springs Road (and after passing Barrell Springs Lane), turn right on the gravel B-1000 Road (2WD), also known as BL-ML Road. Drive past the lower trailhead (toilet available), keep right at the Samish Overlook fork, and park at Blanchard State Forest's upper trailhead. (The Lily Lizard Trail also connects the trailheads.) Discover Pass required (purchase in advance).

THE HIKE

From the kiosk (EMS checkpoint W) at the north end of the upper parking lot, begin a counterclockwise loop by heading up the gentle B-1000 Road and passing a gate. Within 15 minutes, go by a gravel pit on the left and earn a sweet vista of Mount Baker on the right. In Xwlemi'chosen, the language of the Lummi Nation, the glaciated stratovolcano is known as Kwelshán.

A half-hour (1.6 km/1 mi) north of the trailhead, just after the road goes over a creek, turn left on the Alternate Incline Trail (1.9 km/1.2 mi). The path weaves up through ferns, devil's club, Oregon grape, Douglas-firs, and western red cedars. A rusted rail, old cables, and stumps with springboard notches attest to the area's history of train logging.

Go straight through a four-way junction (checkpoint T). Shortly thereafter, come to the Lily Lake turnoff (and the start of the British Army Trail). Before going left on the Lily Lizard Connector Trail, detour right to check out peaceful Lizard Lake, which has swimming potential and beavers, and

Samish Bay from the North Butte.

its campground. Head south on the Lily Lizard Connector for 500 m (0.3 mi), quickly encountering an immense, moss-capped erratic in the shady woods.

Make a hard right on the North Butte Trail (300 m/0.2 mi). Unlike the rest of the trails on our loop, which are shared with mountain bikers and horse riders, this one's hiking only. Look for western cauliflower mushrooms on the forest floor. Clamber up meta-igneous rock to the clifftop viewpoint on the North Butte (2 hours up; 48°37′46″ N, 122°24′26″ W), just north of the off-trail summit of Blanchard Mountain, after 4.4 km (2.7 mi) on foot.

Oyster Dome is the forested knob in the foreground of the satisfying Salish Sea landscape. Guemes Island (Qweng7qwengila7 in Xws7ámeshqen, the language of the Samish Nation), Cypress Island (Séyenglhnelh), Vendovi Island, Sinclair Island, and Orcas Island (Sx'wálex') lie beyond Samish Bay.

The trailhead is 2 hours (5.6 km/3.5 mi) away on our counterclockwise loop. Return to the Lily Lizard Connector, and head south. At Lily Lake, turn right to stay on the west shore, then detour left to visit the horse camp. Take the Lily Lake Trail farther south, then follow it left (at checkpoint V). (Right is the Oyster Lily Trail, which provides access to Oyster Dome.)

Keep left at the Max's Shortcut junction, and join the Pacific Northwest Trail for 600 m (0.4 mi) of its 1,900-km (1,200-mi) journey from the Continental Divide to the Pacific Ocean. Leaving the PNT, turn right on the Lily

Lizard Trail and descend for 4.2 km (2.6 mi). Go left at a junction with the Lily Max Connector Trail. Parallel B-2000 Road until the path deposits you on B-1000 Road. Turn left and walk the final steps to the upper trailhead.

Blanchard Mountain is the southernmost peak of the Chuckanut Mountains, a range of foothills linking the North Cascades to the Salish Sea. The Washington State Department of Natural Resources manages Blanchard State Forest. All-terrain vehicles, fireworks, motorbikes, shooting, and wood cutting are prohibited. Dogs must be leashed. Camping and fires are allowed only at designated sites.

STOP OF INTEREST
BOW-EDISON FOOD TRAIL

Hitting another trail might not be your idea of après-hike fun. However, the Bow-Edison Food Trail is just the thing for hungry hikers with a penchant for local food. The self-guided tour features quaint bakeries, cheeseries, eateries, and farms in the lovely lowland between Blanchard Mountain and the Skagit River. On Interstate 5, south of Bellingham, take Exit 236 and go west on Bow Hill Road. Stop by Bow Hill Blueberries (15628 Bow Hill Road) or Samish Bay Cheese (15115 Bow Hill Road), and pick up a map of deliciousness. The latter establishment is also a stop on Skagitonians to Preserve Farmland's Talking Fields tour, which aims to inform the public about agriculture in the Skagit River delta. Find out about restrictions on bringing food into Canada by consulting the Canadian Food Inspection Agency website.

WELCOME PASS

Take a ridge walk and say hello to Mount Baker

Distance: 9 km (5.6 mi)
Time: 5.5 hours (out and back)
Elevation gain: 1,010 m (3,310 ft)
High point: 1,750 m (5,743 ft)

Difficulty: ■
Maps: USGS Mount Larrabee; Green Trails 13SX Mount Baker Wilderness
Trailhead: 48°54'49" N, 121°42'01" W

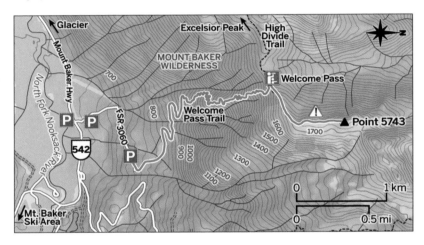

DUE TO its comparatively low elevation, Welcome Pass thaws out earlier in the hiking season than many other destinations in the Mount Baker Wilderness. As described, this trip ascends the High Divide Trail to the pass, then strikes off for the nearest high point. Once in the subalpine, yellow glacier lilies delight and so do the views of Mount Baker (3,286 m/10,781 ft)—the iconic stratovolcano known as Kweq' Smánit (white mountain) in Lhéchelesem, the language of the Nooksack Tribe.

GETTING THERE

Vehicle: From the Canada-U.S. border crossing at Sumas, head south on State Route 9 (Cherry Street). Turn left onto SR 547 (Front Street). Follow SR 547 for 17 km (11 mi) to a roundabout. Take the second exit. Go east on SR 542 (Mount Baker Highway). Pass the Glacier Public Service Center (10091

Mount Shuksan (Shéqsan) from the ridge.

Mount Baker Highway) in 17 km (11 mi). Continue 19.5 km (12 mi) farther. Turn left onto unsigned Welcome Pass Road (Forest Service Road 3060). For 2WD vehicles, a few parking spots are available on the right side, near the bottom of the road. Alternatively, park in the highway pullout just before the turnoff. High-clearance vehicles can drive to the trailhead at road's end.

THE HIKE

Find the Welcome Pass trailhead kiosk at the end of FSR 3060 (740 m/ 2,430 ft), 1.2 km (0.7 mi) from the highway. Set off north on a shady old road-bed lined with northern maidenhair ferns and Sitka columbine flowers. In 20 minutes, cross a creek to river right. Say bye to the gentle road, and start up the stiff, tight switchbacks under cover of forest, including old-growth trees.

Enter the Mount Baker Wilderness, a congressionally protected area within Mount Baker–Snoqualmie National Forest, 30 minutes from the trail-head. Wilderness regulations limit party size to 12—a good rule of thumb for all backcountry areas. Larger groups must physically and logistically divide into separate parties and remain at least 1.6 km (1 mi) apart. Bunchberry, Oregon grape, round-leaved violet, Siberian miner's-lettuce, and western trillium plants, and golden jelly cone fungi are found on the forest floor.

Encounter the first meadows, 2 hours in. Earn vistas of Mount Sefrit, Ruth Mountain, and Mount Shuksan (Shéqsan; 2,783 m/9,131 ft) watching over the head of the North Fork Nooksack River (Chuw7álich).

After less than 2.5 hours (3.4 km/2.1 mi), burst through timberline just before a wooden signpost marking the end of the Welcome Pass Trail portion of the High Divide Trail (1,540 m/5,050 ft; 48°55′39″ N, 121°42′43″ W). The High Divide Trail continues left to cross over to Excelsior Peak and the Excelsior Pass trailhead. With yellow glacier lilies looking svelte, Tomyhoi Peak (Put-lush-go-hap) looming to the north, and Mount McGuire (T'ami-yehó:y) lurking across the international boundary, Welcome Pass is a gladly received viewpoint.

Nevertheless, it's worth pushing on for 40 minutes (1.1 km/0.7 mi) up the ridge immediately to the northeast. Go right and keep to the obvious single track to preserve the gorgeous subalpine flora. Stay well back from cliffs and cornices on your left. Hit the crest and savour the mellow ridge walk north.

A flat-topped boulder marks Point 5743 (3 hours up; 1,750 m/5,743 ft; 48°56′06″ N, 121°42′21″ W). Floral highlights include fan-leaved cinquefoil, queen's cup, and Sitka valerian. The closest peak conceals Yellow Aster Butte in the northeast, but Goat Mountain (Yi7íman), Nooksack Ridge (Smámt-lek), Mount Shuksan, and Mount Baker's Rainbow, Sholes, and Mazama Glaciers are on full display east and south. Carmelo Crater, Sherman Crater, and the Dorr Fumarole Field are situated on Baker's upper reaches; the latter two features are sites of hydrothermal activity.

Return the way you came. Marvel at the virtually rootless and rockless Welcome Pass Trail surface, its condition in stark contrast to the usual state of many southwestern B.C. trails. Pro tip: Hikers going downhill yield to those moving uphill. Bikes, drones, and fires are prohibited in the Mount Baker Wilderness, as is shortcutting trails and switchbacks. Horses are allowed August to October, and llamas in any season (no kidding).

STOP OF INTEREST
NOOKSACK FALLS

At Nooksack Falls, the North Fork Nooksack River (Chuw7álich to the Nooksack Tribe) dives 27 m (88 ft), with two segments, into a dramatic canyon. It's the site of a historical hydroelectric plant, switched on in 1906. Built by the Whatcom County Railway and Light Company, the power plant was largely conceived to generate electricity for interurban rail lines. Visit the waterfall via Wells Creek Road (Forest Service Road 33), 11 km (7 mi) east of the Glacier Public Service Center. Heed safety signs and stay behind fences.

Descending to Welcome Pass.

LAKE ANN

Reflections of Mount Shuksan

Distance: 13 km (8.1 mi)
Time: 4.5 hours (out and back)
Elevation gain: 300 m (980 ft)
High point: 1,480 m (4,860 ft)

Difficulty: ■
Maps: USGS Shuksan Arm; Green Trails
13SX Mount Baker Wilderness
Trailhead: 48°51'00" N, 121°41'10" W

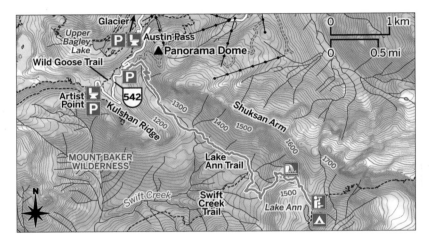

THE VIEW from Lake Ann is all about Mount Shuksan (2,783 m/9,131 ft), the breathtaking greenschist fortress known as Shéqsan in Lhéchelesem, the language of the Nooksack Tribe. Mountaineers tread the Lake Ann Trail on the way to climbing the Fisher Chimney route, first ascended in 1927. Day and overnight hikers should be content with eyeing the postcard massif—particularly its striking Summit Pyramid, Upper Curtis Glacier, and Lower Curtis Glacier—from a distance.

GETTING THERE

Vehicle: From the Canada-U.S. border crossing at Sumas, head south on State Route 9 (Cherry Street). Turn left onto SR 547 (Front Street). Follow SR 547 for 17 km (11 mi) to a roundabout. Take the second exit. Go east on SR 542 (Mount Baker Highway). In 17 km (11 mi), visit the Glacier Public Service

Mount Shuksan (Shéqsan) from Lake Ann.

Center (10091 Mount Baker Highway) on the right and purchase a Northwest Forest Pass. Continue 36 km (22 mi) on SR 542. Beyond the Austin Pass picnic area and Heather Meadows Visitor Center (toilet available), find the Lake Ann trailhead on the left.

THE HIKE

Located in Mount Baker–Snoqualmie National Forest, the well-loved Lake Ann Trail—part of the Pacific Northwest Trail—starts in Austin Pass, the saddle between Mount Baker (Kweq' Smánit; 3,286 m/10,781 ft) and Mount Shuksan. Although the hike's high point, right before the lake, is a mere 30 m (100 ft) above the parking lot's 1,450 m (4,760 ft) elevation, the trail bottoms out at 1,180 m (3,870 ft) in between. So save some energy for the uphill finale.

Lake Ann itself lies in the Mount Baker Wilderness, just outside of North Cascades National Park. Wilderness regulations stipulate a maximum party size of 12. Hikers are asked to use blue bags, available at the trailhead, to collect, pack out, and dispose of solid human waste (in trash bins, not pit toilets). Abiding by Leave No Trace principles is the expected practice here.

From the trailhead kiosk, take the rocky path through pink mountain-heather. Ignoring a gravel road on the left, keep right to find the trail register and another information board. The forest takes over as the trail descends. Soon enough, exit the woods and enter a gorgeous subalpine basin at the

Mount Baker (Kweq' Smánit) and the Lake Ann Trail.

headwaters of Swift Creek, between Shuksan Arm and Kulshan Ridge. Cross creek beds on boulders, and follow a path cleared through a rock field. Striking cliffs and talus aprons line both sides of the basin.

Topped by Huntoon Point, Kulshan Ridge lies on the northeast rim of the Kulshan caldera, the eroded remnant of a catastrophic pyroclastic eruption 1.15 million years ago during the early Pleistocene. Filled with rhyodacitic ignimbrite, the Kulshan caldera rivals the size of the famous Crater Lake caldera at Mount Mazama in Oregon. (Kwelshán is the name of Mount Baker in Xwlemi'chosen, the language of the Lummi Nation.)

Track through mud, and return to shady trees. Come to a signposted junction (48°50′01″ N, 121°39′27″ W) in a meadow, 3.9 km (2.4 mi) from the trailhead. The Swift Creek Trail strikes off to the right, taking the long-distance Pacific Northwest Trail with it. Stewarded by the Pacific Northwest Trail Association, the national scenic trail runs 1,900 km (1,200 mi) from Glacier National Park on the Continental Divide to Olympic National Park on the Pacific Ocean—traversing Montana, Idaho, and Washington.

Leaving a three-month PNT thru-hike for another year, forge straight ahead on the Lake Ann Trail, boulder-hop a creek, and start gaining elevation. Blooms include arctic lupine, edible thistle, partridge-foot, pink monkey-flower, Sitka columbine, subalpine daisy, and tiger lily. Pass a large boulder in a meadow, staying off a closed path to the right. Zigzag up a boulder field, which is home to pikas, and follow the rocky trail through the heather. Look left to see a waterfall plunging over a cliff above. Gaze west at Mount Baker, Coleman Pinnacle on Ptarmigan Ridge, and Table Mountain, a 300,000-year-old stack of pyroxene andesite lava flows.

Crest the windy saddle, and enter the boulder-strewn cirque of Lake Ann. Make a descending traverse to a fork by the east lakeshore (2 hours one-way; 48°49'40" N, 121°38'36" W), 2.6 km (1.6 mi) from the Swift Creek Trail junction. Head a few steps left for an excellent view of Mount Shuksan, with its redoubtable glaciers, waterfalls, couloirs, and pinnacles. Listen for the ominous sound of falling ice. The right fork leads to tent sites and the lake outlet. Take a load off and stay a while. A dip in the subalpine lake is chilling but invigorating. Return via the same scenic route.

Bikes, drones, fires, and snowmobiles are prohibited in the Mount Baker Wilderness, as is shortcutting trails and switchbacks. Dogs must be leashed in the Heather Meadows area. If staying overnight, please stick to existing campsites.

STOP OF INTEREST
PICTURE LAKE

Landscape photographers flock to Picture Lake, for good reason. Try your hand at snapping the perfect postcard photo of Mount Shuksan (Shéqsan to the Nooksack Tribe) reflected in its waters. The 800-m (0.5-mi) wheelchair-accessible Picture Lake Path features a viewing scope and interpretative panels. Find the Picture Lake trailhead just down State Route 542 (Mount Baker Highway) from the Heather Meadows Visitor Center. (Northwest Forest Pass required. Dogs must be leashed.)

HIDDEN LAKE LOOKOUT

A dreamy hike to an old fire tower

Distance: 12 km (7.5 mi)
Time: 6 hours (out and back)
Elevation gain: 1,020 m (3,350 ft)
High point: 2,100 m (6,890 ft)

Difficulty: ◆
Maps: USGS Eldorado Peak, Sonny Boy Lakes; Green Trails 48, 80
Trailhead: 48°30'51" N, 121°13'17" W

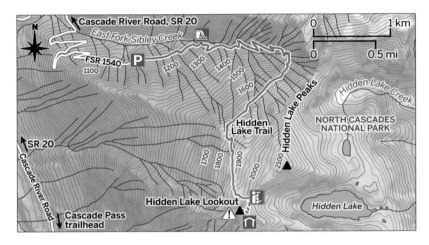

PERCHED PRECARIOUSLY atop a rocky pinnacle, the Hidden Lake Lookout bears resemblance at first glance to a fortress in J.R.R. Tolkien's Middle-earth. Scanning the North Cascades, it's not difficult to imagine the beacons of Gondor bursting into flame across the horizon. On the sought-after Hidden Lake Trail, reality measures up to fantasy. Whether you stop at the pass overlooking Hidden Lake or scramble up to the old fire lookout built in 1931, it's a dreamy hike you won't soon forget.

GETTING THERE

Vehicle: On Interstate 5, north of Burlington, take Exit 232. Head east on Cook Road, going straight through a roundabout in Sedro-Woolley. At the second roundabout, turn left on State Route 20 (North Cascades Highway). Go straight at a third roundabout. After the SR 530 junction in Rockport,

Hidden Lake with Forbidden Peak and Boston Peak.

continue east on SR 20 for 13.5 km (8.4 mi). In Marblemount, where SR 20 turns left, go straight onto Cascade River Road and across the Skagit River bridge. Turn left onto Sibley Creek Road (Forest Service Road 1540), signed for the Hidden Lake Trail, 15.5 km (9.6 mi) from SR 20. Drive up the steep, narrow gravel road (high-clearance 2WD) for 7 km (4.3 mi) to the small parking lot at the end. If it's full, park on the shoulder lower down, without blocking the road.

THE HIKE

From the trailhead (1,080 m/3,540 ft), which lies in Mount Baker–Snoqualmie National Forest, head east on an old roadbed. Find the trail register, where you step across the first creek. Cross a larger creek, and enter the cool, open forest. Commence switchbacking under subalpine fir. Skirt an avalanche path, 15 minutes in. At a switchback, trees obscure a waterfall on the east fork of Sibley Creek. After a muddy section with long boardwalks, cross the creek on a plank.

After a half-hour, break through timberline and burst into exuberant subalpine meadows—thick with wildflowers and abuzz with bees and butterflies. Bring your field guide! The rainbow includes American bistort, bracted lousewort, fan-leaved cinquefoil, orange agoseris, pink monkey-flower, small-flowered penstemon, and Siberian miner's-lettuce. Cross and recross brooks as you zigzag up the meadows under the rocky Hidden Lake Peaks.

Descending the Hidden Lake Trail.

Begin a long, luscious southward traverse, 1.5 hours in. Take care crossing steep snow patches and streamlet gullies. Early in the season, an ice axe is advisable. Negotiate occasional boulder patches. Verdant meadows please the eye every which way. Putting forward Sherman Peak and the Boulder Glacier, Mount Baker looms majestically to the northwest. The northern-most volcano in the conterminous U.S. is known as Teqwúbe7 (snow-capped mountain) in the Lushootseed language of the Skagit people. Baker's last eruption was 6,700 years ago.

After two hours, the switchbacks resume. The braided and eroded path ascends through heather and boulders. Stay on the main trail; don't con-tribute to the sprawl. Earn your first sighting of the old fire lookout atop the southernmost of the Hidden Lake Peaks. Pass through the treeline and into the alpine, with more and more of the glorious North Cascades coming into focus. Follow the odd cairn and snow up through the rocks—slabs on the left, boulders on the right—to arrive at the pass (2,000 m/6,560 ft; 48°29′48″ N, 121°12′14″ W), after 3 hours on foot.

Welcome to North Cascades National Park and the Stephen Mather Wilderness. (Group size is limited to 12. No dogs, drones, feeding wild-life, fires, or hunting.) From massive boulders, gaze down at Hidden Lake (1,747 m/5,733 ft), the heavenly blue tarn filling the granitic cirque far below. The backdrop—pointy Forbidden Peak and serrated Boston Peak (2,711 m/ 8,894 ft)—is tremendous.

Up to the pass, this hike is rated "moderate." To continue to the lookout, 20 minutes away, follow cairns across and up the steep slope south of the pass, making use of ledges. Scramble up boulders to gain the southeast ridge. Turn right and pick your way through the big rocks to the summit (3.5 hours up; 48°29′44″ N, 121°12′18″ W).

The small fire lookout, last staffed in the 1950s, is a magical spot, featuring historical U.S. Forest Service artifacts and old guest registers. Two U.S. Geological Survey reference marks dated 1939 are found outside. Known as Tda-ko-buh-ba to the Sauk-Suiattle Tribe, Glacier Peak (3,213 m/10,541 ft) commands the southern horizon. The active dacite stratovolcano last erupted 1,100 years ago. When you manage to pull yourself away from the superlative panorama, head back down the way you came.

Overnight stays in the cramped lookout are first come, first served, with priority given to volunteer work parties. If you sleep there, please make a donation to the Friends of Hidden Lake Lookout. A backcountry permit is required to camp in North Cascades National Park. Hikers are asked to use blue bags to pack out solid waste. Leave No Trace methods are imperative here.

STOP OF INTEREST
HENRY THOMPSON BRIDGE

In the town of Concrete, an elegant old bridge spans the Baker River, just upstream of its confluence with the Skagit River. Built in 1916 to link parts of the town on either side of the river, the Henry Thompson Bridge is an open-spandrel arch made of—you guessed it—reinforced concrete. Two local manufacturers donated the cement. The bridge replaced a wooden truss structure condemned by the county engineer. It was added to the National Register of Historic Places in 1976. From State Route 20 (North Cascades Highway), 13.5 km (8.4 mi) west of the SR 530 junction at Rockport, head north on North Dillard Avenue to visit the bridge.

CASCADE PASS

Dazzling scenery from start to finish

Distance: 13.5 km (8.4 mi)
Time: 5.5 hours (out and back)
Elevation gain: 750 m (2,460 ft)
High point: 1,860 m (6,100 ft)

Difficulty: ■
Maps: USGS Cascade Pass; Green Trails 80 Cascade Pass
Trailhead: 48°28'32" N, 121°04'30" W

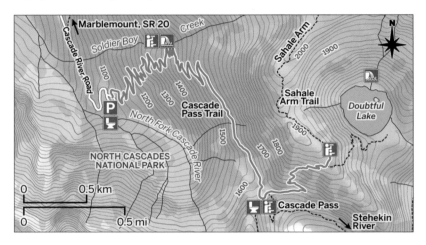

TODAY, HIKERS flock to Cascade Pass to spot mountain goats, smell the wild-flowers, and marvel at lofty glaciers and waterfalls. However, humans have been drawn to this passage through the Cascade Range for millennia. Consequently, a hike on the Cascade Pass Trail entails following in the footsteps of Upper Skagit hunters and traders, gold prospectors, land surveyors, and wagon road builders. Reputedly the most popular day hike in all of North Cascades National Park, this exceptionally rewarding trail serves up dazzling scenery from start to finish.

GETTING THERE

Vehicle: On Interstate 5, north of Burlington, take Exit 232. Head east on Cook Road, going straight through a roundabout in Sedro-Woolley. At the second roundabout, turn left on State Route 20 (North Cascades Highway).

The North Cascades from the Sahale Arm Trail.

Go straight at a third roundabout. After the SR 530 junction in Rockport, continue east on SR 20 for 13.5 km (8.4 mi). In Marblemount, where SR 20 turns left, go straight onto Cascade River Road and across the Skagit River bridge. The road turns to gravel (2WD), 16 km (9.9 mi) from SR 20. Drive to the end, at 36 km (22 mi), and arrive at the parking lot (toilet available). Except in heavy snow years, the road is open by late June.

THE HIKE

The scenery at the Cascade Pass parking lot (1,110 m/3,640 ft) is awe-inspiring to say the least. Stare up at towering Cascade Peak and Johannesburg Mountain, and their glaciers, snow caves, and waterfalls. Read the interpretive panels for insight on the area's geology, geomorphology, and history. Set off east on the well-graded Cascade Pass Trail, and climb a couple dozen switchbacks. Devil's club, pinesap, queen's cup, and salmonberries grow in the shady forest.

Within an hour, earn a down-valley viewpoint and detour left at a bend in the trail to see a fan waterfall on Soldier Boy Creek. The switchbacks end, after 1.5 hours on foot. Head southwest on an ascending traverse full of eye candy. Spot pocket glaciers on The Triplets and Cascade Peak across the valley of the North Fork Cascade River. Cross a number of brooks, breach timberline, go across a rockslide with pikas, and enter subalpine meadows with hoary marmots.

Sahale Mountain and Doubtful Lake from the Sahale Arm Trail.

The array of wildflowers is staggering: common butterwort, Davidson's penstemon, edible thistle, green false hellebore, mountain arnica, Sitka columbine, spreading phlox, subalpine daisy, yellow mountain-heather, etc. Cross a large talus slope, perhaps encountering lingering snow.

Arrive at Cascade Pass (48°28′03″ N, 121°03′33″ W), after 2 hours (5.5 km/ 3.4 mi) on the trail. Peer up at Mix-up Peak, Magic Mountain, and Pelton Peak, and down the U-shaped valley of Pelton Creek. Eye the slopes above for mountain goats. (Never approach wildlife.) Boulders provide seating and a U.S. Geological Survey benchmark reports the elevation (1,643 m/5,392 ft). Please heed the signs imploring you to stay off the meadows. The composting toilet to the right is only for solid waste; hikers are asked to urinate on bare rock or trail.

Head left momentarily, along the Skagit-Chelan county line, to find a signposted fork. The Cascade Pass Trail goes right, descending to the Pelton Basin campsite and the Stehekin River. However, take the left fork for the Sahale Arm Trail to gain a higher perspective. Cross a boulder field and creek, and switchback up steep meadows blooming with partridge-foot, red paintbrush, and yellow glacier lily. Soar above the pass. Round a bend and— boom—see Sahale Mountain (2,646 m/8,680 ft) looming large ahead.

Hit a fork (3 hours up; 48°28′14″ N, 121°03′06″ W) in the alpine, 1.2 km (0.7 mi) from the pass. The Sahale Arm Trail continues left and up the ridge to the Sahale Glacier campsite (2,320 m/7,600 ft); the right path drops down to Doubtful Lake (1,641 m/5,385 ft), which buzzed with gold-mining activity in the late 1800s. Wander either way for views of the waterfalls streaming down Sahale Mountain's cliffs to the clear, aquamarine gem of a lake. Once sated with the enthralling scene, retrace your steps to the trailhead.

Doubtful Lake (via Doubtful Creek) and Pelton Creek both drain into the Stehekin River, which flows into Lake Chelan. *Stehekin* is an anglicization of *stxʷíkn'*—which means "the way through" in nxaʔamxčín, the language of the Chelan, Entiat, Moses-Columbia, and Wenatchee tribes. Archaeologists have found ancient stone microblades and cooking hearths in the Cascade Pass area. (Do not remove objects, dig, or disturb the ground.)

The Cascade Pass Trail lies in the Stephen Mather Wilderness. Group size is limited to 12. No bikes, dogs, drones, feeding wildlife, fires, hunting, or shortcutting switchbacks. Camping is restricted to designated sites and requires a much-in-demand backcountry permit.

STOP OF INTEREST
ROCKPORT STATE PARK

Nestled between Sauk Mountain and the Skagit River is an ancient forest estimated to be 400 to 600 years old. Walk the Evergreen Trail to commune with the sky-scraping Douglas-fir trees of Rockport State Park (51905 Highway 20). Take the Skagit View Trail for a look at a part of the congressionally designed Skagit Wild and Scenic River System. In 1935, Sound Timber Company sold the park property to the State of Washington for a dollar. Find the park 1.9 km (1.2 mi) west of the State Route 20–SR 530 junction at Rockport. (Discover Pass required. Dogs must be on leash.)

BLUE LAKE

Home of the golden larches

Distance: 8 km (5 mi)
Time: 2.5 hours (lollipop)
Elevation gain: 305 m (1,000 ft)
High point: 1,935 m (6,350 ft)

Difficulty: ●
Maps: USGS Washington Pass; Green Trails 50 Washington Pass
Trailhead: 48°31'08" N, 120°40'27" W

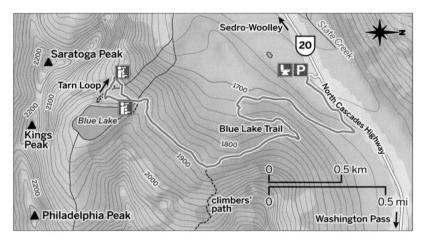

THE WATERS of Blue Lake are a beautiful cerulean, and charmingly reflect the granitic towers of Liberty Bell Mountain and the Early Winters Spires. However, the subalpine larches take centre stage in autumn, when their pale blue-green needles turn golden yellow. The popular, family-friendly Blue Lake Trail is found between Rainy Pass and Washington Pass, in Okanogan-Wenatchee National Forest and Chelan County. It's best hiked late July to early October.

GETTING THERE

Vehicle: On Interstate 5, north of Burlington, take Exit 232. Head east on Cook Road, going straight through a roundabout in Sedro-Woolley. At the second roundabout, turn left on State Route 20 (North Cascades Highway). Go straight at a third roundabout. After the SR 530 junction in Rockport,

Subalpine larches at Blue Lake.

continue east on SR 20 for 102 km (63 mi). Beyond Rainy Pass (road closed in winter), turn right into the busy parking lot at the Blue Lake trailhead (toilet available). Northwest Forest Pass required (purchase at the trailhead).

THE HIKE

The Blue Lake Trail begins behind the vault toilet (1,630 m/5,350 ft). Fill out the trail register, and cross the first of several boardwalks. The wide path parallels the highway for a bit, gently rising under the conifers. Cross a boulder patch in the woods. In 20 minutes, arrive at an open area with downed trees. Gaze at colourful wildflowers and Cutthroat Peak across the State Creek valley. Negotiate some mud, and dive back into the woods.

Pass boulders, and enter the magical realm of the subalpine larch, after 45 minutes on foot. These beloved trees grow near timberline and bear deciduous needles that positively glow between late September and early October. You might startle a spruce grouse. A climbers' path exits to the left at a small cairn, providing access to rock routes on aptly named Liberty Bell Mountain (2,353 m/7,720 ft) and the Early Winters Spires (2,380 m/7,807 ft). In 1946, Fred Beckey, Jerry O'Neil, and Charles Welsh logged the first ascent of Liberty Bell via the southwest face.

Stay right with the Blue Lake Trail, and traverse southwest through larches and heather meadows, with vistas of Whistler Mountain and Cutthroat Peak. Stay on the main trail, and walk in single file. Respect restoration

Cutthroat Peak from the Tarn Loop.

area closures on both sides of the path. "As few as 25 boot steps can kill a plant that may be centuries old by crushing fragile stems," an interpretative sign informs.

Fork right to cross the outflow creek. Go left at the next fork by the remains of a log cabin (48°30′30″ N, 120°40′20″ W). Emerge on a rocky promontory next to the logjammed outlet of Blue Lake (1,906 m/6,254 ft), an hour (3.6 km/2.2 mi) from the trailhead. Blue Lake Peak, Philadelphia Peak (2,332 m/7,651 ft), Kings Peak, and Saratoga Peak form a horseshoe ridge at the head of the glacially carved cirque. Stocked cutthroat trout inhabit the tarn. Whisky-jacks may swoop in to try to share your lunch. (Don't feed wildlife!)

Keep your eyes peeled for mountain goats—sometimes called goat-antelopes—which have evolved to thrive in steep, rocky terrain. The annual rut climaxes in late November and early December. Within a few hours of birth, goat kids start to climb. These ungulates (hoofed mammals) are drawn to mineral licks—and salty urine—in summer. Hikers are asked to urinate on rocks or bare earth at least 46 m (50 yd) away from trails.

Back at the cabin fork, continue south on the 15-minute Tarn Loop (600 m/0.4 mi). Fork left to proceed clockwise and gain the best vantage yet of Liberty Bell Mountain, Concord Tower, Lexington Tower, and the Early Winters Spires. Split by faults, these pinnacles belong to the Golden Horn

Batholith, a 48-million-year-old igneous intrusion. Turn right at a junction to go round the upper pond and earn additional Cutthroat Peak views. Complete the loop, and head back down the way you came.

Blue Lake falls in the basin of the Columbia River, to which it drains via State Creek, Bridge Creek, the Stehekin River, and Lake Chelan. The Columbia River is known as nq̓ʷtn̓atkʷ in nxaʔamxčín, the language of the Chelan, Entiat, Moses-Columbia, and Wenatchee tribes, which today are represented among the Confederated Tribes of the Colville Reservation.

Pack it in, pack it out. No bikes, camping, drones, fireworks, or shortcutting trails or switchbacks.

STOP OF INTEREST
WASHINGTON PASS OVERLOOK

At 1,669 m (5,477 ft) above mean sea level, Washington Pass is the highest point on State Route 20 (North Cascades Highway). The road through the mountain pass is closed every winter due to dangerous avalanche conditions. Visit the Washington Pass Overlook, 1.9 km (1.2 mi) east of the Blue Lake trailhead. A short trail features interpretative panels and outstanding views of the gap; Kangaroo Ridge, the Early Winters Spires, and Liberty Bell Mountain; and subalpine larches. West of the Blue Lake trailhead, the Mexico-to-Canada Pacific Crest Trail crosses the highway at Rainy Pass (1,480 m/4,855 ft).

ACKNOWLEDGEMENTS

YOU'VE PROBABLY HEARD the ancient proverb: It takes a hiking club to publish a guidebook. For starters, I'm grateful to everyone who made it possible for me to write not just one but two hiking guides without owning or driving a car.

Special thanks to Jaime Adams, Jacqueline Ashby, Patrick Hui, Sarah Palmer, and Joan Septembre. Many thanks also to Esther Brysch, Julius Brysch, Stefan Brysch, Verena Brysch, Roberto Castro, Dawn Coers, Jason Cusator, Richard Egolf, Susana Egolf, Bob Hare, Laszlo Hulicsko, Alexandra Juzkiw, Maria Kelly, Connie Lacasse, Amanda Lewis, Ella Li, Noel Memije, Grace Pizzuti, Lyda Salatian, Mary Simmonds, and Svetlana Tkacova.

The Wanderung Outdoor Recreation Society, founder Steve van der Woerd, president Andy Gibb, secretary Paul Taylor, and the club's directors, trip organizers, and participants have my sincere appreciation for their contributions to many a hiking adventure and for enthusiastically supporting the release of *105 Hikes In and Around Southwestern British Columbia* in 2018.

Of course, none of this happens without the brilliant work of Rob Sanders, Jennifer Croll, Nayeli Jimenez (who won gold and bronze medals at the 2019 PubWest Book Design Awards for her work on *105 Hikes*), Lara LeMoal, and the whole squad at Greystone Books. It was a distinct pleasure to collaborate again with peerless editor and living trail encyclopedia Lucy Kenward. Credit goes to Steve Chapman of Canadian Map Makers for the excellent topographic cartography. Thanks to copy editor Erin Parker for going over the text with a fine-tooth comb.

Without the unsparing support of Oliver Hui-Reid and Nicole Reid, this book might have been a journey without a destination. I'm appreciative of Karen Tam Wu, Kelly O'Connor, Melyssa Hudson, and all of

The summit cairn on the South Needle.

my climate-chilling coworkers at the Pembina Institute; Charlie Smith, Travis Lupick, Tammy Kwan, and Gail Johnson at the *Georgia Straight*; Oliver Lazenby at *Mount Baker Experience*; Tori Ball at the B.C. chapter of the Canadian Parks and Wilderness Society; and Lydia Kwa, Charles Demers, Cara Ng, Tara Henley, T'uy't'tanat–Cease Wyss, Michael Coyle, Taryn Eyton, and Kristine Krynitzki for help or encouragement along the way.

Indigenous toponyms were learned from First Nations' land-use plans, environmental assessment submissions, dictionaries, and mapping projects; anthropological books and papers; the work of Kwi Awt Stelmexw, the Squamish Líl'wat Cultural Centre, and Stó:lō Research and Resource Management Centre; and many other reliable sources. The remarkable accomplishments and efforts of Indigenous language activists, educators, researchers, and speakers should be commended and supported.

I'd like to salute legendary guidebook authors Mary Macaree, David Macaree, Jack Bryceland, Dawn Hanna, Harvey Manning, Ira Spring, and Craig Romano for setting the high bar to which I aspire. Much respect to AdventureSmart, the Alpine Club of Canada, Avalanche Canada, B.C. Mountaineering Club, B.C. Search and Rescue Association, Burke Mountain Naturalists, Chilliwack Outdoor Club, Coquitlam Search and Rescue, Federation of Mountain Clubs of B.C., Galiano Conservancy Association, Hope Mountain Centre for Outdoor Learning, Leave No Trace Center for Outdoor Ethics, North Shore Rescue, Powell River Parks and Wilderness Society, Ridge Meadows Outdoor Club, Trails Society of B.C., Washington Trails Association, and Wilderness Committee for all of the important work that you do.

Lastly, thank *you* for reading this guidebook. I hope it leads you down new paths, as it did for me.

Hike	Distance	Time	Elevation Gain	High Point
1. Elsay Lake	18 km (11.2 mi)	10.5 hours	610 m (2,000 ft)	1,260 m (4,130 ft)
2. South Needle	18 km (11.2 mi)	8 hours	1,060 m (3,480 ft)	1,163 m (3,820 ft)
3. Kennedy Falls	10 km (6.2 mi)	5 hours	140 m (460 ft)	450 m (1,480 ft)
4. Dam Mountain	12 km (7.5 mi)	5 hours	1,075 m (3,530 ft)	1,349 m (4,430 ft)
5. Twin Sisters (The Lions)	15 km (9.3 mi)	9 hours	1,430 m (4,690 ft)	1,654 m (5,430 ft)
6. Petgill Lake	10 km (6.2 mi)	5.5 hours	625 m (2,050 ft)	770 m (2,530 ft)
7. Slhánay̓	5 km (3.1 mi)	4.5 hours	630 m (2,070 ft)	660 m (2,170 ft)
8. Echo Lake	7.5 km (4.7 mi)	7 hours	905 m (2,970 ft)	910 m (2,990 ft)
9. Crooked Falls	6 km (3.7 mi)	4.5 hours	465 m (1,530 ft)	520 m (1,710 ft)
10. Helm Lake	26 km (16.2 mi)	9.5 hours	940 m (3,080 ft)	1,765 m (5,790 ft)
11. Cheakamus Lake	14.5 km (9 mi)	4 hours	145 m (480 ft)	890 m (2,920 ft)
12. Singing Pass	23.5 km (14.6 mi)	7 hours	1,040 m (3,410 ft)	1,730 m (5,680 ft)
13. Decker Mountain	12 km (7.5 mi)	6.5 hours	600 m (1,970 ft)	2,421 m (7,943 ft)
14. Wedgemount Lake	12.5 km (7.8 mi)	8.5 hours	1,165 m (3,822 ft)	1,920 m (6,300 ft)
15. Semaphore Lakes	5.5 km (3.4 mi)	3 hours	315 m (1,030 ft)	1,659 m (5,440 ft)
16. Marriott Basin	10.5 km (6.5 mi)	5.5 hours	710 m (2,330 ft)	2,110 m (6,920 ft)
17. Blowdown Pass	8.5 km (5.3 mi)	4 hours	490 m (1,610 ft)	2,160 m (7,090 ft)
18. Gotcha Peak	10.5 km (6.5 mi)	6 hours	780 m (2,560 ft)	2,450 m (8,040 ft)
19. Gott Peak	12 km (7.5 mi)	6.5 hours	840 m (2,760 ft)	2,511 m (8,240 ft)
20. Diez Vistas Trail	13 km (8.1 mi)	6 hours	460 m (1,510 ft)	555 m (1,820 ft)
21. Dennett Lake	16 km (9.9 mi)	7.5 hours	750 m (2,460 ft)	1,070 m (3,510 ft)
22. East Canyon Trail	19.5 km (12.1 mi)	6 hours	170 m (560 ft)	330 m (1,080 ft)
23. Mount Nutt Viewpoints	10.5 km (6.5 mi)	5.5 hours	970 m (3,180 ft)	1,130 m (3,710 ft)
24. Statlu Lake	13 km (8.1 mi)	6 hours	300 m (980 ft)	630 m (2,070 ft)
25. Chadsey Lake	10 km (6.2 mi)	5 hours	510 m (1,670 ft)	660 m (2,170 ft)
26. Taggart Peak	10.5 km (6.5 mi)	4.5 hours	770 m (2,530 ft)	796 m (2,610 ft)
27. Pierce Lake	11.5 km (7.1 mi)	6 hours	1,080 m (3,540 ft)	1,400 m (4,590 ft)
28. Greendrop Lake	12 km (7.5 mi)	5.5 hours	340 m (1,120 ft)	970 m (3,180 ft)

Hike	Distance	Time	Elevation Gain	High Point
29. Flora Pass	11 km (6.8 mi)	5.5 hours	1,110 m (3,640 ft)	1,740 m (5,710 ft)
30. Radium Lake	17 km (10.6 mi)	7.5 hours	920 m (3,020 ft)	1,510 m (4,950 ft)
31. Eaton Lake	8.5 km (5.3 mi)	5.5 hours	920 m (3,020 ft)	1,350 m (4,430 ft)
32. Hozomeen Lake	12.5 km (7.8 mi)	3.5 hours	330 m (1,080 ft)	880 m (2,890 ft)
33. Mount Lincoln	3 km (1.9 mi)	3.5 hours	595 m (1,950 ft)	660 m (2,170 ft)
34. Yak Peak	5.5 km (3.4 mi)	6 hours	840 m (2,755 ft)	2,039 m (6,690 ft)
35. Zoa Peak	8 km (5 mi)	4 hours	620 m (2,030 ft)	1,869 m (6,130 ft)
36. Ghostpass Lake	17 km (10.6 mi)	10 hours	810 m (2,660 ft)	1,465 m (4,810 ft)
37. Punch Bowl Pass	17 km (10.6 mi)	6.5 hours	1,020 m (3,350 ft)	1,770 m (5,810 ft)
38. Poland Lake	16.5 km (10.3 mi)	5.5 hours	480 m (1,575 ft)	1,840 m (6,040 ft)
39. Derek Falls	9 km (5.6 mi)	3 hours	170 m (560 ft)	1,385 m (4,540 ft)
40. Mount Killam	13.5 km (8.4 mi)	5.5 hours	840 m (2,760 ft)	844 m (2,770 ft)
41. Mount Elphinstone	13 km (8.1 mi)	6 hours	1,060 m (3,480 ft)	1,266 m (4,150 ft)
42. Mount Hallowell	16.5 km (10.3 mi)	7 hours	1,050 m (3,445 ft)	1,231 m (4,040 ft)
43. Mount Galiano	13.5 km (8.4 mi)	4.5 hours	300 m (980 ft)	300 m (980 ft)
44. Bodega Ridge	8 km (5 mi)	3.5 hours	130 m (430 ft)	250 m (820 ft)
45. Extension Ridge	13.5 km (8.4 mi)	4 hours	185 m (610 ft)	255 m (840 ft)
46. Mount Benson	6.5 km (4 mi)	4.5 hours	730 m (2,395 ft)	1,019 m (3,340 ft)
47. Lookout Mountain	18.5 km (11.5 mi)	5.5 hours	660 m (2,165 ft)	816 m (2,677 ft)
48. Lost Lake	15 km (9.3 mi)	5 hours	405 m (1,330 ft)	430 m (1,410 ft)
49. Chuckanut Ridge	16.5 km (10.3 mi)	6 hours	565 m (1,850 ft)	590 m (1,940 ft)
50. North Butte	10 km (6.2 mi)	4.5 hours	405 m (1,330 ft)	670 m (2,200 ft)
51. Welcome Pass	9 km (5.6 mi)	5.5 hours	1,010 m (3,310 ft)	1,750 m (5,743 ft)
52. Lake Ann	13 km (8.1 mi)	4.5 hours	300 m (980 ft)	1,480 m (4,860 ft)
53. Hidden Lake Lookout	12 km (7.5 mi)	6 hours	1,020 m (3,350 ft)	2,100 m (6,890 ft)
54. Cascade Pass	13.5 km (8.4 mi)	5.5 hours	750 m (2,460 ft)	1,860 m (6,100 ft)
55. Blue Lake	8 km (5 mi)	2.5 hours	305 m (1,000 ft)	1,935 m (6,350 ft)

STOPS OF INTEREST

FURTHER READING

Baldwin, John. *Exploring the Coast Mountains on Skis: A Guide to Ski Mountaineering.* 3rd ed. Vancouver: John Baldwin, 2009.

Bates, Dawn, Thom Hess, and Vi Hilbert. *Lushootseed Dictionary.* Seattle: University of Washington Press, 1994.

Beckey, Fred. *Cascade Alpine Guide: Climbing and High Routes.* Vol. 3, *Rainy Pass to Fraser River.* 3rd ed. Seattle: Mountaineers Books, 2008.

Bourdon, Marc. *Squamish Hiking: Hiking Trails From Horseshoe Bay to the Callaghan Valley.* Squamish: Quickdraw Publications, 2017.

Bryceland, Jack, Mary Macaree, and David Macaree. *103 Hikes in Southwestern British Columbia.* 6th ed. Vancouver: Greystone Books, 2008.

Crerar, David, Harry Crerar, and Bill Maurer. *The Glorious Mountains of Vancouver's North Shore: A Peakbagger's Guide.* Victoria: Rocky Mountain Books, 2018.

Culbert, Dick. *Alpine Guide to Southwestern British Columbia.* Vancouver: Dick Culbert, 1974.

Fairley, Bruce. *A Guide to Climbing & Hiking in Southwestern British Columbia.* West Vancouver: Gordon Soules Book Publishers, 1986.

Galloway, Brent D. *Dictionary of Upriver Halkomelem.* 2 vols. University of California Publications in Linguistics. Berkeley: University of California Press, 2009.

Gunn, Matt. *Scrambles in Southwest British Columbia.* Vancouver: Cairn Publishing, 2005.

Halliday, John, Alice Purdey, Mary Macaree, and David Macaree. *109 Walks in British Columbia's Lower Mainland.* 8th ed. Vancouver: Greystone Books, 2019.

Hanna, Dawn. *Best Hikes and Walks of Southwestern British Columbia.* Rev. ed. Edmonton: Lone Pine Publishing, 2006.

HBC Trail Book. Hope: Hope Mountain Centre for Outdoor Learning, 2018.

Hui, Stephen. *105 Hikes In and Around Southwestern British Columbia*. Vancouver: Greystone Books, 2018.

Kahn, Charles. *Hiking the Gulf Islands of British Columbia*. 4th ed. Madeira Park: Harbour Publishing, 2018.

Litzenberger, Lyle. *Burke and Widgeon: A Hiker's Guide*. Port Coquitlam: Pebblestone Publishing, 2013.

McLane, Kevin, and Andrew Boyd. *The Climbers Guide to Squamish*. Vol. 1, *Squamish Rockclimbs*. Squamish: High Col, 2018.

Mountain Trail Guide for the South West Mainland Area of British Columbia. 4th ed. Vancouver: Federation of Mountain Clubs of British Columbia, 1972.

Mountaineering: The Freedom of the Hills. 9th ed. Seattle: Mountaineers Books, 2017.

Richardson, Allan, and Brent Galloway. *Nooksack Place Names: Geography, Culture, and Language*. Vancouver: UBC Press, 2011.

Romano, Craig. *100 Classic Hikes: Washington*. 3rd ed. Seattle: Mountaineers Books, 2016.

Sept, J. Duane. *Common Mushrooms of the Northwest*. Rev. ed. Sechelt: Calypso Publishing, 2012.

Scott, Andrew. *The Encyclopedia of Raincoast Place Names: A Complete Reference to Coastal British Columbia*. Madeira Park: Harbour Publishing, 2009.

Shewchuk, Murphy. *Coquihalla Trips & Trails*. Rev. ed. Markham, Ontario: Fitzhenry & Whiteside, 2007.

Squamish Nation Dictionary Project. *Skwxwú7mesh Snichim–Xweliten Snichim Skexwts: Squamish-English Dictionary*. North Vancouver: Squamish Nation Education Department; Seattle: University of Washington Press, 2011.

Stoltmann, Randy. *Hiking Guide to the Big Trees of Southwestern British Columbia*. Vancouver: Western Canada Wilderness Committee, 1987.

Varner, Collin. *The Flora and Fauna of Coastal British Columbia and the Pacific Northwest*. Victoria: Heritage House Publishing, 2018.

Visalli, Dana, Walter Lockwood, and Derrick Ditchburn. *Northwest Mountain Wildflowers*. Surrey: Hancock House Publishers, 2005.

INDEX

Note: Hike details are indicated by page ranges in **bold**

ABOUT THE AUTHOR
AND PHOTOGRAPHER

Zoa Peak. Photo by Joan Septembre

STEPHEN HUI has been hiking, backpacking, and scrambling in British Colum-bia's Coast Mountains for more than 25 years. Hui's first book, *105 Hikes In and Around Southwestern British Columbia*, was a #1 B.C. bestseller. His outdoor writing and photography have appeared in the *Georgia Straight*, where he was the web editor and technology editor, as well as in the *Toronto Sun*, *Le Journal de Montréal*, *Where Vancouver*, and *Mount Baker Experience*.

Born and based in Vancouver, B.C.—in the territories of the Musqueam, Squamish, and Tsleil-Waututh First Nations—Hui works for an environmen-tal organization and serves as the vice-president of the Wanderung Outdoor Recreation Society. *Destination Hikes In and Around Southwestern British Columbia* is his second book. Hui's third book, *Best Hikes With Kids In and Around Southwestern British Columbia*, is forthcoming.

A portion of the author's royalties from this book will go to the Hope Mountain Centre for Outdoor Learning to support trail building and maintenance.

105hikes.com

📘 @DestinationHikes	🐦 @StephenHui
📷 @stephenhui	✉️ stephen@105hikes.com
🎵 @105hikes	💬 #DestinationHikes